SUFI VISION & INITIATION

SUFI VISION & INITIATION

Meetings with Remarkable Beings

Samuel L. Lewis

Edited by Neil Douglas-Klotz

RUHANIAT
PRESS

Sufi Vision and Initiation:
Meetings with Remarkable Beings
Ruhaniat Publications
Copyright 1986, 2013 Sufi Ruhaniat International

3nd Edition 2015

Grateful acknowledgement is made to the Marin Independent
Journal of San Rafael California for permission to reprint
portions of articles from its issues of May 13, 1957, January
21, 1961, and April 13, 1961.

The photos on pages 312, 348 and the back cover are by
Mansur Johnson.
©1998, 2015 Mansur Johnson

Cover Design by Hauke Jelaluddin Sturm.

ISBN 0-9881778-5-4

Library of Congress Control Number 2013934649

Acknowledgements for the 1986 First Edition

This book would not have been possible without the support of the students and friends of Samuel Lewis and of the work carried out through the Sufi Ruhaniat International, most of whom never knew Murshid while he was alive. This book is dedicated to them. May the "way of peace through breath" continue and prosper for the benefit of all beings!

Grateful acknowledgement is also made to Hassan Herz, for his invaluable advice on the original design and typography as well as support and feedback through the two years of active production. To Wali Ali Meyer, whose extensive interviewing of those who knew Samuel Lewis provided the basis for much of the background that put Murshid Sam's own writings in perspective. To the late Moinedin Jablonski, Samuel Lewis's successor at the Sufi Ruhaniat International, who performed the final proof reading and whose editorial comments improved this book. To Ishmael Ford, who indexed the book on short notice as a labor of love and to Zarifah Demcho, the sales manager for SRI at the time of publication, who communicated patiently with those eagerly awaiting the book though its many production delays.

Acknowledgements for the Third Edition

Life is in an ongoing process of change and impermanence. This book came out long before our current digital, print on demand and e book world. As the inventory began to dwindle Padme Blackwolf and Raphael Birney made the decision that the narrative and transmission of this book needed a place in our 21st century world of global connection and hopefully emerging planetary spirituality. Grateful acknowledgements to Dr Neil Douglas-Klotz for his initial creation of this book and the new forward. Many thanks to Hauke Jelaluddin Sturm for his beautiful new cover design. We hope this book continues to inspire many seekers to bring more love, harmony and beauty to our world.

Contents

Appendix

Foreword

THE AIR WAS BEMISTED BY A PUNGENT SMOKE-CLOUD, THE onions had burnt. With frying pan in hand, Sam (sometimes known as Murshid S.A.M.) was inviting me for supper, all at the last minute. I had a previous engagement, but the convivial host was irresistible and the whole place was wrapped in an atmosphere of enchantment. That was in the 60's, with flower-kids strewn about the place embracing. On the previous occasion, I had taken the liberty to describe the Dervish dances I had witnessed in the East. Within a matter of days, the Dances of Universal Peace were born in the West under the impulse of that magical pied-piper, Murshid Sam, much to the dismay of the old-timers and mainstream of conventional society. But the Dances came to stay, and so does the indelible memory of their pioneer, veteran in the art of carrying the experience of the meditation on the divine attributes right into the body.

Pir Vilayat Inayat Khan
Sufi Order in the West

Preface to the Third Edition

The project that became Sufi Vision and Initiation began as a simple work of service almost 40 years ago. It evolved into an incredible personal journey.

When I came to the Ruhaniat Sufi community in 1976, my teachers, Murshids Moineddin and Wali Ali, recognized an unregenerate intellectual, albeit with professional editing and writing skills. Rather than tell me, "stop all that," they put me to work.

One of the first projects Murshid Wali Ali gave me was to compare a galley version of Murshid Samuel Lewis' unpublished book The Lotus and the Universe with the original in order to check whether the editing done by the prospective publisher was accurate and faithful to the original. This involved two things: first, comparing, word for word, the original and the galley. In the pre-computer era, this was the editor's equivalent of Marpa asking Milarepa to build and then take apart a stone tower three times. Second, I needed to look up all of Murshid's references to people, places and events to see whether the changes that the publisher had made were accurate. Again, no Internet. The 'search engine' was me in the library using my research skills learned as a journalist.

In addition, Murshid wrote the book in response to Arthur Koestler's The Lotus and the Robot (1960) and made many references to it. So I read this book as well. Essentially, Koestler tried to make the case that all mystics are either phonies or charlatans, and that Western science and secular culture had all of the answers we need today.

After many months' work, I reached several conclusions: 1) The editing was very inaccurate. The editor had changed Murshid's words and references willy-nilly, seemingly from ignorance about what Murshid was talking about. It would be better to start from scratch.

2) Koestler's book was already long out of print, and no one seemed interested in it, or his approach to debunking mysticism. On the contrary, *The Tao of Physics* (1975) had just been published, and the interest in the connection between science and mysticism was very high.

3) The polemical parts of Murshid's book were not very strong, and since Koestler was not really "on the radar," there seemed little reason to publish the book in its original form. On the other hand, the book contained many wonderful stories that Murshid relates about meeting and studying with his spiritual teachers, including Hazrat Inayat Khan, Nyogen Senzaki, Sokei-an Sasaki and others.

I then set out to discover whether he told these stories elsewhere in his writings and to find the best examples. That took me into his letters, of which Murshid kept carbon copies to serve as his diary. At the time I did my research, the letters were housed in multiple file cabinets in the basement of the Mentorgarten, Murshid's home in the Precita district of San Francisco. As I described in the introduction to the original edition of Sufi Vision, I felt drawn to compile Murshid's spiritual biography told in his own words rather than as "hagiography."

It was a long project that involved sorting through and deciphering the second and sometimes third carbon copies that Murshid kept of his correspondence. I came to recognize Murshid's various typewriters, as well as his typing eccentricities. For instance, one of his typewriters habitually skipped a space after the letter "h." This led to several mistaken readings that had crept into some early printed excerpts from his letters. For instance, Murshid reports that one of his Pakistani teachers appointed him as a representative of "Ch_isti" Sufism in the West, which was edited into "Christian Sufism."

Many times, I found references in Murshid's writing to letters or documents that were missing from the file. I began to use what I called "editorial dowsing," basically, breathing "Use us for the Purpose that Thy wisdom chooseth" and then letting my heart and hands do the searching through the file cabinets, trying to think as little as possible. Amazingly, I was invariably led to a missing document that had been misfiled, or in one case was printed on the reverse of an entirely different document (probably to save paper).

Again, in an era when computer scanning and OCR were only expensive dreams, compiling all of the texts involved typing them slowly into an early laptop computer with a screen five lines long, which saved files onto cassette tapes, about 10-15 typed pages at a time.

Then there was the question of editing Murshid's grammar or syntax. As those who have read him know, he had his own way of punctuating sentences and using words like "Now" at the beginning of some of them. As a journalist, I had transcribed many interviews from tapes and adhered to the theory that the printed text should re-create the subject's speech pattern and rhythms as much as possible (this was the so-called "New Journalism" approach of Tom Wolfe and others in the 1970s). I began listening to tapes of Murshid, then reading all of Murshid's texts aloud, getting into his speech and breath rhythm, and letting him direct me. The work gradually became much easier, and I began to receive a very deep inner connection with him. [For those grammarians who notice that the punctuation in Sufi Vision is still "non-standard," I was using the grammatical theory of Rudolf Flesch, one of the early proponents of "readability" and co-creator of the Flesch-Kincaid Readability Test, which is now embedded in much word-processing software.]

The whole project lasted almost ten years, from start to finish. Two days still stand out for me.

First, in 1978, I was becoming disheartened by how long the whole process was taking. Late that year, along with 12 other mureeds, I went on a pilgrimage to Turkey, Pakistan and India to find the teachers of Murshid S.A.M. who were still alive and receive their blessing. Murshid Moineddin had asked us to do this, because he expected to die shortly of kidney failure, and he wanted Murshida

Fatima Lassar, who was then his successor, to receive the blessing of Murshid's teachers.

Towards the end of the trip in February 1979, we met Pir Barkat Ali of Pakistan. From Murshid's correspondence with him, as well as from what people told us, the Pir was very conservative, and we had all learned the Salat prayers of Muhammad in order to be able to pray with him. He lived in the jungle outside Lahore in a little village called Salarwala, where he had established an eye hospital for the benefit of the community. When Barkat Ali met us, as Murshida Fatima later described, he became Murshid Samuel Lewis. Not "acted like" him, but actually became him in a process that can only be described by the word fana. You can see a photo of him giving the darshan of Murshid S.A.M. in this book. He was also on silence.

Over the next several hours, he laughed and played with us, herding us around his mosque complex and generally baffling his followers. At one point, he took us into the mosque itself and began to throw pieces of bread to us. Then he brought out a typewriter and put it in front of me. He mimed dictating a letter and motioned to me to type. Of course, there was no paper in the typewriter, but I got the message.

Later he took us into his office, which was part of what you could call his "Qur'an refuge." He had put out the word for people to send him old, disused Qur'ans, which he lovingly rebound and then gave away to anyone who needed one. He wrote a message to us to say that if we prayed for something in the presence of all these Qur'ans, it would surely come true. I had already learned that praying for things was a mixed blessing, because you might get them. So I just prayed, "Use us for the Purpose that Thy Wisdom Chooseth." Really, at that point, I had no idea what was best for me or where my life was going.

After we returned, a year of so later, I was looking through the drawers of a bureau in the Mentorgarten office one afternoon and found, tucked away behind some folders, several cassette tapes. One was dated "October 2, 1968" and was a talk by Murshid that had never been transcribed. On it, he says:

I'm involved in two revolutions. One of them was when I told Ruth St. Denis:

"Mother, I'm going to start a revolution."

"What is it?"

"I'm going to teach little children how to walk."

"You have it! You have it! You have it!"

The second is to say the Lord's Prayer in Aramaic.

Murshid had started the Dances of Universal Peace and Walks. No one could remember him doing anything with the Lord's Prayer in Aramaic. This became a seed that I couldn't remove from my head or heart, which set me on a path of discovery that still continues today.

The one deficiency in *Sufi Vision* is the brevity of some of the excerpts from 1967 until Murshid's passing in 1971. Mansur

Johnson's wonderful book *Murshid* (2006) has rectified this by giving us the context for a more complete selection of Murshid's letters during this period as well as a personal and moving description of what life with Murshid S.A.M. was really like-- including the pain and struggle.

The diligence of later archivists and the generosity of the Sufi Ruhaniat International also brought another development in recent years: the scanning and archiving of most of the papers of Murshid Samuel Lewis, which can be found online at www.murshidsam.org. If it had been available in my day, it might have cut years off doing Sufi Vision. Or maybe not, given that the editing process became linked with my own personal process.

If you read Sufi Vision and Initiation, you might wonder if the types of experiences Murshid Samuel Lewis describes are still possible today. Are there really 'remarkable beings' to meet and remarkable experiences to have? Having travelled around the world over the last 36 years, I can tell you that there are. However, the spiritual path is not for the faint-hearted, and it is not Disneyland. If you're willing, like Murshid, to take on seemingly impossible projects in the name of service, to learn from both love and pain, all doors are open to you.

Ya Fatah! May Allah preserve Murshid's secret!

Saadi Shakur Chishti,
Neil Douglas-Klotz
Edinburgh, Scotland
August 2012

Editor's Introduction

IF YOU TRAVEL TO SAN FRANCISCO'S MISSION DISTRICT, AND then go a little further south, you may find yourself in a small patch of green called Precita Park. Along the south side of the park, across from a children's playground, will be a green house with a wooden carving of a heart with wings over the door which says "Mentorgarten." If you gain admittance to the house, you will find, where the garage should be, a finished Dance room and behind it an office. In the office sit six file cabinets filled with the largely unpublished writings of Samuel L. Lewis, aka Murshid S.A.M., Sufi Ahmed Murad Chisti, He Kwang Zen-shi.

At first (and second and third) glance, the sheer volume is overwhelming. Much of the writing is in the form of letters to scientists, politicians, religious leaders, professors, Sufis, Buddhists, Yogis, combinations of the above and others who defy description and could best be termed "friends."

Many people know Samuel Lewis from the film *Sunseed*, as the initiator of the joyous dancing and music depicted therein, as the man who could give the Islamic call to prayer from the top of a hill over the din of dirt-bikers in the background, who could dictate letters rapid-fire and play solitaire at the same time, who came across with an electrifying presence of love and peace.

Others may know him from his epic poetry, as contained in *The Jerusalem Trilogy* or *Crescent and Heart*, which relays a message of universality and an attempt to convey the essence of the world's religions in order to promote better understanding among them.

Perhaps, however, more people know him from direct experience through the Dances of Universal Peace, a form of spiritual folk dance that carries the intent of his poetry into minds, hearts and bodies through music and movement. These Dances have grown, expanded and spread around the world since his passing in 1971.

One thing that Murshid Samuel Lewis never finished was an autobiography of his experiences in the US and the East with various spiritual teachers: yogis, saints, dervishes, zen masters, priests — many of whom figure prominently in the history of contemporary mysticism.

Nine years ago, this project began with the understanding of putting together one man's spiritual autobiography from fragments of diaries, papers, articles and unpublished books.

Over that time, while gathering and editing the materials, one became more and more convinced that to extract only the "spiritual" from a life that included many other dimensions was to give a limited picture of a person whose depth of both joy and suffering can be felt in all the poetry, articles, letters and Dances. This was not "another guru book."

About one of the Sufis whom Samuel Lewis met in Pakistan, he said, "He was the most perfect ordinary human being I ever met." About his friend Swami Ranganathananda, he used to say, "Do you want to meet a *real* man?" and Mother Krishnabai, he said, had the highest realization of anyone he had met. What these persons had in common with Murshid Samuel Lewis was their ability and willingness to carry their spiritual realization into the most dense elements of life, to "get their hands dirty," whether that meant collecting trash, cleaning out sewers or planting flowers by the side of the freeway. At the same time, they could also commune and communicate with everyone from presidents to priests to paupers.

Ten years ago Lama Foundation (where Samuel Lewis is buried) published a volume called *In the Garden*. That book is a collection of stories about "Murshid S.A.M.," poetry and practices by him and excerpts mostly from his later diaries. It was lovingly compiled by his new-found family, the "New Age" people of the late sixties. As a tribute and sampler of his way of teaching at the end of his life, it may never be surpassed.

As Samuel Lewis warned, however, whenever a person is idolized to any degree, there is the danger that progress will stop on the part of the idolizers. We may experience new things by seeing through another's eyes, but in the end we must live our own lives. The being of love and light that showed himself in *Sunseed*, in the poetry and other writings and in the early Dances is only surpassed by the being as he is now. We may never hope to surpass him, we can only hope to surpass ourselves.

Over the past ten years, the blush has come off the "New Age" rose. Many who were involved as idealistic youths are clawing for survival as careerists or trying to make a family work over the long haul. It is clear that if there is to be a "New Age," we need to talk less, ideate less and "earthify" more.

It is right in the middle of this very dilemma that we find Samuel Lewis in the major portion of this book—his journeys to the East. For those who wish to walk (or dance) in the footsteps of Murshid Samuel Lewis, some attention could be paid to how he integrated the "liabilities" of his childhood, his here-and-now life skills and spiritual vision during this period. Somehow (by grace or effort?) all of Murshid's disparate life threads pulled together in an active way.

This happened before he became "the spiritual teacher of the hippies"; during this "homecoming"—the last eight years of his life here—he was most actively engaged in transmitting the fruits of his hard-fought victory to his new family. It would be a mistake to say, "Go and do thou likewise." It might be more in keeping to say, "Go and do thou your own way."

A word about the title of this book: in the mid-1960s Samuel Lewis wrote a college term paper called "Vision and Ritual in Sufism." In this paper he relates his own experiences and maintains that while vision can live without ritual, the opposite is not true. That is why there has been a rejection of lifeless rituals by many who have sensed the primacy of vision. On the other hand, a ritual can help to embody a vision and communicate it to others.

In his own life Samuel Lewis regarded vision—and its reponsibilities—very seriously. According to his Sufi teacher, Hazrat Inayat Khan, this meant testing the vision through direct action in the world, or what has been called "taking a step in an unknown direction." This is the real meaning of initiation, regardless of ceremonials called by the same name.

For Samuel Lewis these initiations took many forms. Some helped to make the Sufi teachings more accessible to greater numbers of people. Others helped to bridge the gap between intellectuals and mystics. High on his list were the challenges to feed the world's hungry, and to create viable and enduring sympathy among the world's different religions and cultures.

Constant during these outer tasks was his endeavor to bridge his own internal gaps. He often quipped, "My secret is controlled schizophrenia." But the practical components of this dynamic balance included work in Golden Gate Park as a gardener, and on highway road crews planting median strips, financially supporting adopted godchildren over the years, cooking meals for his disciples in the late 60s, stops at the butcher shop to pick up chicken necks and beef bones for the cats and dogs at his homes in San Francisco and Novato—the list goes on.

For the mystic, initiation leads to "meetings with remarkable beings"—not just human beings, but plants, animals, soils, rocks, trees, atmospheres and souls who have passed the tests of earth. As Samuel Lewis notes, real meetings are mergings; they change the parties involved while leaving them more fully themselves.

Murshid S.A.M. loved to play with established titles, and I think he would approve of this modification of Gurdjieff's well-known book. In response to Arthur Koestler's *The Lotus and the Robot*, for instance, he wrote his *The Lotus and the Universe*—much of which is included here.

This volume was edited and compiled by one who never knew Murshid Samuel Lewis in the flesh. The editor, even after a professional career of 12 years, was in a quandary many times as to how to proceed. Many of the materials—third or fourth carbons—are largely illegible. Others have been lost or misfiled despite the careful efforts of various librarians. In each case, the editor was "guided" to a lost paper or misplaced letter or unlabeled tape recording that supplied a missing link. In addition, he was able to build on the research and efforts of scores of others who were (and are) touched by this being.

One began with a feeling of awe and finished with a feeling of inevitability. It may seem presumptuous to say that Samuel L. Lewis did, in fact, write his own book, but it is true. The Sufis believe that there is a link between student and teacher which can be be demonstrated even in the physical absence of the teacher. As the Song of Solomon says, "Love is as strong as death." If this book demonstrates anything, it is "I am the vine and ye are the branches thereof." Alhamdulillah! (Praise God!)

Now, do you want to meet a *real human being?*

Neil Douglas-Klotz
Saadi
Karma Tashi Wosel

I. CALL TO THE QUEST

Samuel L. Lewis at age 31 (1927)

CHAPTER ONE

Book Excerpt:

Dedication and Introduction
(from *The Lotus and the Universe*)

Dedicated to the living memory of
President Sarvepali Radhakrishnan and Mataji Krishnabai of India,
Sheikhs Abusalem Amria and Mohammed Desoughi of Cairo, UAR,
Pir-O-Murshids Sufi Barkat Ali and Dewal Shereef of Pakistan,
Roshi Sogen Asahina of Engakuji, Kamakura, Japan.

Dedicated in Love, Peace and Devotion to Those with whom
I am, world without end . . .
Dedicated in Love, Peace and Devotion, to Those before whom
I am not, world without end . . .

by Samuel L. Lewis of San Francisco, California,
also known as Sufi Ahmed Murad Chisti

Beloved Ones of God:

This work is an effort to bring people of goodwill closer together in understanding, especially those of the Asian continent together with those of other continents. It has been stimulated in response to a number of books about the Orient, often written by those who have little acquaintance with the knowledge or peoples used as subject matter.

Others besides scientists know that a single swallow does not make a summer. Yet today one is led to believe that while a scientist may require two hundred trials before coming to any conclusion, many non-scientists take only a single event to reach two hundred conclusions. This reveals egocentricity.

We are besieged by multitudes of books in which the word "Zen" appears in the title without authorization. The Anti-Defamation League of Jewish People has done a splendid job in preventing such occurrences within their realm. The Oriental, not being a dualist, faces this world as it is. True, there are some excellent books being written by the real Zen masters, but their readership is small when contrasted with that of the total of current literature.

Arthur Koestler, in his book *The Lotus and the Robot*, seems to have moral integrity, but without understanding of esotericism and mysticism. This much cannot be said of all the writers. The term "Dharma Bums" is particularly offensive; one does not know how offensive it is. Much misunderstanding also results from emotional prejudices which are based on lack of real historical background, as is the case of reactions to the Prophet Mohammed and the religion of Islam. We do not believe that before God there is any East or West, North or South.

The people to whom this work is dedicated are all living in this year (1963), though originally one of the names appearing in the opening page was that of the late Swami Ramdas of Anandashram, South India. His recent death has been felt by more people in India —and elsewhere—than our cultural and spiritual leaders realize . . .yet.

The idea of a mystic writing on mysticism is not new. In some lands—though not in the United States—only scientists whose knowledge is operational (that is, based on direct experience) are permitted or expected to tell of their experiences.

There is no reason why the same policy may not be acceptable in more bizarre endeavors.

Samuel L. Lewis
Sufi Ahmed Murad Chisti
Rev. He Kwang, Zen-Shi

CHAPTER TWO

Editor's Note:

Childhood
and Early Life

Samuel Leonard Lewis was born October 18, 1896 at 2:20 a.m. in San Francisco. His father Jacob was a Vice President of the Levi Strauss Company. His mother was Harriet Rosenthal, the daughter of Lenore Rothschild of the international banking family. A family tradition is that Lenore's first husband, a man by the name of Krause, invented the copper rivet in Levi's jeans and became fabulously wealthy therefrom.

By all accounts, Samuel's childhood was not a happy one. His parents literally did not speak to each other for 25 years and used their two sons, Samuel and his younger brother Elliot, as intermediaries, according to a surviving cousin Mary Lou Foster. She tells the following story of visiting the family in 1946:

"Even for a simple thing like 'Would you please pass the cream,' it was communicated between the sons from one parent to another, and depending upon what space the sons were in, one might ask his mother or ask the other son — it was like his (the father's) son and her (the mother's) son."

This family dynamic led to an intense enmity between the brothers, which was only resolved just before the passing of both (Elliot died in March, 1970, 10 months before Samuel.) Since Samuel was the first-born, his father had high hopes of his going into business, or if not that, of at least going into orthodox religion. When it became apparent that his interests were more universal, his father was very disappointed. Part of the disappointment may have also been due to the fact that Elliot did not develop into a businessman either; he lived at home his whole life and, according to Foster, frittered away his family's money as a "sportsman."

Foster said that she did not really get to meet Samuel until after Elliot's passing, because of the "lies" that had been told about him by his brother. Having inherited the family home upon Elliot's passing, Foster said that she cleaned out various pictures of Samuel and other relatives that had been defaced and mutilated. According to both Foster and Samuel, it was his brother who turned his mother against him after his father's death. Samuel had been reconciled with his father just before the latter's death in 1954. His father had finally agreed to send him back to school in 1949 (Samuel was then 53) and on his deathbed had given him his gold watch. According to Foster this incident, as well as the fact that Jacob tried to disinherit his wife (illegal in California) touched off a bitter and ugly court battle over the terms of the will that saw Samuel's mother disowning him in court (apparently Elliot wanted Samuel disinherited).

Originally, Samuel had been his "mother's son." Samuel maintained that he had been conceived out of wedlock and that neither his mother nor father ever forgave him for that. His mother denied this, according to Murshida Vera Corda, who met Samuel in 1937. She recalls one interchange with his mother as follows:

"You'd have to hear Fuchsia (Harriet) on the piano to believe it. She had the strength of three men, and all of it came out on those keys. It was tremendous power in those little hands and this little bird-like alive, vital person who would bang away and stop in the middle and say, 'Vera, come here. Did you know my son is named Samuel; do you know why. . . . You know, they said he was born out of wedlock, but don't you believe it. He is — he was born a prophet and he came in the spiritual body first.'"

In body type, Samuel was originally much more like his mother: delicate bone structure, thin, short (he was about 5'2", she about 4'8"). His brother Elliot was built more like his father: strong masculine features, heavy bone structure. As Samuel describes it, his body and constitution began to change as a result of the Sufi practices as well as working

6

as a gardener and laborer in Golden Gate Park, for the State Highway Department and elsewhere before the reconciliation with his father allowed him to go back to school.

The reader will find only hints of Samuel's family history in his writings. From a family systems point of view, this is not surprising, considering what the level of communication was as he was growing up. According to Foster, broken homes were the rule, not the exception, in the family tree: divorce, sadism, hate, insanity were all part of it. "He would have to have been a saint to come out of the hate that his environment consisted of and to have so much love for so many people, and to be able to instill love in other people," said Foster.

As far as we know, there is only one person to whom Samuel Lewis definitely told his whole family history. That person was the late Dr. Blanche Baker, a psychiatrist to whom Samuel went for therapy in 1958 to help clear the effects of childhood and the development of what he called a "left-handed masochism." Samuel later recounted that he told Dr. Baker he would give her $200 unless she agreed, after hearing his history, that his was the worst story she had ever heard. If that was the case, he would ask that the therapy be free. "I got it free," he said [see entry in the last section, October 2, 1968.]

A student of psychology might ask: did Samuel Lewis become involved in spiritual matters so early in life because of his family situation or in spite of it? A student of metaphysics or consciousness might talk about "karmic cause and effect." Toward the end of his life, Murshid Samuel Lewis considered that his soul had chosen to come in early, to be misunderstood, in order to prepare the way for the coming generation that would begin to signal a "New Age"; he could understand the "generation gap" first hand, because he had lived it from birth.

The best answer to the "family question" might be another question, this time from Samuel quoting his Zen teacher Nyogen Senzaki: "Is the Zen monk bound by the law of Causation or is he outside of Causation? The Zen monk is ONE with the Law of Causation." To either ignore or overemphasize one's "unpleasant" history does not allow for *the full humanity of an individual—a world of many parts learning cooperation and wholeness.*

Neither of the first two pieces are dated. The best estimate, from internal evidence and style, would be that they were written between 1923 and 1946.

Jacob Lewis

CHAPTER THREE

Early Paper:

Intimations of Immortality from Juvenile Reminiscenses

UNTIL I WAS 15, I DISTINCTLY REMEMBER HAVING BEEN IN A KIND of wood. It was gloomy there, being like a perpetual four o'clock in the afternoon, lacking the bright light of the sun, but not being in darkness. This, I feel, is the condition of the soul, and the afternoon of the soul continues until about the age of seven when the sun of the soul sets, and we are enshrouded in darkness (until the "New Birth.")

As a positive proof of this: when my great-grandmother, who first told me of God, would mention Him to me, I always saw a great sky of white or light—no sun in it, and no figure or being or anything anthropomorphic or in form. The man-like God, or the veiled God or mist, or God in symbol came later, particularly after Sunday school studies.

Returning to the wood. There were three of us closely associated. We had been exiled—my chum and his sweetheart and I. We had been leaders of a great group of reformers of some kind, destined to free humanity, but passing through the realm of the Usurper, we had been deprived of our power and I had lost all my wealth and my wife (or sweetheart) besides.

These two souls with me, I feel, were Maurice and Minnie [relation unknown—ed.]. In my last visions of this wood (which continued as mentioned before, until I was about 15) I remember a few souls having gathered around us, and a sign that we would again be leaders in a great movement and recover our position, power, wealth and I my soul-mate sometime, somehow.

On one side of this wood there was an open space, but it was also gloomy there and entirely bare and flat, almost like a dry mud flat. Both the flat and the wood extended a long distance back to a land of greater light, memory of which gradually disappeared, but which I must have remembered until I was about 12. However, it was from this land that souls came and they were not permitted to return that way. All the traffic was in one direction, and I should call it downward in the same sense as if all traffic had to go to the South Pole, which is at the bottom of the earth.

(It is interesting to note that this South Pole is actually the South Pole of the mystics (or *Nadir* or *Sifar*) and the opposite movement has been called the Northern movement.)

Before we had been exiled into the world of gloom, we had been given some choices; some of these choices were actually repeated to me during my youth. One of them was the choice between truth and suffering on one hand, and pleasure and plenty on the other. When the Usurper offered me this choice, it seems that at first our entire band deserted us, won by stealth or trickery, and only Maurice, Minnie and I, it would appear, held out, although later a few discovered the treachery of the Usurper. (This group continued growing until "birth." I believe that, from the ages of 3 to 15, I went through a great deal of suffering over this memory, which I am now mentioning for the first time. The fact that I was to be separated from my wife-to-be, whoever she is, is further explained by some of the details below.)

The land where the Usurper overthrew our power was, I would say, a sort of 2 or 3 in the afternoon of the soul, where it was warm and bright and there were meadows. There was much playing and feasting and dancing. I had evidently been a great dreamer and idealist, for I would not join in the games, and it was in this way that my band left me, drawn by pleasure.

This is rather interesting, for when I was in my late teens, I was in the Socialist movement and had a fair amount of influence among the young folks; then I lost my power through the machinations of a young man who introduced dancing and dancers and used this means to overthrow me. This same youth also caused Maurice a great deal of trouble then and afterwards, playing a part in this world as the Usurper did in the former world. Later, H. Spencer Lewis and also one other person played similarly in the lives of Maurice and myself.

It seems that in the former world, I had therefore taken an aversion to dancing, and this played a part in this life. At the same time, I have always loved to watch good dancing, and sometimes I feel that I shall marry a dancer. I do not know God's Will in this matter at all, but it is not necessary to know.

Before entering the world of the Usurper, we had been in a much brighter world, memory of which only remained in early childhood, as with Wordsworth, but I am sure many more children have this experience than is commonly believed.

This Land of Light was where souls receive their instructions before birth. I was at the top of this class (later, I was invariably at the top of my classes in school), but the idea of "school" is somewhat a misnomer. We learned *directly out of the light with our breath,* and this breath came in not only through the nostrils, but through every pore of the body. This learning was the same as food; we lived on it, and learning, living, eating and breathing were all one and the same process.

In that land, there was no idea of parentage, but of brother and sister, and perhaps sweetheart and even husband and wife. We travelled in bands, but I do not remember much and that not very clearly. However, I shall relate a few memories, all of which can be explained by doctrines given in "The Phenomenon of the Soul," and "The Soul, Whence and Whither" [by Hazrat Inayat Khan—ed. note].

Sister: In that land, I had both a brother and sister. For many years after coming to this plane, I continued to dream of a sister younger than myself, but older than my brother. This continued until I was about 12. I had already met the girl who was adopted the following year, fulfilling the conditions; also most of the dreams, if not all, materialized in the following years.

In the Land of Play, as I call it, the girl was about 1½ years and my brother 3 years younger than I, but there were no parents. In this world, the periods were considerably shortened.

English Language: I was evidently born with a knowledge of the English language, for as soon as my mother repeated the alphabet, I repeated it and was reading before I was 3. I read history at 4 and completed the Old Testament at 6. Now as regards reincarnation, there is this peculiarity: I have always felt that if I lived on earth before that I was a Jew, and yet every memory I might have brought has been with England or the English language.

For instance, when I was 13, I had to write a story in English class and wrote in detail the first half of "The Lady of the Lake," which I had never read. The teacher thought I had copied it, although I never heard of it and knew nothing of Scott. This could be explained that I met him on a higher plane, where I also most likely met at least one Sufi poet on the downward course to earth.

Messiah: I always believed in the coming of the Messiah, and for a long time felt that I would meet him, and that the great work for which I had been a leader (on the earlier planes) was connected with him. I often rehearsed conversations with the Messiah, and later, after I was 18, with a Master. But when I awoke to the realization, it was almost impossible to reconcile the dreams and musings with the objective reality. In fact, this has been the wonder of my life.

Morals: Closely associated with the last (no doubt) is the reason why I did not indulge in dancing, sex, smoking, etc. I had evidently been given very complete instructions on these points before incarnation. I have never received any guidance on such matters from my parents.

There were also some other intimations which came during childhood.

Choice: I was several times given a choice as to whether I should have my worst sufferings early in life or later. I chose to have them earlier. Now, while this choice was given to me in this life, part of it—that my wife was to remain unknown to me and not revealed until after certain events—belongs to the group of memories, rather than intimations.

Philosophy: When I was 15, it came very definitely— suddenly at first, but often repeated—that I would be a philosopher. At the time I had but the vaguest idea as to what this word meant, and a few years later I actually scorned studying the subject. This was an initial form of spiritual experience, in some way connected with the *djinn* [mental genius or artistic—ed.] period of development through which youth goes. I already knew at the time that I was to pass through my adolescence without meeting my sweetheart—very painful—and that my career would be tragical for some time. This made that year particularly hard, and it was not until I was 18 that I recovered from that mood, only to fall in time (from the material point of view, at least) into a worse condition.

This was the last intimation, I believe, when I began my spiritual studies at 18.

Note: At 18, for entirely different material reasons, but certainly connected with spirituality, I began with Theosophy and "Morals and Dogma of Masonry" and Comparative Theology. Already at 13 I knew about spiritism and psychic research, and evidently earlier about magic and alchemy.

CHAPTER FOUR

Early Paper:

In Quest
of the Super-Miraculous

Scene I. The World's Fair, San Francisco, 1915.

Youth comes to the Palace of Education. "Lord, I know nothing, show me." He places his hands on his forehead, moving each in the opposite direction as if to empty his mind and walks in. He walks in as if a Socrates and asks and asks and asks.

Then he meets the Theosophists. "All religions are right. They differ on the outside when taken exoterically, they agree on the inside if taken esoterically. All religions are from God. There are seven planes of existence, the lower ones experienced in life after life, the higher ones only by sages and the illumined."

The youth is satisfied. He thinks he has found The Way.

Scene II. November 1919. This way has proven only intellectual.

He is on Sutter Street in San Francisco, looking at a display of books. He is unaware, but soon he is upstairs facing a little dark-haired lady. She is Jewish.

"You can explain the Kaballah?"

"Yes, and all religions."

"What is Sufism?"

"Sufism is the essence of all religions. It has been brought to the West by Hazrat Inayat Khan."

Scene III. June 1923.

It is night. It is morning. Hazrat Inayat Khan is coming. The youth is in a hurry. The train draws closer. Inayat Khan sticks his head through the smoke-stack. Youth jumps out of his body. Inayat Khan jumps into his heart. Youth jumps into his heart. The two hearts rush and blend and become the Infinite Whole.

Scene IV. The next day.

It is noon, the Summer Solstice. Youth enters the Clift Hotel. He is summoned to see Pir-O-Murshid Inayat Khan. There is nobody there, only a tremendous light. "Come, don't be afraid."

Youth walks on and sees a man and experiences joy. The Quest of the Super-Miraculous becomes real.

Rabia Ada Martin

II. JOURNEY INTO SUFISM

Pir-O-Murshid Hazrat Inayat Khan

CHAPTER FIVE

Book Excerpt:

Pir-O-Murshid
Hazrat Inayat Khan
(from _The Lotus and the Universe_)

LATE IN 1919 I FOUND MYSELF VERY SUDDENLY STANDING BEFORE a lady in an office loft in San Francisco. The lady was Murshida Rabia A. Martin, a qualified Sufi teacher and senior disciple of one Inayat Khan, whom I was blessed to meet later on. The term _murshid_ means director or teacher. Rabia was the name of a great woman saint of Iraq whose tomb has been visited by many people for over a thousand years.

Earlier studies and researches had brought the writer to the conclusion that common interpretations of religion were either incomplete or incorrect; there must be some deeper meanings in them. Murshida Martin then took me on three journeys:

A.) the mysticism of the Old Testament;

B.) the esoteric study of Comparative Religion, and

C.) the Sufic discipline.

But though disciplined, she encouraged investigations into the mysticisms of all faiths and was a good friend of Dr. M.T. Kirby (my early Buddhist teacher), just as her teacher the Pir-O-Murshid later became a good friend of Nyogen Senzaki.

Among the Sufis, _ishk_ (love), _ilm_ (wisdom) and _shahud_ (direct experience) are what count. As has been said, "Sufism consists of experiences and not premises." (Al-Ghazzali). Historically, Sufis came later than other schools of mysticism, and both historically and esoterically, they can be traced to _and_ through Mohammed. But as

Professor Titus Burckhardt has pointed out, one does not learn mysticism or esotericism except through direct experience.

It is not our place here to write a biography. The family of the Pir-O-Murshid has continued to see that his books are published, and perennially there are shorter or longer sketches of his life and personality.

Hazrat Inayat Khan was born in Baroda state in India and came from a family of musicians. This family was also long associated with Sufis. Largely through the art of music, the mystics of Islam and Hinduism had mingled and intermingled, each making impressions on the other. The first autobiography of Hazrat Inayat Khan appeared in his own "Confessions of a Sufi Teacher" [presently in print as part of Vol. 12 of *The Sufi Message of Hazrat Inayat Khan* — ed. note].

He came to America in 1911 and gave the *bayat* (pledge of initiation) to Mrs. Ada Martin, who immediately became a Murshida with the sobriquet of "Rabia." He entrusted her with a considerable body of teaching which was not, however, put to general usage, for after establishing himself in London, he began to systematize his work along other lines.

In his early days, the teachings were based on two interconnected methods. One has to do with *zikr* (remembrance) and involves a long series of disciplines and practices called *ryazat*, all of them having for their purpose the remembrance of God at all times, in all places, under all circumstances. Perhaps in some form or other all the Sufi and Dervish orders utilize it.

The other method dealt with self-effacement, called *fana*. This has three distinct grades or stages: *fana-fi-sheikh, fana-fi-rassul, fana-fi-lillah*. In *fana-fi-sheikh*, one practices self-effacement by holding the ideal of the living teacher before him and practicing whatever has been imparted to him. It can go on indefinitely. At the same time, the experiences of Sufism carry one through what are called states (of consciousness) and stages (of evolution) or "stations."

Fana-fi-rassul means effacement in the human ideal. To most or all Sufis, this is Mohammed, but even "Mohammed" takes on various

20

meanings, until one reaches the interpretations offered by Ibn-al-Arabi and Al-Jili (in his "The Perfect Man.") And *fana-fi-lillah* means effacement in the universal, or beyond name-and-form, or the direct experience of God.

All of these were and are living experiences of which there are many examples and exponents, but there is a strange chasm between those who have experienced and the intellectuals who are busy translating or interpreting.

Pir-O-Murshid was first given bayat in the Chisti School, which bases spiritual development on music. Its chief center is at Ajmir, India, where the celebrated Moineddin Chisti is interred. But by the time he left India, Inayat Khan had received the training in what may be called "Four School Sufism," which is to say, in the Chisti, Kadri, Sohrawardi and Naqshibandi Schools. The Sufism that was presented to the West was basically a synthesis of these.

Hazrat Inayat Khan went to Europe at the invitation of composers such as Debussey and Scriabin, and for some time he carried on the dual career of musician and spiritual teacher. During World War I, his headquarters were in London; afterwards they were transferred to Geneva, Switzerland, with much of his time spent between there and Suresnes, near Paris. He visited the States in 1923 and 1926, returned to Europe, and from there travelled to India where he died in February 1927.

The meeting with this man was a wonder. It was preceded by certain types of dreams and visions which our Western culture must someday learn to re-evaluate and explain. Then occurred a more cosmic experience of *union* which seems to be common to certain types of mystics. But when I entered the room to meet him in 1923, there was no man there, only a great body of light.

Hazrat Inayat Khan was not the first man authorized to present Sufism in English, but he seems to have been the first to do something effectively. The famous Sir Richard Burton had been appointed as a Murshid, and some Muslims expected him to become a missionary. But certainly common religion of any sort did not appeal to him.

Hazrat Inayat Khan taught us that religion has three stages: faith, love and knowledge. So long as religion remains bound to faith and proceeds no further, it can be caught in the web of egocentricity. We have plenty of literature concerning love and plenty of literature that has arisen because of love. The lesson to be learned here is to extract love from time and link it to eternity. And when we become aware of this eternity, we begin to have the real knowledge (called *Marifat*).

The other aspect of Sufism besides that of Cosmic Monism (*Tauhid, Ahadiat*) is that of the acceptance of a Spiritual Hierarchy. This has not only been presented by J.P. Brown in his *The Dervishes*, but also by E.W. Lane, who was a pioneer Orientalist. As the intellectuals took over the teaching of Orientalia, this aspect of Sufism has been ignored. And yet it is this aspect of Sufism which both unites all the Orders and separates them from the generality of Muslims.

There is plenty of material in Sufic literature regarding the saints. Even in this age, books are being published concerning men who have lived in the twentieth century.

Here we come to another great division between the real Sufis and what has been called "Islamic Philosophy"—stemming mostly from Europeans. Practically all Sufis regard either Hazrat Ali or Abdul Kadir-i-Jilani of Baghdad as the greatest of saints. True, Moineddin Ibn-al-Arabi either declared he might be the "seal of the saints" or his commentators have said so. But throughout the length and breadth of the Islamic world, these two—Hazrat Ali and Abdul Kadir-i-Jilani —stand out. Not only is this so in popular opinion, but also in occult experiences.

The general teachings given by Hazrat Inayat Khan were first mentioned in an early work of his called "A Sufi Message of Spiritual Liberty" [presently in print as part of the *Sufi Message of Hazrat Inayat Khan, Vol. 5* — ed. note]. All of his instruction was a detailed expansion of what appears in this work. It covers in outline many facets of mysticism and spiritual development. But, of course, it is at best a sort of laboratory manual; it is not even a cookbook.

In 1925, I had a complete breakdown, went into the wilderness and there experienced a number of visions and states of consciousness quite common to Sufis.

The writer's experiences of 1925 were explained by Pir-O-Murshid when he visited Los Angeles in 1926, and a number of confidences were given, largely drawn therefrom. His death the following year saw the disintegration of the Sufi Movement and the efforts of personalities who had not gone through the higher mystical states to take over leadership. In this they failed, though at this writing (1963) his son Vilayat Inayat Khan is making a valiant effort to restore the Movement.

My own journey in fana-fi-sheikh began on February 5, 1930, exactly three years after Inayat Khan's death, when the Pir-O-Murshid appeared to me and helped me "from the other side" to write the commentaries on his esoteric works, that is, his lessons for mureeds (initiated disciples). This was a provision in the constitution of the Sufi Order.

It is also an illustration of love. We love one another insofar as we are part of one another, or blended with one another. Indeed, love cannot have a definition; defined love is incomplete love, it is love's shadow. We *become* the other, or as Jesus Christ said, "I am the Vine and ye are the branches thereof." This is the relation of the teacher to the disciples — ever, always.

No doubt during the coming years, there may be more complete biographies of Hazrat Inayat Khan. But his followers must learn that there are many mystics, many Sufi teachers, and that not all mystics are Sufis and not all who call themselves "Sufis" or "Dervishes" are mystics. We must learn, all of us, that "in God, we live and move and have our being" (Acts 17:28).

CHAPTER SIX

Editor's Note:

The First American Sufi Khankah—Kaaba Allah

As Samuel Lewis describes in the following section, many of his early spiritual experiences with the Sufis centered around Kaaba Allah, a retreat center and group living house (called a khankah) which was located in Fairfax, California. What were originally two houses were nestled up against Mount Tamalpais, near what later became the Marin Municipal Water District preserve. Behind the two houses, up the hill, was a large outcropping of rock which was dedicated by Hazrat Inayat Khan as Pir Dahan (the Voice of the Prophet). He, and others, felt that this spot had a special vibration and significance, some of which is detailed in Samuel Lewis's article called "Baraka (Blessing)—Direct Experience at the Rock Pir Dahan." The area surrounding this rock was also the site of his 1925 retreat and early Sufi visionary experiences, which are detailed next.

We do not have any diaries of Samuel Lewis from this early period, except for remnants of his retreat diary from 1925 in a collection he called his "scrapbook." We do know that he lived and worked as a gardener-caretaker at Kaaba Allah on and off from 1925 to 1949. At that time, one of the houses burnt down, destroying a huge esoteric library and most of his papers and books. Piecing together information from old friends and his later writings, we know that Samuel Lewis also lived during this time in Los Angeles (where he studied with Nyogen Senzaki and Ruth St. Denis). Around 1939 he lived at a "bohemian" tent-shack community called the "Dunes" near San Luis Obispo where he knew poet-mystic Hugo Selig, astrologer Gavin Arthur and scientist-adventurer Bryn Beorse (who was also an early disciple of Hazrat Inayat Khan). Samuel undoubtedly also lived with his parents during some part of this period, since he was seen there by other relatives.

The burning of one of the Kaaba Allah houses in 1949 served as a crisis and turning point in many respects for Samuel Lewis. From 1926–44, he had attempted to protect and defend his first Sufi teacher Rabia Martin according to Hazrat Inayat Khan's directions (detailed in the following writings). In 1944, Rabia Martin died of cancer, after turning over the Sufi properties (and her organization) to Meher Baba, whom she had become convinced was the "Avatar" of the age. She appointed Mrs. Ivy Duce as a Murshida and her successor to carry this out. Meher Baba felt that he was empowered to "re-orient" Sufism and began an organization suitably named. During this time, Samuel Lewis decided to try to work with Meher Baba within the organization, even though he felt that the "Message" of Hazrat Inayat Khan was being lost through its "reorientation." This we have from his disciple and close friend, Murshida Vera Corda. She related that many people were outraged that Rabia Martin had turned the organization over to a total stranger and chosen as successor someone who had never lived or worked at Kaaba Allah. Part of the problem, she said, was that Murshida Rabia Martin began to rely on Samuel for his visionary capacity instead of developing her own. Then she began to doubt him and had no way to confirm or deny through her own experience. Murshida Vera Corda said that she chose to dissociate herself from the organization when it was turned over to Meher Baba.

In 1946 Samuel Lewis had more visionary experiences of Hazrat Inayat Khan (detailed at the end of this section) during which he felt the Pir-O-Murshid turned him over to Jesus and Mohammed for further guidance. The fire in 1949 served as one of the "last straws," so to speak. Samuel had already become known as a troublemaker in the Baba Sufi organization and was, in addition, blamed for the fire. He thereafter moved elsewhere in Marin County and began attending City College of San Francisco following the reconciliation with his father.

During happier times, the Fairfax khankah was an oasis for many

25

young people who came there to pray, work and share meals, according to Murshida Vera. She described some of the scenes there from the mid- to late '30's:

> In those days of great poverty in the Depression, you could go there, as many times we did, without food all day. Samuel would never see that you got something to eat first. First he would take you on a hike, pick an herb here and there to give you, and talk to you. And soon you ended up on the rock (Pir Dahan) and sat down with him. Then he would transcend you out of the flesh totally and into the spiritual body. You would have marvelous experiences with him — some spoken, some in meditation, some merely holding his hand and watching the sunset from the rock. You would come down totally filled. You would not feel hungry, weak or depleted. You would feel a fulfillment of all of your bodies — spiritual, mental and physical — complete harmony. Then you entered for your evening meal, and you weren't even thinking about physical food. . . .
>
> Murshida Martin was extremely generous — those of us who did not have the money were never kept away from Kaaba Allah. When you were assigned to your room you found on the inside of the door your assignment for the weekend. Samuel made these assignments and somehow he had it planned for you to use your energies in a way that you would gain something in the spiritual body, no matter what. You might be working on the rock pile, digging up bamboo, planting fences, digging the earth.
>
> There was a great work going on at Kaaba Allah. At one time, we were leveling the ground where the clotheslines were, which was the only flat area on the grounds. This was a great place where we could do our dancing and games. We played lots of games with the younger children. Samuel's games were always in a circle, big group things that pulled everybody in. If you went down there, you got hauled into it and had a great old time. We took down the clotheslines, which made the old ladies [who lived at Kaaba Allah]

roar, so that we had an even bigger area of hard-packed dirt. Bare feet felt great in it. . . .

On Sunday morning, all the young people would gather together with Samuel and we would visit a church of his choice in Fairfax: Methodist, Baptist, Pentecostal, Catholic, Quaker, Jewish. We visited every church in the area. We were taught that a Sufi enters any house of God and behaves as that denomination behaves. He honors God in that manner. And we learned by experiencing these different congregations, the love of God expressed in so many different manners. But always behind it, at the heart of it, was one truth, one message.

You were prepared ahead of time. Samuel would tell us how to behave before we entered. He would say, "These are the manners, your manners of worship. They have nothing to do with your talking to God. When you talk to God, you speak one language, remember that." When we came back, Samuel would give us the heart of that message in that religion's own texts. Then he would also quote Hazrat Inayat Khan so that you would see that this was also the same message, in a different age, in different words, in a different teacher. . . .

You ate supper and left on the Sunday night train. It was usually beginning to get dark when we would sit down to supper. Everyone had packed before this, and following supper you went back to the meeting room and we walked single file up to the chapel. There we had the last of prayers — short prayers and mostly the zikr again was sung. You left after the zikr in silence. Everybody kissed everybody, said goodbye, but it wasn't in language, it was in gesture. Usually the three oldest disciples, the three old ladies, always stood together in the doorway and said goodbye as we went down to go back to the city.

CHAPTER SEVEN

Excerpt from Papers:

The Retreat of March 1925

TOWARD THE ONE,
THE PERFECTION OF LOVE, HARMONY AND BEAUTY,
THE ONLY BEING;
UNITED WITH ALL THE ILLUMINATED SOULS,
WHO FORM THE EMBODIMENT OF THE MASTER,
THE SPIRIT OF GUIDANCE.

In the Name of Allah, the Merciful and Compassionate, and in the
Name of all the Messengers and Prophets and all the Sufis-in-Chain,
beginning with Mohammed, the Seal of the Messengers.

On March 10, 1925, Samuel L. Lewis of San Francisco left his
family home and the city of his birth to go to Kaaba Allah, a Sufi retreat near Fairfax, Ca. He had been in pain for years. Doctors had
done nothing for him except to apply medicines and charge accordingly. There was not an organ in his body properly operating. He had
been forced into debt by wealthy parents who demanded accounting
of every cent he earned, while indulging his brother Elliot in any and
all enterprises, honest or questionable, provided they bring in financial returns. (It is not necessary to go into these complexities; the
terms used by sociologists are extremely confusing. In any event his
father apologized on his deathbed, and Sam is in excellent financial
circumstances for a retired man, due to a combination of his own
efforts and the receipt of family inheritances long overdue.)

By a series of circumstances not easily explained, Samuel had met
Murshida Martin, a Sufi teacher, in September 1919, and six weeks
later encountered one Reverend M. T. Kirby. Kirby's spiritual name

was Sogaku Shaku, and he had been a disciple of Shaku Soyen, who brought the real Zen Dharma Transmission to this country, first in 1893 and then in 1906. Dr. Kirby and Murshida Martin became friends, and Sam studied both Zen and Sufism without conflict. In 1923, he introduced Nyogen Senzaki, another disciple of Shaku Soyen, to Pir-O-Murshid Inayat Khan, and they both initiated each other, so to speak. Thus, when he went into seclusion, he had already had some training both in Sufic practices and meditative Zen.

He was too weak to carry books with him, so he only brought copies of the works of the Sufi poet Hafiz, a notebook, and foods. He was put on a special diet by Rabia Martin, one based on teachings and directives of Hazrat Inayat Khan. This was the basic *khilvat*, or seclusion diet, very much akin to that used by Sufis in seclusion all over the world.

It was with difficulty that he mounted the steps above Forrest Avenue in Fairfax. He fell down when he reached Kaaba Allah, 133 Hillside Drive. This was the last time he ever fell down in his life, and much has happened since 1925.

The first few days, he was too tired for anything but meditation and Sufic practices. But he was able to read a little. On the third day, he completed the reading of Hafiz as the sun was setting. The rays of the sun fell on the book, and as he finished the last page two doves suddenly appeared, circling his head, cooing.

That night, as he was doing his spiritual practices, he felt a presence, and he was sure it was Khwaja Khizr. There are many legends of Khwaja Khizr. Even some Western occultists have accepted the reality—of the legends. When it comes to *events*, that is something different. If you believe in legends you are "saved," but if you propose that your belief is based on actual experience, that is a sure sign you are a pretender and damned.

There was a recurrence of this appearance of Khwaja Khizr on the following night and on the next also. He offered poetry or music. Sam chose poetry. On the third night of the appearance, there was a long argument—why was the poetry chosen and not the music? It is not necessary to detail this, but if anyone wants it, it can be given. Actually, it was not a choice. It is merely a different story. Years later, the music did come, and it is coming, and with it the Dance, but these are different stories. After the third night, Sam began writing incessantly.

At the end of ten days, all the health and vigor were restored, and Sam prepared an initiatory ceremony for noon, March 21, the equinoxial hour. It must be said here that Murshida Martin had been a teacher in occultism, especially what is called "Martinism" before she became a Sufi Murshida, and she transmitted some of this knowledge to her early disciples. One prepared a ceremony with concentration, and in turn Shiva, Buddha, Zoroaster, Moses and Jesus appeared. Then Mohammed appeared, but double (on the left and right) and on horseback. All the others came singly. Then the six Messengers of God, so to speak, formed a circle and danced and became one, and as they danced, the Prophet Elijah appeared and bestowed a Robe.

This is the Robe, not a Lloyd Douglas fiction. The same Robe was bestowed in vision by Khwaja Moineddin Chisti at Ajmir, India in 1956 and by Amir Khusrau at Nizamuddin Auliya in New Delhi in 1962. And when Ahmed Murad, as he was then called, returned to Pakistan after that, he was given this Robe, actually. He has it in his possession now. It is functional. It has been recognized by Sufis who are Sufis.

The disciple was supposed to remain in seclusion 10 days with an additional day before and after. But owing to his exaltation, Sam kept quiet for 14 days until he met Murshida Martin and reported to her. He told no one else until 1926 when he again met Pir-O-Murshid Hazrat Inayat Khan at the Beverly Hills Hotel in Los Angeles. The above was the subject for the first interview. Murshid asked him to write this up and keep it as a record, and it was also the basis for the five interviews which followed.

CHAPTER EIGHT

Excerpt from Scrapbook:
Writings from the 1925 Retreat

Allegory
At night, Friday-Saturday, March 13-14.

First Impression:

A certain Great King had a very beautiful daughter whom he wished to marry to one of the kings of the earth. So he summoned a herald with a message he was to carry. The herald visited the court of a king, who was so glad to receive an envoy from the Great King that he ordered a banquet prepared in his honor. Then he loaded the herald with presents and built a statue in his honor and sent him away. But the Message he heard not.

Second Impression:

A certain Great King had many daughters. And they were exceedingly fair and of marriageable age. Wishing to marry them to the kings of earth, he summoned a herald, telling him that whosoever married one of his daughters would have a dowry whatsoever they desired. So the herald visited the court of one of the kings who was so glad to receive an envoy from the Great King, that he rejoiced and ordered a great banquet and prepared a holiday for all his people in honor of the envoy. Then he loaded the herald with presents and built a statue in his honor and sent him away. But the Message was heard not.

Then the Great King sent him to another king with a like result. So the Great King sent in his stead other messengers from time to time. And some of the messengers were stoned, and some were tortured and driven away by the people. And some kings were so honored at receiving a messenger that they warred with one another as to who was entitled to the greatest honor for having received the greatest envoy.

But few were those who first listened to the herald and his message and then went to the Great King. And they that went found his daughters so exceedingly fair that they gave up their kingdoms and dwelt at the court of the Great King, where sorrow came to them no more.

Allegory II

Night of March 15:

A man once founded a large business with many branches and departments, and every now and then he sent one of his sons to visit one of these branches or departments. And each son would do his work faithfully, rewarding the competent, encouraging the backward and bringing peace and harmony wherever he went.

Time passed and the sons were no more. Then the business did not prosper. Each department or branch thought itself most important and would not cooperate with the other branches. The Sales Department listened not to the Production Department, and the Purchasing Department listened not to the Accounting Department nor would the Chicago Branch cooperate with the San Francisco Branch.

Now one of these sons had a son, and when this son saw how affairs were going, he visited each one. And he found that the departments and branches still revered the memory of his father and uncles, but had forgotten their admonitions and considered that the brother that had visited them was superior to the other brothers. Then this one said: "They were brothers, my father and my uncles, and all wanted to carry out the wishes of my grandsire—listen and see if their instructions were not the same." But they would not, even though the business was not prospering. And though the new head of the firm tried hard, so bitter was the opposition and so hard were his struggles that he died.

And when he died, all saw how good he was, and that since conditions were bad, they might take his advice though he had gone. And this they did, and the business prospered exceedingly thereafter. And him whom they ignored in life, they honored in death.

(Must this be with thee, O Pir-O-Murshid?)

Hafiz

Written 3/16/25 at 1:30 p.m.

"Hafiz." What a joy to utter the name! What a thrill in the heart. I have never had a vision of him and hardly read a line of his poetry, yet—picture him and what do I see? Smiles! One big smile, bearing joy to all who greet him. He is like sunshine, bringing comfort and courage. In my days of darkness he was with me, guiding me, encouraging me, showing me the way, always smiling, always cheerful. When I look at the beautiful trees and pleasant meadows of sunny California, I picture him in his rose garden at Shiraz and feel that, had he not been born where and when he was, this country with its lovely scenery and beautiful weather would have brought inspiration to his heart, and ode upon ode would have resulted.

Allons, Hafiz! To study your works together!
***

I hear the blue birds twittering in the trees,
The leafy branches fluttering in the breeze,
While I sit here, musing at my ease,
Thinking of thee, Hafiz.

The trees around me spring has clothed in green
On hillside and in lovely vale between,
A typical lovely California scene,
Reminding me of thee, Hafiz.

And now to study and to read thy book,
Neath shelt'ring trees and in this lonely nook,
For though alone, God has not forsook me,
Nor thee, Hafiz!
***

Hafiz is always young. Not a boy or youth, but in early manhood. He has the spirit and enthusiasm of the child and youth with the wisdom of experience.

The Maypole
March 17, 1925

What a source of happiness the Maypole is: what a joy it brings to children! No competition here, but each for all and all for each, all pulling together. Grab a ring, let's start, hold on tight and run!

Just a little and then you swing up in the air and out into space, going round and round, up and down, every now and then touching the earth, every now and then rising upward toward the sky. Self is forgot—you are not several souls joining in a game, you are part of one whole. If but one of you try breaking this charm, 'tis broken and 'tis known by all. So all keep in harmony, swinging in rhythm.

Come, brethren, let's join in the Maypole of Life. Forget yourself and seize this ring He has given to you. 'Twill bring you peace and happiness inconceivable. We are going to start—come and join us, rising and falling together in the Cosmic Dance!

Initiation
"Peace on Earth, Good Will Towards Men"
March 21, 1925, 9:00 a.m.

My dearest Murshida,

Here in your wonderful room I sit, awaiting the hour of noon, when the signs of the cross shall be made in the heavens, and the sun pass over the equator. This lovely room with its spiritual atmosphere

34

—here where I have sat in meditation, morning, noon and night for the last 12 days—an atmosphere of calm and peace. Once when I fled here when someone came to the grounds, my strength and courage were not only renewed, but doubled like that of the giant Antaeus in the story of Hercules. At night, if there was any fear, fear itself grew afraid when I neared the threshold and stronger and stronger I became in body, heart and soul. There seems to be a sign over the door: "Abandon all *fear* ye who enter here."

Yet not one hour have I been alone. God said—and it is noted in the diary—that an angel with a flaming sword stood outside, and only those who could see, could pass. So the birds remained and other creatures and humans never disturbed me. "You have nothing to fear but yourself." And God Himself has been with me. Even now I was not to start writing until the hour of nine, and when a voice from the silence said "Begin," I thought I lacked at least five minutes. But I found the hour had passed by two minutes. Time and again have I known the time.

And not only this, but in the matter of food, fuel, matches, and so forth, my doubts proved false. I thought I did not have enough wood and went out Thursday and brought some in. And how vain! My original stock of wood will last several days more if I should stay. And the same applies to food and matches.

I have brought with me every word I have written in diary, articles, poems and essays to lay them this morning on the altar of Him alone Who is Creator. Step by step have I risen, to find myself in Him. Every prophecy or hint in the diary has been realized. He offered me poetry or music. I chose poetry, and while these may not be works of art, therein there is a promise and there is an inspiration. I have felt at times like a mosque, with my head as a dome reflecting the light from underneath. I have felt as a circle with a point inside. Facing the south, the point is God; Hafiz in front of me; Pir-O-Murshid to the left, the Rab [Fabre D'Olivet—ed. note] to the right, and you behind me. And each one of you always took the same post. When the Murshid and Rab came together, they were on either side. And it seemed that Pir-O-Murshid stood on the left, nearest my heart. When the inspiration came from God, it came through my heart, but when Pir-O-Murshid was there, he seemed to be whispering in my left ear. His nearness to my heart brought love. You seemed to be behind or even in me, my very backbone, giving strength and courage. Hafiz was in my forehead, holding the mirror there that the light from within might be reflected without. And the Rab on the right side seemed to be guiding my hand, even using it himself.

Murshida, I have been shown by the Grace of God, as you can see and read, the possibility of being "a light unto the Gentiles and a glory unto thy people Israel." My words first seem like a baby trying to speak, and day by day the inspiration increased until suddenly I say "The Art of Creation." And if I have not gone more deeply into the Truth, it is because I myself have asked God to guide me slowly and make my steps sure.

Last night, it seemed as though Christ Himself were with me, giving me the instructions He gave to His disciples when sending them forth and repeating ever and anon, "Be wise as serpents and harmless as doves." So long as I remain true to God, I feel I can reflect His Light and help to spread the Message, to go to Los Angeles or anywhere. "The Lord is my shepherd, whom should I fear?" I am ready to teach the New Testament and explain much of the Old with God's help and under your direction.

I can see now the relation between Moses, Fabre D'Olivet, Murshid and the Tarot in regards to creation. *Bareshith bara Elohim hashamayim Vihaarets:* "In the First Principle God Created the Selfsameness of the Heavens and the Selfsameness of the Earth." And what is meant by *reshith* or "principle'? This is what Fabre D'Olivet calls "Providence" and Pir-O-Murshid "Love." And the "Heavens"—this is what F.D. calls "Will" and Pir-O-Murshid "Harmony." This is the action of vibrations, energy. And "Earth"? This is what F.D. calls "Destiny," but Pir-O-Murshid calls "Beauty." The principles correspond identically and can be proven scientifically.

And the more I have pondered, the more I found that the Prophet

Mohammed Himself was expressing the greatest principles of science in words: that God is Love and He is Beauty and so forth. I am beginning to see further into the great declarations of Judaism and Islam, to see behind the philosophy of Plato and Pythagoras in ways I could hardly dream of. When I first came here I placed Pir-O-Murshid's picture over Fabre D'Olivet's and said the Rab looked pleased. And that has seemed to be the key to all thereafter.

Not long after you left for your trip around the world, I broke the rosary and meditated without it. The night after I determined to go to Los Angeles and go into *purdah* (seclusion) beforehand, I looked and it was fixed. Many times I wanted to fix it, but could hardly bear to look at it. And whether it was fixed by my mother or an Unseen Hand, I care not. But it was a sign, and from that night until now I have been growing, growing in a way to give you comfort. I trust I have not failed, that I shall be pure in heart and remember God. Knowing the Law, how much greater my sin, if I obey not.

"Truth is now on earth." Truth has always been on earth despite deluders who say that it has been kept from man except at certain ages and in secret ways. "When the disciple is ready, the Master appears"; God has always looked after His children. The mysteries have never been lost and never will be lost, but their outward form may change. Today one joining the Church of Universal Service is really being initiated into the Lesser Mysteries.

My future—that is in God's hands. It is now four and one-half years since I began studying with you and five and one-half since we met. I have always wished to carry on the work of the Rab, and it may be so. I have also desired to continue the true American Philosophy of Emerson and Whitman—to serve the Jews and Americans first in humanity—then others. Now I leave all these things to God, yet feeling that if I keep my covenant with Him, my wishes will come true.

The gift of poetry is entirely from Him. I have never cared for poetry, but I feel more and more the spirit of the Sufis, and I almost can say, "with God's help and Hafiz" I may succeed.

You will note in my diary about my name. I feel I have realized my name: *Samuel—Shemuel:* "In the name of the Lord." Even "the word or the voice of the Lord." *Leonard:* "Leon" is a lion; "-ard" from *Arduus,* (Lat.), valiant. Valiant as a lion.

Initiation comes from the Latin and means "a beginning." Beginning of what? Beginning to live and express oneself. Everyday have I read much from the "Gayan" [of Hazrat Inayat Khan— ed. note] and step-by-step realized it. I feel I am ready to begin, Murshida. I feel I can say "God bless you" to others as you have said it to me.

My meditations have been like the cleaning of machinery at night so the factory will produce more during the day. I have needed little sleep. My brain has been as a servant, working at certain hours, not allowed to work at other times and often getting tired while working. Much of what I have written may hardly be legible, but the inspiration was so great at times, my hand flew and the writing may have suffered. I have not read my diary or articles over except to make two small changes in poems.

Needless to say, I shall enjoy Pesach (Passover) and Easter this year. I have lived Pesach and Easter. God has blessed me with the finest weather. From the moment I entered and the rain stopped, I felt Him in the air. If you read any of this or say anything to the mureeds (Khalifa excepted), tell them that the door is open. I have not had many visions or phenomena, but the greatest of phenomena has been the opening of the door of my heart, and I have felt like Walt Whitman, without a grain of conceit: "I am so full of good things. . . .I never knew I contained so much goodness." For I have found I contain God and all Goodness is in Him.

Soon I enter into my last meditation before the sun crosses the equator. I again thank you with all my heart and soul and mind for your benefits and blessing and to Him above be all honor and glory forever. Amen.

Faithfully and sincerely,
Your Mureed and disciple in Israel,
Samuel

[Editor's note: Thereafter followed the initiatory ceremony and experience described in "The 1925 Retreat," earlier in this section. Most of the diaries which Samuel Lewis refers to were destroyed by a fire in 1949. All the papers in this section were found in his "Scrapbook," including the next two, which are dated as immediately following the retreat when he moved to Los Angeles.]

The Hay Ride!

March 29, 1925

Come boys! Come girls! Let's go for a ride.
They're hitching on the horse, they're piling on the hay.
Soon the wagon will be filled and we'll be off.
Climb in now, and be careful and be sure you get way up on top.
Climb in now and select a nice, soft spot for yourself.
The fare will be nothing and all can ride who will.
Nestle in now and keep your "eyes front." We're off!
Off we go down the highway, isn't this fun?
There we strike a bump and bounce way up into the air.
There we strike another, but it doesn't hurt a bit,
For back we fall into the nice soft hay.
We can sing and laugh and play along this hayride,
We can look at the beautiful scenery along the roadside,
We can mock the passing travelers on foot and they can do naught
    to us,
We can halloo to all the passing traffic and yell and shout as we may.
Isn't this fun? Why the more bumps, the better time we have.

You think because I am sitting along the front seat, I'm the driver;
And though it may be I hold the reins a bit, I'm not the driver.
'Tis true I helped you on the wagon and hitched the horses,
But the reins I hold not, I tell you, the reins I hold not.
Could you but see the driver? What manner of man is He?
I can't describe the driver well, but use your imagination.

He has the beard of a prophet and the eye of a saint,
A smile from Him brings Peace and Joy to your heart,
His one glance bids to your troubles, "Flee, begone —
We would not have you here, get you hence."
Yet were it not for the driver, we could not enjoy this ride.

Come and sit with me by the side of the Driver.
Come and listen to His talk, His cheering words,
Come and listen to His message and His advice,
His anecdotes, His pleasant tales of His long past.
What a wonderful time we are having with the Driver!
Our destination is Los Angeles, the city of Angels,
The home of the Saints, the land of Happiness!
Let us drink our fill of Happiness while we may, boys and girls.
Listen to the words of the Driver and look ahead,
The bumps will hurt you not and you may ride through life,
Laughing and chattering on the road to Happiness!

Letter

March 31, 1925

My dear Aunt:

I have slept well these last two nights and am feeling pretty good, but last evening I almost broke down. I keep on learning so many bad, if not terrible things about my brother, that I can hardly understand where he could have gotten such wickedness into his system. While I was pondering on these things and listening to the radio, some club took charge of the program (KFI, Los Angeles) and began putting on sentimental songs about "mother." That was just about the last thing to put pep in me, so I had to go to my room.

Well, I have learned one lesson, and that is: if I feel very good or very bad, try to write poetry. I tried, and although I did not succeed very well, got the following in blank verse:

A PRAYER FOR MY FATHER!

God give him strength to fight, though hard the fray.
God give him the courage to bear the battle's blows;
Guide him in these hours of darkness and despair;
Show him the light, and Lord, please lift the veil
That he may see a step or two ahead.
O Lord, I pray Thee lighten his burdens a little,
A little that, though stormy be the way,
Though terrors seem to encompass him about,
Disperse the clouds, and let a ray of sunshine
Pierce the gloom. O God, may the end be now in sight,
An end to these torments and these tortures;
Though time be needed, let the time approach
When he may have peace and rest, though years pass by
Before he leaves his mortal frame and enters
Into a world where sorrows abide not.
O God, give me strength to aid my father.
May my next years bring happiness to his heart,
Make me a source of pride and joy to him,
And may the future show the way
That he may see in me a son of his,
And I see and treat him as my father.
O God, give him hope, and may Thy Mercy
And Thy Grace rest upon him even as I write.
May he have that faith which leads to Peace,
That faith in Thee, remover of all pain
And sorrow, Source of all that's good.
O God, help my father, I repeat again,
Give him strength and courage, from this day forth. Amen

This may not be good poetry, but I always put down what comes.
Sometimes I have had very good inspirations, and at other times, not
very good. Prayers, so far, have come in the same rhythm as this.

I shall be in town Sunday to attend the final symphony concert. I presume Hertz will play in the Hollywood Bowl this summer, and if so, I expect to attend regularly.

We had quite a rain up here, but this morning it is very nice.

Well Auntie, I must to work. I trust you are feeling better now, but it certainly is a Hell we are going through.

With love, I remain,

Your nephew,
Samuel

Surviving building of the former Sufi Khankah in Fairfax.

CHAPTER NINE

Excerpt from Papers:

Six Interviews with Hazrat Inayat Khan

[Editor's note: As Samuel Lewis mentions, the initial reports of his six meetings with Hazrat Inayat Khan in 1926 were either lost in a fire in 1949 or discarded by functionaries of the Sufi Movement in Europe who took over the organization after Hazrat Inayat Khan's passing. Between 1967 and 1971, he compiled several different drafts of these meetings, expanding upon different topics in the history of Western Sufism. The following is mostly taken from the earliest available manuscript, with additional explanations from later drafts.]

772 Clementina St.
San Francisco 3, Calif.
26th March 1967

Beloved Ones of God:

It is fitting on this Christian Day of Resurrection to start a record—a rather poor one after 40 years—of "Six Conversations with Inayat Khan." These meetings were never sought by the writer, and the very fact that they were requested by the Pir-O-Murshid earned for the writer the ill-will of the then-secretary, a pattern which has been repeated many times. Recently, a Vietnamese Buddhist master, coming to this city, sought this person before all others. One awoke this morning with the appearance of Lord Isa (Jesus) who said, *"This is Very Significant."* So feeling the blessings of heaven, one will proceed realizing all the way—without humility—that time and age have dimmed the records.

One does not remember any longer the exact six meetings in order. One's records were destroyed in a fire in 1949 immediately after some of these records were forcibly seized by a person pretending to be a Sufi, having a following who call themselves "Sufis," but who do not attempt to practice *La Illaha El Il Allah* (There is no Reality but God, the Only Being).

I.

The meetings were held in the Beverly Hills Hotel in the year 1926. The first one was the most significant to the reporter. In the year 1925, one had come to the end of one's tether and had gone into the wilderness to die, he thought. Instead, he was completely resurrected and learned, for the first time, the Principle of Death and Resurrection, of which this Day is significant. Briefly, there were encounters with Khwaja Khizr at the beginning, and with the Mursaleen (Chain of Prophets) at the end with Lord Mohammed appearing in double capacity, the other Messengers singly, and one was vested with a special Robe.

The whole history of the first *khilvat* (spiritual retreat) of the writer was told to Pir-O-Murshid. All records are gone. Three times was it submitted to various descendants of Hazrat Inayat Khan in Europe and discarded. The failure of the Message of God in Europe, and to some extent in America, has been due to too much "Message" and no God, and in the end to personality emphasis. Pir-O-Murshid said, "Heart speaks to heart and soul to soul." This is for those whose ears and inner beings are opening—or opened.

Pir-O-Murshid listened and told me to write. But in the next meeting, something happened, and it will stand as a testimonial, an unfortunate testimonial against those who worship the Teacher and discard the Teaching, a habit which is universal and only brings misfortune. La Illaha El Il Allah.

II.

As I entered the room for the second interview, Pir-O-Murshid stood up and motioned to me, took my hands in the spiritual manner and said, "I initiate you for the sixth time in the Sufi Order." Later when I looked up Hazrat Inayat Khan's early records, I found he had initiated me as "Sufi." One dare not take that appellation, and it was only years later, receiving such initiation openly from Pir-O-Murshid Sufi Barkat Ali that one could use it. This appellation was also confirmed by Pir Dewal Shereef, President of the Board of Directors, Islamabad University. It has been accepted in Asia by many Pirs, many schools.

Practically everything of this second interview, and much of the later interviews, was rejected by presumably "good" people, and this substantiated what Hazrat Inayat Khan said to me at the time as well as what actually happened later.

I was at the time a rather frightened young man but had another "veil-lifting experience" (in the home of Roderick White on Garden Street in Santa Barbara) which indicated potential—or more than potential, assurance—of the spiritual advancement of this person. What followed during this interview so shocked everyone when I later told them that its contents and those of the following interviews were rejected, excepting by Mr. Paul Reps who was stationed outside the door during all but the last interview, when he was inside.

Before we sat down, Inayat Khan said to me, "Samuel, I am going to ask you a favor. I want to speak to you as man to man. I am not Murshid; you are not mureed. We are just men. If we cannot act as men, it will not help me. Can you act to me as man to man? If so, let us shake hands and then we can sit down and talk as man to man."

We did so and sat down. "How many loyal mureeds do you think I have?" he asked.

"Oh, I guess about 100."

"I wish I had 100. But how many do you think, at the least, loyal mureeds I have?"

45

"Well," I said, "I don't believe it, but just to give an answer, I would say 20."

"I wish I had 20! I wish I had 10!" Then he arose in full majesty and yelled at me out loud, "I wish I had 10!" Then he lifted his right hand, and using the index finger of his left hand, pointed to the middle of it and yelled, "I wish I had 5 loyal mureeds. Samuel, can you believe it, I have not as many loyal mureeds as I have fingers on one hand."

By that time, the chair in which I had been sitting toppled over like in a Hollywood movie, and I was sitting on the floor, totally amazed. But, by this action and by his loud speech, I received the full magnetism of his baraka or blessing, and I believe I still have it.

He then told me the story of his search for one honest man whom he could trust. It was only after years that he found one Mr. E. DeCruzat Zanetti to whom, he said, he gave all trust, no compromise. He told me, and repeated later in the course of further interviews, that in case of any difficulty I should write to him.

This was never believed. Neither the disciples of the East (Europe) or the West (America) accepted it. Then he began telling me some things which were also told to Pir-O-Murshid Hasan Nizami on his (Hazrat Inayat Khan's) deathbed. These fall into two classes, the first on succession, the second on the Sufi Order.

He began telling me that he wished me to defend Murshida Martin of San Francisco, who had been my original teacher (1919–1923) and in another vein after that. I was to stand by her and protect her, but see to it that she never defended herself. He went over that again and again. He said he expected trouble, and that I was to write to Mr. Zanetti in Geneva about what he told me.

Murshida Martin was then under attack by several people. She had had the *fana-fi-rassul* with Mohammed soon after she met Hazrat Inayat Khan. She had had a long training in European Occultism and in Comparative Religion. But during the years I knew her, although she was a Murshida, I know of only one or two experiences on her part in *fana-fi-rassul* and one in *fana-fi-lillah*. This was much more than others experienced. (I was not initiated into *fana-fi-sheikh*

46

until 1930 when Hazrat Inayat began to appear to me "from the other side.")

I was told, over and over again:

A. Pir-O-Murshid Inayat Khan intended that Murshida Martin be his successor.

B. She was never to defend herself on any occasion and positively never in public.

C. She was to divest herself of all right to handle funds.

This was the history. The aftermath was terrible.

The first thing that happened after the death of Hazrat Inayat Khan was my removal from the Board of Trustees which handled the funds. Never after that until the disassembling of the *khankah* (in Fairfax) which Pir-O-Murshid blessed was I ever permitted to say a word about finances.

The funds were handled by a Board of Mureeds with the Murshida, but with the advice and consent of her family, and never was any undertaking done without the family. When this person refused to countenance private deals in which her family benefited, he was never forgiven, ever.

It must have been this spirit which was felt in Europe, where the vast majority of disciples refused to accept Murshida Martin as successor to Pir-O-Murshid Inayat Khan. But they surely felt the *nafs* [ego — ed.]. It is to one's great regret that Murshida Martin always insisted on defending her nafs in public, and this led to her downfall.

True, when she visited Pir-O-Murshid Hasan Nizami in New Delhi, he proclaimed her as successor to Hazrat Inayat Khan. There were deliberations and newspaper notices, and she was accepted — or at least respected — in the undivided India. But none of this had the slightest effect in Europe.

Still, if we have to see life from the standpoint of another as well as of ourselves, the outlook is that there is nothing that can be called exactly right or exactly wrong.

Later on in life — much later than the above events — when an outsider came along and insisted that Rabia give up public self-defense and control over funds, she did so without a whimper. She could not do that at the dying request of her own Pir-O-Murshid, but for an outsider she did that. Her death was a tragedy.

III.

This had to do with the papers for the disciples. There were several rules and constitutions in the short career of Pir-O-Murshid Hazrat Inayat Khan. At that time, he had papers called "Gathekas" for non-mureeds (some of them later published in *The Unity of Religious Ideals*), "Gathas" for the first three years and "Githas" for the next three years. He gave me some instructions about them. There were further instructions at other meetings.

The Sufi Movement had been envisioned as covering twelve grades, but the last degrees were for teachers only. Only if there was a "full graduation," the person became either a Khalif or its equivalent, but that was outside the immediate instructions.

Pir-O-Murshid told me how he wanted these things handled. He made me *esoteric* but not *exoteric* leader in Los Angeles. That is to say, my authority was limited to the teaching of disciples, the training of applicants and their first *bayat* (initiation). There was little in this meeting which did not extend to others elsewhere.

IV.

The Sufi Movement was to be divided into three sections, and this also appears in the literature called "The Sufi Message." There was to be: a) the *Sufi Order*—for mureeds and spiritual instruction, which was the heart and soul, and without which there can be no Sufism whatever; b) the *Universal Worship*—a ritual including scriptures of all faiths, which was connected with the Universel temple and which became organically active but socially ineffective; c) the Brotherhood, which was to be the intellectual side of the teaching to bridge the gap between mysticism and universal culture.

48

According to the teachings of Sufi mysticism—and this has nothing to do with anything from India—there are developments in the sciences of Breath which enable the adept to see into the future, to ascertain the purposes of life, and which can be used by an enlightened teacher to direct the progress of disciples toward the accomplishment of those purposes for which he was born. Hazrat Inayat Khan felt—and no doubt he was right—that this person was essentially an intellectual, and he directed him toward the integration of the mystical and the intellectual.

He went into exact details and told me to work with Miss Sakina Furnee in Suresnes, France, but if anything happened to her, I was to take over the Brotherhood work. She did retire on Pir-O-Murshid's death. This appointment was never recognized in Europe and has been de-emphasized in America.

It is very difficult, although times are changing, to present in the Western world a picture based on mystical attainment which transcends all religious separatism. Still one has gone on trying to bridge the gap between mysticism and general culture, and the last few weeks show, that if one persists for forty years, he will surely succeed. But this success comes when there is no practical, working Sufi Movement.

Now one has reached a complexity, because the young—to whom one was not originally sent—accept his spiritual prowess; and at the same time there is increasing acceptance of this person all over the world as one bridging the gap between the intellectual and mystical worlds. If Sufi Ahmed Murad Chisti has any rights as "Khalif" or "Murshid," these came from Pirs outside the Sufi Order of Hazrat Inayat Khan.

One would prefer to work in and with one of the various constitutions laid down by Hazrat Inayat Khan. Long after he had left the world, he asked that the disciples, particularly in Europe, either restore the constitutions—any one of them—that he had given, or have a visible constitution which could be seen by others. Instead there have been nothing but unsubstantiated ego-claims, as if there was no Universal God.

It is notable after all these years that what Pir-O-Murshid gave instructions in is coming to pass. Pir-O-Murshid said, "Neither can I be broken nor God, but the one who would break me, he is broken."

Shortly after the death of Hazrat Inayat Khan in 1927, the writer encountered the late Ali Khuli Khan of the Bahai Movement and asked him what would be the difference between seven hundred conflicting religious sects and seven hundred conflicting universal brotherhoods. The question was not answered, and today we see the rise of an ever-larger number of verbal universal brotherhoods, mutually exclusive.

But Hazrat Inayat Khan, contrary to both his legal successors and to disciples, proclaimed that universal brotherhood would form of itself. And he also told his quondam disciple Mr. Paul Reps that there were far more people who were not his disciples who were closer to the Message of God than the so-called "Sufis." The well-known Paul Reps, who will again be mentioned, will probably confirm this and especially confirm that the New Age young people are going to bring real brotherhood; none of the legal entities, either the Sufi Movement or other entities, can ever bring universal brotherhood.

V.

This had to do with the science of commentaries. Originally, this had been part of the general teachings. There was an Esoteric Constitution (there were several) which distinctly called for commentaries. Each person to become Khalif was supposed to write a commentary on the "Gathas," the first three years instructions, and each Murshid on the "Githas," the next three years instructions. While this was explicit in the Esoteric Constitution, years later when I saw a copy the section had been removed.

[from 1970 draft:] One read later in records which have since been suppressed, that the Gathas and esoteric papers belonged to and belong to the Sufi Order and not the Sufi Movement. The Sufi Movement was organized to facilitate the outer workings for the Sufi

Order, a matter which has been investigated further by Pir Vilayat Khan, who received full recognition from the Chisti Order in India. This validates any claim he may make, regardless of the actions and attitudes of any legal entity calling or mis-calling itself "Sufi" or anything else.

The descent of *baraka* [blessing] and similar operations (which are found in the mystical processes of perhaps all faiths) continue to go on. God, so to speak, does not consult any legal group as to whom He may bless or manifest to. There is no *bayat* to any legal entity. There may be a *bayat* to a representative of the Sufi Order—Sufi Order not Sufi Movement—or to Teachers of the seen or unseen, who do not consult with legal entities as to who is worthy or unworthy. (End of section of 1970 draft.)

VI.

Pir-O-Murshid asked me to study all his constitutions, all his records and submit findings to Mr. Zanetti in Geneva. This was not an easy task. The records were scattered. Murshida Martin had a "Book for Murshids" which she put away for safety, and at her death nobody was able to find it. But at her death, one found a lot of scattered miscellany in strange places. These covered the complete *ryazat* (spiritual practice) of Hazrat Inayat Khan.

This last was the most important of all the meetings. Pir-O-Murshid went over everything with patience. I have since found several attempts on his part for a constitution. One was based on prowess in *zikar*, never completed. Another on advancement in *hal* (mystical state) and *makam* (station). Another on different bases. Many of the principles are found in Volume X of *The Sufi Message*, now published. For practical purposes this volume includes everything needed for a Sufi School in any and all parts of the world.

However, there are now many efforts on the part of those who have some prowess in *hal* and *makam* to come together, realizing the unity of all Knowledge, the passing of the importance of national boundaries, and the coming of a movement toward the Brotherhood of Man.

This has been written rather hurriedly in face of a number of dramas and climaxes surrounding the writer and it is hoped that at some leisure time, or in *khilvat* if possible, one can submit a more sober report. At this writing, Pir Zade Vilayat Khan seems to have assented to his father's wishes about this person being a leader in "Exoteric Sufism."

There are many means by which problems can be solved. The tragedy is a school of Sufis discarding one after another the esoteric sciences which could be used to settle problems, and resorting to ego-reasons, or rather just ego, then justified, instead of to Allah.

The rise of a new generation, not to say culture, that wishes Divine Experience directly and not personalities and personalisms means, inshallah, that the Truth *(Hikmat)* will manifest despite all the arguments, unsubstantiated statements and claims of all persons. This includes those of the writer himself, who is not without faults. But in a law court, an eye-witness is permitted the box, not on his private merits or demerits but on whether he has been witness to events causing litigation.

Around 1946, the writer entered into *fana-fi-rassul.* Although this came from Mohammed, the Khatimal Mursaleen [Seal of the Chain-of-Prophets], it was followed almost immediately by a similar experience with Jesus (Isa). And on this day, it was the appearance of Lord Jesus which has prompted the report at this time.

With all love and blessings to whomsoever reads this and to whomsoever has access thereunto.

Faithfully,

Sufi Ahmed Murad Chisti
Samuel L. Lewis

CHAPTER TEN

Early Paper:

Baraka (Blessing)— Direct Experience at the Rock Pir Dahan

IN THE SPRING OF 1926 SUFI INAYAT KHAN VISITED THE PROPER—ties at Fairfax, California, and named a certain rock *Pir Dahan* (the Voice of the Prophet), and the house of meditation *Kaaba Allah* (this house is no longer in existence). I was in Los Angeles at the time, but the man who brought Inayat Khan to Fairfax is the same Saladin Paul Reps who has recently visited Hasan Nizami in India.

The psychic and mystical events and the baraka [magnetism of grace—ed. note] experienced by myself (and a few others) in the building of Kaaba Allah, would resemble a fairy tale. I did find some parallels in Efleki's *Lives of the Adepts* and in Palladius' *Lives of the Solitaries*, which I shall refer to in another paper.

1. *Elsie Norwood*, now living 65 Ramsdell St., San Francisco. Shortly after the demise of Sufi Inayat Khan in 1927, Mrs. Norwood, who has been a clairvoyant and disciple in both Sufism and Vedanta, claims she saw on the rock Pir Dahan, all the great prophets of all ages greeting Sufi Inayat Khan, and the Buddha was the greatest in maintenance of the pure spiritual state. She had this vision steadily over a long period.

A. I wrote this experience in poetic form and presented it to the Rev. Ishida, Zen monk and tea-master, who was then a guest of Nyogen Senzaki, the Zen Master in San Francisco, and he was so pleased he gave me a tea-ceremony in honor thereof [see paper "Dharma Transmission" later in this book—ed. note].

B. Several years later, when I was in difficulty and went to see Mrs. Norwood, there was with her a clairvoyant from Stockton, California. This lady asked me to come the next day, at noon, when she looked at the rock and told me what she said was my spiritual future. The chief difference was that she saw Jesus Christ as the leader, as against Buddha in Mrs. Norwood's report.

2. *Nyogen Senzaki*, Zen monk and, to me, Master; friend of Watts and Spiegelberg. A friend of many year's standing. Visited Fairfax one year to commemorate Sufi Inayat Khan's passing, went to the rock and immediately entered samadhi. He reported it had the highest vibration of any place he had known in America.

3. *Sabin Orgler*, Jewish mystic, visited the rock in 1932. Same general experience as Mrs. Norwood and the psychic, except that he saw Moses in place of Buddha and Christ, as above. All saw "angels ascending and descending."

4. *Vera Zahn*, 11 Hilliritas St., San Francisco. Disciple in Sufism with some psychic faculties. Always felt the vibrations and had various experiences there.

5. *Theodore Reindollar*, long resident of Marin County. Visited Tlemcen during the war as my representative. Returned to Fairfax in 1947 and claims rock is in full possession of baraka. A disciple of Sidi Adah in Tlemcen, where he has been staying.

6. *Samuel L. Lewis*. Some of my reports in writing and poetry, some very exact prophecies (some not so much). In September 1940, one night at 10:30, went to rock to offer prayer and sacrifice (of sleep, etc.) to pray for the safeguarding of the city of London. Placed myself before the tabernacle, which had been built at my direction to "house" the baraka ("shekinah" theory). Heard a voice from Heaven: "Go back, go to sleep and forget everything. If you can absolutely relax and sleep London will be saved. London is saved." That week the Germans suffered their first terrific losses in bombing flights.

—Samuel L. Lewis

CHAPTER ELEVEN

Excerpt from Scholarly Paper:

Experience of Fana (Effacement)

THERE IS ALWAYS A QUESTION IN SUFISM AS TO HOW FAR THE individual performs and how far he is subject to Grace. The theory, as appears in *Kashf al-Mahjub* of Al Hujwiri and other books is that one's station (*makam*) is the result of one's effort, but one's state (*hal*) is the result of Divine Grace.

Fana-fi-Sheikh: In February 1930, I went into seclusion to commemorate the third anniversary of Hazrat Inayat Khan's passing; he appeared to me in quite physical form and began communicating in what we might call a telepathic fashion. In 1926, when I had called on Hazrat Inayat Khan at the Beverly Hills Hotel to report on the 1925 retreat, he sent for me constantly, and there were six interviews. One of these concerned the science of commentary. Indeed, just before his death in February 1927, he sent a letter of praise and approval for the first efforts. But after he appeared in 1930, it seems that the major portion of these commentaries were nothing but direct mental transmissions from the teacher.

From that point on until 1945, one felt an increasing awareness of the Pir. This did not often produce any emotional effects, which are quite common. The records were in two forms: the commentaries and the diaries. Most of the diaries were destroyed in a fire on the night of December 31, 1949. These included a tremendous amount of auguries, which the public would call "prophecies." Some of these foretellings were prophetic and these were in a book which was saved from the fire. They make Nostradamus and Blake look like amateurs, but they are nothing, absolutely nothing compared to the sayings of the great Saints, Christian and Islamic.

Fana-fi-Rassul: There is a tradition that the Prophet Mohammed had lost a certain tooth. And there is one school of Sufis in North Africa where the initiation ceremony consists of knocking out that tooth.

I was living in semi-seclusion in the woods of South Carolina in 1946, and every day Hazrat Inayat Khan would appear. One day while brushing my teeth, a tooth fell out, the very one missing in the Prophet's mouth. Hazrat Inayat Khan appeared and laughed and laughed. The next day Rassul Mohammed appeared. During the following period, both Jesus Christ and Mohammed appeared intermittently. I have "seen" Jesus in so many guises. True or false, he has never appeared to me looking like Galahad, but in human form exactly as Khalil Gibran pictured him. But seldom has he appeared in human form and the last times as the Spirit of Guidance.

Once one has contacted the Messengers of God, one will never confuse them. They are at the same time both the incarnation or humanization of the Spirit of the Universe, yet different from each other. Therefore the Arabs (or Mohammed) have given them special names. And before the Christians object to this, Jesus is known as *Ruh-i-Allah,* or "The Spirit of God."

In my own particular life, the expressions have come out in poetry, and occasionally in music and dance. But if one gives Buddha any name it is "The Voice of the Silence." A great elevation is often accompanied by a great rejection. For after the appearance of these Messengers came "the Dark Night of the Soul." During this period, Swami Ramdas appeared to me at work and predicted he would see me in 52 weeks. When I told people who had known him, I received the usual derision, but in exactly 52 weeks he came.

CHAPTER TWELVE

Editor's Note:

The Early Days of Sufism in America

As the reader will have noted, the period of time following the passing of Hazrat Inayat Khan in 1927 was fraught with confusion and dissension for the various Sufis who claimed to continue his work. Most of the controversy revolved around who the "successor" was (or would be) and how would the "organization" be run. These two issues — successorship and organization — seem to have plagued most of the known Sufi orders around the world during the 1200-1300 years that the eternal wisdom has been known as "Sufism."

In the case of Hazrat Inayat Khan, many people witnessed him blessing his son Vilayat as his successor. At the time of his passing however, Vilayat was only a boy. The issue then became, who was to take over "in the meantime." The late Bryn Beorse (Shamcher), one of Hazrat Inayat Khan's early disciples and a friend of Samuel Lewis, believed that if Hazrat Inayat Khan did appoint Rabia Martin as his successor, it was only in a caretaker capacity. However, the European disciples had their own ideas and also did not get along with Rabia Martin, Shamcher said. The above is a simplification. The entire history is as tortuous and complex as one would expect an intra-family dispute to be.

One of the essences of Sufism is that, as Samuel Lewis was fond of quoting, it is based on "experiences, not premises." Which seeds grow into plants from the many sown can only be known by time (or the "proof of the pudding . . ." in other terms). The proof, in this case, came much later and sprouted for the world to see in the work of Murshid Samuel Lewis and Pir Vilayat Inayat Khan in the late 1960's.

Two people who have provided some additional perspectives on this early period of Sufism in the West are the above-mentioned Bryn Beorse and Paul Reps (co-author with Nyogen Senzaki of Zen Flesh, Zen Bones), *another early disciple of Hazrat Inayat Khan. Reps provided the following understanding:*

Inayat Khan was the most remarkable man I ever met. It was as if one's soul were speaking all the time. When we would ask him something, he would say "Call me Inayat," because he was completely humble and completely at peace, relaxed and concentrated at the same time. His eyes looked right through your forehead all the time when he talked to you. And yet, he was completely at ease and said nothing for himself; he was always letting you do the talking and drawing you out. But he was certainly practicing what we might now call "Sufism," the mind on the breath or however you want to interpret it.

This presence, with this great gentility and kinglike bearing simply overcame those who had never seen anything like it. They were very much impressed and extremely touched by his sympathy for them and felt, "Here, at last, is the one person who understands me thoroughly." And feeling that way, with such love, they began to feel, "Now I am really right." And the contact and the message dug so deep into their system that they felt, "I am really right, but all the other people may be wrong." And so all of these various appointees and representatives of Sufism in different countries began to have that kind of feeling. They began to get at odds with each other. . . .

Inayat Khan felt very deeply, "I must put God first. I must turn to the Only Being, because these Westerners are not doing this and this is what they need." That's what he expressed and this is what is called his "Message." But his Message was his Being, the way he felt about it. It might have been the greatest Message ever; it might have been the Message for the times. It was certainly a most beautiful expression which then people began, strangely enough, to quarrel over. . . . Unlike other teachers, the teaching was humble instead of assertive. However, he had all of these initiates which he gave various ranks to, and they fought so much that, upon leaving for India, he said that if he came back again to the Western world, he wouldn't have anything to do with these ranks. You see, because it was misused. . . .

I think he realized his life was short. I asked him once, "Murshid, why do you organize?" He said, "To reach more people." He was searching for ways to reach people. Now we have a guru on every street corner, but it's easy for them to reach people because people — young people — will come to them. . . .

Shamcher Bryn Beorse gave another version in an interview before he died in 1979:

In Suresnes after Inayat's passing, four of his former disciples came and said that 'I' was appointed leader, because Inayat had spoken to them in such terms and said, "You are a great sovereign, you will do so and so. . . ." And so they expanded on that in their own consciousness to the fact that they were the one leader. And of course all of them were equally wrong. The idea that one person is the successor, or personifies a teacher is always wrong. No spiritual teacher ever had a successor, or can have one. When a disciple feels he is fulfilling the mission given to him by his teacher, then he feels a successor. In that sense, every teacher has had successors, plural. Some of these successors may be, from the eternal point of view, even greater than the teacher, who knows? But they are not the same as the teacher; they don't represent him in all spheres and in all senses. But if anyone claims to be the One Successor, then he repudiates a great number of disciples, perhaps in some cases everybody but himself. . . .

Sam is a genuine mystic, as good as they come and as good as they have ever come. Personally I see no difference, at least not a lot, between for instance, Hidayat (Pir-O-Murshid Inayat Khan's youngest son) or Jesus Christ or Sam or Inayat Khan or Vilayat Khan, when it comes to spirituality — and some of you people. Some people get onto the stage as the Great Messenger, but a lot

59

of people are just as great messengers without being on the stage as that. The aim of the Sufi, of course, is to see that greatness in every man, and the relative greatness of the dogs and the cats and the cattle and the elephants. The same with the Sufis abroad. Sam seems to have fallen in with them and to be a reborn great Sufi. I walk around and see some great and some I think are not so great. Then something comes up in my mind quickly about their difficulties and their problems and I go away half smiling and half weeping.

Receiving citation for unknown work done for U.S. Army Intelligence in World War II.

III. JOURNEY INTO BUDDHISM

Nyogen Senzaki

CHAPTER THIRTEEN

Editor's Note:

He-Kwang's Zen

Samuel Lewis pursued a simultaneous study of Sufism and Zen from 1919 until his death in 1971. The first three chapters in the section are taken from his book The Lotus and the Universe, *which he began in 1963 to counter Arthur Koestler's* The Lotus and the Robot. *At the time, there had been few published books on Buddhism or Zen in the West by anyone who had actually undergone the Zen disciplines. This situation has happily changed over the past 20 years.*

At the time, however, Samuel Lewis felt that he had to, in the strongest terms, counterpose his own experiences against Koestler's opinions, which included the following:

"Taken at face value and considered in itself, Zen is at best an existential hoax, at worst a web of solemn absurdities. But within the framework of Japanese society, this cult of the absurd, of ritual leg-pulls and nose tweaks, made beautiful sense. It was, and to a limited extent still is, a form of psychotherapy for a self-conscious, shame-ridden society, a technique of undoing the strings that tied it into knots. . . .

"Mankind is facing its most deadly predicament since it climbed down from the trees; but one is reluctantly brought to the conclusion that neither Yoga, Zen nor any other Asian form of mysticism hcs any significant advice to offer" (from The Lotus and the Robot, *Arthur Koestler).*

The last chapter in this section, "Dharma Transmission" was started in 1966. Here in a very different style, Samuel Lewis — the Reverend He Kwang — as much shows his Zen as talks about its history in America.

CHAPTER FOURTEEN

Book Excerpt:

In Search of Satori
(from *The Lotus and the Universe*)

Zen for the West by Professor Sohaku Ogata.

WE BEGIN HERE WITH A REFERENCE TO A BOOK, NOT WITH A quotation. A quotation may seldom help us to attain *satori*, that is to say, enlightenment or samadhi. A book may not be of much use either, but if we must have books, this is an excellent one.

An earlier generation was much concerned with the privilege of defaming a certain religion or race, and not even the last World War has removed from the face of the earth the assumed liberty of defaming. (Only, at this writing, we are defaming peoples other than the Jews and religions other than that of the synagogue.) To the writer, all defamation of peoples, races and religions is morally wrong and will bring both social and personal retribution.

The following incident is true. A gentleman built a beautiful garden in Santa Barbara. It attracted much attention and many people (including the writer) came long distances to see it. It was called a Japanese garden, or occasionally (whenever the late Mr. Hearst had an outburst) an Oriental garden. A Japanese ambassador who came to Los Angeles decided to visit the place. The owner proudly conducted him around.

"What do you think about it?" he asked.

"Wonderful, wonderful," replied the ambassador, "We have nothing like this in Japan."

This well applies to much of the material paraded as 'Zen' before the American public in books, lecture courses and even in some university studies.

Among the minor speakers at the Columbia World Exposition in Chicago in 1893 was Master Shaku Soyen. He gave the first presentation of Zen Buddhism to America, and for a long time Zen meant nothing but meditation and meditation-practices, not lectures, not doctrines of any kind.

Shaku Soyen received a cordial welcome in San Franciscc and was invited to return in 1906. At that time he brought with him two monks of his Rinzai School—Daisetz Suzuki and Nyogen Senzaki. Both of them were linguists and scholars, though the former became famous therefor and the latter hid his light under bushels.

The Rinzai (Chinese Lin-chi) School was brought to Kamakura centuries ago by Master Eisai (also famous for his contributions to Tea Ceremony and art). It is a school of rigor which especially appealed to the nobility and samurai, the warrior caste. It still flourishes, though far outnumbered in membership and strength by the Soto School, which is more democratic and milder (or more compassionate). But both are meditation schools; both speak about Dharma and Buddhism, and meditation is the means, not necessarily the end.

Shaku Soyen published his now little-known *Sermons cf a Buddhist Abbot* [recently republished by Samuel Weiser, Inc.—ed.]. If he had only had the "foresight" to have used the word—nay the magic word—Zen in the title, it might now be a best seller. Instead, it is not even on the required reading lists of many institutions purporting to give instructions in Buddhism or Zen.

Another early influence toward imparting Zen to the West was the famous lady writer L. Adams Beck (Elizabeth Barrington). Although her later books were devoted to Buddhism and Zen, her outlook always seems to have been cosmic and beyond sectarianism. It was she who first arranged to bring the Reverend M. T. Kirby (Sogaku Shaku) to America to give the first public lectures on Zen after those of his Master (or Roshi) Shaku Soyen.

Kirby was a monk by nature and psychologists could no doubt have a field day studying him. He was a scion of a fairly prosperous English family, but from early youth was inclined toward monkery. He joined a Roman Catholic order, but it proved too "worldly" for him (so he said). He thereafter went to Japan, with the example of Lafcadio Hearn before him, became converted and studied under the great Master.

Like most Westerners and like nearly all university graduates, he had a terrible time trying to control his ego and his mind. Scholars either do not understand that the mind can be in a state of rest or they do not want it. It is like wishing to have your cake and eat it, too.

Monks in Zendos have been divided into (A) "Rice-bags," who have come to escape the turmoil of life and have a place to stay; (B) "Sutra-reciters," whose delight is in the intellect, and (C) those with a real insight into Dharma.

Kirby had already gone through the "rice-bag" stage, but controlling his mind was almost too much. Some Rinzai monks *seem* to be tinged with sadism. That is on the outside, for the Rinzai students recite the Four Vows of the Bodhisattva, and there is no absolute differentiation between oneself and another. The Teacher really takes it upon himself to see that all devotees advance in the Dharma, and it is no child's game. Only when the pupil succeeds may the teacher rest. So processes of discipline are taken very seriously.

Kirby had been raised in comfort. Suffering and tribulation were hardly known to him. He was trying to rise above difficulties he had never had to face. How could he go through the Buddha-experience if pain, poverty and disease were so foreign?

But instead of finding peace in the Zendo, our brother was finding everything else. The Master seemed to have become more and more impatient, more and more angry, more and more apt to administer "thirty blows"—actually.

After one severe thrashing, Kirby could stand it no more. He fled down the hill, threw his arms around a tree and sobbed in utter despair. In that instant, *it happened*—the satori experience, the reality.

I was a very young man when Kirby told me his story. In those days, we in California pictured Tibet as the land of the Masters and the Himalayas as particularly holy. There was no distinction between magic and wonder-working and spiritual development. If you could perform phenomena, you must be especially advanced, it was thought.

At the same time, the Japanese had come here and introduced their Pure Land Buddhism. It was nothing like the folk-mythology concerning Tibet; it did not even resemble the early teachings which were originally recorded in the Pali language. So Kirby had to face an enormous task. But he was so successful that after a while he received a promotion and went to the Hawaiian Islands. He planted at least the seeds of the Dharma there, and there has been a continuum of instruction in English.

Kirby could speak Japanese. At the time, Japan and Great Britain were allied. There were open conversations in his presence, and he warned me and others over and over again that the Japanese intended to occupy the Islands some day. Who believed him?

Buddhism teaches peace, Buddha teaches joy; the selfless religion opens only to a universal outlook, and here was the Reverend M. T. Kirby involved in Japanese imperialistic politics. He could not give up the Dharma with which he was thoroughly imbued. So he left first Hawaii and then Japan and went to Ceylon where he became a Theravadin monk and may best be known as the teacher of Dr. Malalasekera.

On December 8, 1941, after Pearl Harbor, the British Secret Service took Kirby into protective custody. I vowed then and there that whenever anybody told me that my country, the United States, was in danger, I would go to the authorities. My friends, this leads to no satisfaction. The story of M. T. Kirby was repeated in part in the life of Nicol Smith (author of *Burma Road*) and Robert Clifton (Phra Sumangalo) and others. Before one can inform or warn his country, he should remember the old Greek story about the boy who cried "Wolf!" This has been the attitude toward Americans who have had unusual entrees into exotic societies (unless, of course, they be news-papermen—then we believe anything!)

Kirby left two heritages, which might be called Theravada and Zen Buddhism. Theravada teachings flourish in Southeast Asia and rely on Pali texts. Sometime after Kirby left San Francisco, one Dr. Thompson arrived bringing the whole *Tripitaka*, the canon of Southern or "Hinayana" Buddhism. He also introduced the Siamese cat. The scriptures have to date been put safely away, and there has been little serious study of the historical Buddha in our country, unless it be in universities. The Siamese cat has made Dr. Thompson famous forever.

Kirby introduced me to Beatrice Lane, who later became Mrs. Daisetz Suzuki. This brought me into contact with that marvelous literature of Mahayana which takes one years to scan, many more to study. I believe that she, more than anyone else, inspired her husband in the work which has occupied much of his life.

The next introduction was Dr. Kenneth Saunders. He started out as a Christian missionary and became a deep student of Buddhist and other Oriental art. He gave grand lectures on Angkor and Borubodur, and it was from him I learned about the "Lotus Gospel." He wrote at some length, my dear Koestler, on the Lotus in art, religion and symbology.

I first met the late Nyogen Senzaki early in 1920. Like Dr. Kirby, he had been a student-disciple of that wonderful Shaku Soyen. He occasionally attended meetings at the Hongwanji Temple on Pine Street where Kirby officiated. When that monk departed, he urged me to become friendly with his brother, a friendship which continued until the latter's death in 1957.

At that time, Senzaki-san had two quite different careers. He served as cook and valet and did any work, no matter how menial, to maintain his livelihood. On the other hand, he was a respected linguist and translator, well-versed in languages and literature, and a specialist on the German poet-philosopher Goethe. As a servant, he acted humbly toward everybody; as a scholar, people acted humbly toward him.

Kirby and Senzaki established "Mentorgarten." It was a sort of open forum for Asian subjects, though we did celebrate Japanese folk festivals and Mahayana religious holidays. There was no special emphasis on Zen, but we did have silences, especially at the end of meetings. Anyone who had been to Asia or could contribute from studies of Asian scriptures or direct investigation was welcome. Only one thing was forbidden, and that *absolutely*—speculation.

In our search and spiritual ventures, one of the most interesting of all persons contacted was Robert Stuart Clifton. He came to San Francisco around 1928, then began officiating at the Hongwanji Temple on Pine Street, the same place where I had met Kirby, Senzaki and Daisetz Suzuki.

Two aspects of Buddhism are presented by Hongwanji. It continues the Pure Land teachings, especially as formulated by Saint Shinran Shonin. This is called *tariki* in Japan, meaning salvation through other than self. But it is based on "The Vow of Samantabhadra," which represents the Bodhisattva in an exceedingly high and profound form seeking to save all mankind from misery at any cost. The Pure Land methods are far more widespread than our literature or so-called "study courses" indicate, and neither on Pine Street nor in the Orient did I find the total separation of methodologies that one does in Christianity or even in Hinduism. Both in America and in Japan, Hongwanji promulgates the universal and Pure Land teachings together. And nowhere are there any statistics put forward to prove that any one Way is better than any other Way.

All Buddhism involves compassion: compassion and salvation are not separate. The whole career of Robert Clifton exemplified this. During his lifetime, he had crossed both the United States and the Pacific Ocean many times. He had been to Japan for Pure Land instruction. In New York, he met Sokei-an Sasaki and became convinced of Zen. He later became a novitiate at the Soto Temple in Tsurumi, between Yokohama and Tokyo. His spiritual realization gave him a universal outlook. Later in life, he also passed through the Theravadin discipline (for which he became known) and Tibetan (kept rather secret). He became known as Phra Sumangalo, a leading personality in the whole Buddhist world.

Partly through his efforts, as well as through the cooperation of others, there is now a World Buddhist Fellowship. Buddhists have accomplished what other religions have not: an organization including all sects and interpretations of their faith, a mutual recognition.

It is regrettable that our State Department and press never took this man seriously. We are spending millions of dollars today in efforts — and they are not always successful, either — to obtain an equilibrium of status in Southeast Asia which was ours if we had listened to him. His name will go into history, if not into the press. The *Encyclopedia of Buddhism* will contain objective articles and historical data which our universities will later seek while the public remains ignorant of the true facts of a true Asia.

Did Phra Sumangalo find the "Great Peace?" He did exemplify love and compassion and has been recognized in many lands, by many people. Is this not enough for a "Lotus-man"? He joins that grand array of Americans — Lafcadio Hearn, Townsend Harris, Dr. Higginbottam, Gertrude Emerson and Morgan Shuster — loved in Asia, important in Asia, contributors to history, but not always to "news."

Phra Sumangalo (R. Clifton)

70

CHAPTER FIFTEEN

Book Excerpt:

Zen is Meditation
(from _The Lotus and the Universe_)

"Friends in Dharma, be satisfied with your own heads. Do not put any false heads above your own. Then, minute after minute, watch your steps closely. These are my last words to you."

—Nyogen Senzaki in "The Iron Flute"

ONE CAN HARDLY REPRESS TEARS. TWICE I HAVE SEEN THIS noble man melt—once on a celebration of Shaku Soyen's birthday and again on a celebration of the birthday of my first spiritual teacher, the Sufi Pir-O-Murshid Inayat Khan. With all his development, all his problems, all his sufferings, even being a Bodhisattva did not mean to lose his humanity, ever.

Friends, there is nothing in an emancipated soul which compels him to drop his humanity. The Sufi, the Yogi, the Bodhisattva may spend much effort in watching his footsteps closely; this is beyond the ken of the metaphysician, of the "false head."

Zen is operational. It is based on discipline, practice, experience. _Zen for the West_ by Professor Sohaku Ogata has been mentioned. Sokei-an and Ruth Fuller Sasaki have contributed much. We now have excellent Zendos. Indeed, we even have the Chinese coming out and instructing us in wisdom. We need no more "false heads." "Kill the Buddha"—never. Kill the Mara—yes.

The biography of Nyogen Senzaki is being written by others, whether piecemeal or complete, I do not know. The simple servant I met in 1920 has become a legendary figure. The great doctor of philosophy remains unknown. The Buddha-Dharma claims there is no abiding ego; *sensei* (teacher) used to say: "There is no such person as Nyogen Senzaki."

In 1926, he suddenly dropped all his learning and began to speak in pidgin English. He denied everything else and held us, for a time, strictly to meditation with nothing else but a word or two from Shaku Soyen, and tea. The Bible may teach: "Naked came I out of my mother's womb and naked I shall return thither; the Lord gave, and the Lord hath taken away" (Job 1:21). This is good Judaism, or Christianity—at funeral services. It is good wisdom always. Read "The Gospel of St. Thomas" and you may not be able to distinguish between that Jesus and a Zen Master—it does not matter.

Yes, Senzaki-san gave me *ko-ans*, and gave the others around me ko-ans, too. It is not necessary to discuss them. The aim of the ko-an is Prajna. This is translated as "wisdom" and loses its significance thereby. It may be called the operation of the One Mind. Read "The Sutra of the Sixth Patriarch" and try to prove it—to yourself.

One of the early visitors to the Zendo in San Francisco was the Reverend Ishida, a Soto Zen Tea-Master. This was my first contact with a teacher of this school, and it was noticeable that he seemed more concerned with compassion (*karuna*) than with any other discipline or morality. He performed a Tea-Ceremony and gave us the impressions intended by *The Book of Tea* by Okakura Kakuzo. The "Great Peace" is beyond the distinctions of Taoism, Buddhism or any other spiritual pattern.

The Bodhisattva is patterned after one of the great archetypes that we find in art, in folklore and in ritual, and Master Ishida was, to me, an "incarnation of Samantabhadra," the Bodhisattva of Compassion. His Tea-Ceremony had the same import as a pure Christ (if not Christian) communion.

Some Americans have accepted the tradition that the Dalai Lama is an incarnation of the Bodhisattva of Mercy, Avalokitesvara. Avalokitesvara (Kwan Yin, Kwannon) represents Mercy; Samantabhadra, Compassion; Manjusri, Wisdom; Maitreya, the "future Buddha" and so forth. And then there is Fudo . . . .ah, Fudo!

Fudo is Jesus driving the money-lenders from the temple; Fudo is Jesus castigating the scribes and Pharisees; Fudo is Jeremiah standing before the king; Fudo is Bodhidharma refusing to praise the emperor; Fudo is the wise guide who does not confuse sentimentality with love.

Roshi Furukawa of Engaku-ji, Kamakura, was the very embodiment of Fudo. Many only knew him as a severe mentor, and yet because of him, disciples experienced satori. What good is all the negativity, guised as mercy, if it does not lead to deliverance from sorrow? When the pupil fails, the karma of the failure is on the teacher. Buddhism does not recognize ego-personality, and people are in error if they presume any self-teacher is whipping any self-pupil because of failure. The self-centered man can not comprehend the ways of Bodhisattva.

And yet when I was privileged to visit Roshi Furukawa's temple at Kamakura in 1956, my friend Kiichi Okuda and I were received with open arms and treated as a school boy treats his best pals after a long absence. There was nothing but love and joy.

The Zendo in San Francisco also hosted the Chinese Master, the Venerable Tai Hsu. He was the Chief Teacher of the Chinese Lin-chi School, which corresponds to the Japanese Rinzai. Much milder than the Reverend Furukawa, he was just as adamant on one point—that *speculation* has no place in Buddhist teachings. Here he failed; he did not impress America, which has, alas, only too often accepted both speculation and personality as the doors to what is called "Buddhism."

Tai Hsu and Senzaki-san used to communicate by writing. Our Japanese mentor told us he did not understand Mandarin, but could easily read the Classics. One day the two Buddhists were invited to the house of Mrs. Leila Havens in Piedmont (near Oakland, California). By some mistake, they took the Claremont Avenue train and got off at the Piedmont Avenue crossing in Oakland. Nobody was there to meet them.

Senzaki-san told us that after awhile he became very nervous and walked back and forth in a fidgety manner. Master Tai Hsu looked at him and said: "Isn't this a wonderful day? Look at all the trees in bloom and see the beautiful flowers. How we can enjoy ourselves here!" Our Japanese friend at once apologized. Just then a car that had been sent to look for them turned up and they were quickly escorted to their destination.

The event resulted in a marked change in Senzaki-san's behavior and attitude. He himself henceforth showed less of Fudo and more of Samantabhadra.

Tai Hsu's later career was very tragic. In his organization, the Buddha, the Dharma and the Sangha were not so properly united that the wise or illuminated man controlled the destiny of Buddhism. The tradition that a holy man must not touch money has often resulted in funds being misused on both a large and small scale. The successes of all Tai Hsu's campaigns were frittered away. But he did influence Dwight Goddard, who gave us *The Buddhist Bible* and tried to present the whole of the Dharma to the American public.

In 1923, the Zen Nyogen Senzaki met the Sufi Pir-O-Murshid Inayat Khan in the home of Murshida Rabia Ada Martin in San Francisco. The two men sat down at a table, looked into each other's eyes and both immediately entered into that *samadhi* which so many lecturers tell us about but do not experience themselves. The details have been written in Senzaki's memories. They corroborate Emerson and dismay dualists.

After that, the Zen Master considered himself to be a disciple in Sufism and the Sufi teacher, in turn, regarded himself as a devotee in Zen Buddhism. In the Hadith, the Prophet Mohammed said, "Seek wisdom even as far as China," but the path of the Muslim seeking such wisdom is not always easy, either.

Senzaki-san showed himself to be a universal man in other respects. His favorite quotations were not from Buddhist texts. One was John Tauler's, "The eye with which I see God is the same eye with which God sees me." Another was from Abdul Baha: "People of

the world, you are as branches of the tree and leaves of the branch."
He did not only quote them, he lived them.

Shortly after the Zendo was moved to Los Angeles, I was in severe
difficulties, and when publicly attacked, a former friend who was
functioning as a Buddhist teacher turned on me. At that time, I had
to visit Los Angeles, and when I entered the Zendo, was amazed to
hear sensei (teacher) excoriate this pseudo-Buddhist in no uncertain
terms. It was almost in the language of a Henry Miller. In a short
time, the karma this man had set into operation overtook him and
he disappeared.

At another time, two women I knew were going around Los Angeles spreading vicious gossip about a Vedanta Swami. True, all
Swamis are not masters or saints, and not even every Vedanta monk
has reached a high state. But I found that this particular Swami was
totally incapable of any sort of vice or tort or misdemeanor; that sort
of evil did not appear capable of having a foothold in him.

A personal vindication of the Swami resulted in these women trying
to spread the same gossip about me, and they immediately followed
it up by visiting our Zen friend. As soon as they came to the Zendo
steps, he walked out and greeted them: "Get out or I call the police!"
This was rather a shocker to those who had never heard of Fudo.

"But Mr. Senzaki, you do not know what we have come for."

"Get out or I'll call the police!"

"But Mr. Senzaki, we wish to join the temple and study with you."

In those days, our friend had a battered old hat which he often
wore. He took it from the shelf and walked down the front steps.

"Where are you going?"

"To call the police!"

I never heard from or of these women again, and there was no
more personal gossip about either this person or the Swami.

Not that Senzaki-san always admired the Swamis, either. He called
on another one who gave a sermon on how to "Be Equal-Minded In
Pleasure and Pain." Our Japanese friend said he enjoyed the talk so
much, he would like to have an interview. This was granted.

There was a vase on a table in the waiting room, and just as the door opened for the interview, the monk got up in an awkward manner and knocked the vase over.

"You clumsy fool," cried the Swami, "that vase cost me $200!"

"Oh," said Senzaki, taking out his wallet, "I'm very sorry." To the amazement of the Indian, he showed the wallet that contained hundreds of dollars (at that time), calmly peeled off the amount requested, gave it to the Swami with a flourish and a bow and departing said, "Thank you very much. Now I know the meaning of being imperturbable in pleasure and pain. Thank you very much."

These and many other anecdotes prove that a Zen monk seldom, if ever, behaves like a "Zen monk" of the lecture hall or necessarily like the questionable translations of Chinese tales of centuries ago.

My friend Paul Reps became interested in Senzaki-san shortly after the Japanese went to Los Angeles and helped in the publication of *Zen Flesh, Zen Bones, A Hundred Zen Stories* and other works which are particularly Zennish—not based on speculative enigmas.

Sensei introduced the ko-an teaching. This does not mean—or prevent—a witty saying: "In Zen there are no miracles." Once there is a spiritual attachment, neither time nor space nor conditioned existence (*samsara*) can interfere. Someday one may speak as plainly of occult experiences as of physical ones. I hope someday this will be permitted and welcomed.

Here one can only relate our last conversation with Senzaki-san in 1957. I had returned from Japan the long way, and entering the Zendo, remarked: "When Sam Lewis and Sogen Asahina met, were there one, two or no persons in the room?"

"Have some tea," he replied.

Further conversation was unnecessary. Both of us knew a phase had been completed. The ko-an—nay the ko-ans—had been solved.

If anyone asks, what did Nyogen Senzaki *give* me, the answer is: "Buddha Hridaya (Heart)."

Seek and ye shall find.

CHAPTER SIXTEEN

Book Excerpt:

Learning Zen from Zen Teachers
(from *The Lotus and the Universe*)

"The Cat's Yawn"
—Title of Sokei-An Sasaki's work.

"Some may slander or argue against Zen,
They are playing with fire, trying to burn the heavens in vain,
A true student of Zen should take their words as sweet dew-drops,
And that sweetness will also be forgotten when he enters into the
realm of non-thinking."
—from "Sho-do-ka," translation of Nyogen Senzaki

FRIENDS, BODHISATTVAS:

It is very hard to write those experiences which take one deep into the recesses of personality, or beyond personality. The emotions which accompany or follow meetings with those more advanced in the spiritual realm vary, and one has to express them in terms which cannot convey these variations.

Sokei-An Sasaki was not a Swami Ramdas or Sufi whose love-vibrations permeate the atmosphere. Nor did he show power or beauty or repose; he was in one sense the most ordinary person one could meet and in another sense the most complete. If his followers seem slightly fanatical or devoted, this has been because of the Dharma-Transmission left by him, and no one who has fallen under his influence has ever been the same afterwards.

My first visit to him in New York took place in September 1930. I was then in part a guest of the Roerich Museum, which was the center of many activities. Among them were groups dedicated to Tibetan-Mongolian Buddhism and to the Theravadan teachings (Maha Bodhi Society). It was there that I was first told about Sokei-An, a Zen monk living in New York.

The Roerich Museum tried the impossible: egocentric "Buddhism." There was no Sangha (community of brother/sister devotees) in the usual sense, and soon the individuals were in conflict. Some of this story is too well-known to discuss here. But one of the final efforts of Professor Roerich was to establish a cancer research center in the Himalayas where people seemed to be unusually free from this disease. Unfortunately, even now there has been no proper world survey to ascertain why people in some places do not develop this disease; in other words, there is no etiology (study of causes), yet we still seek cures.

Sokei-An had then only recently opened his Zendo. His teacher was another disciple of the oft-mentioned Master Shaku Soyen. He had learned to amalgamate the verbal and the super-verbal, the intellectual and the Prajna. Fortunately, his teachings have been preserved in "The Cat's Yawn." To me, this is the same as the "Lion's Roar" of the Buddha, the "Wind-Bell" of the San Francisco Zendo (Soto School) or the "Thundering Silence."

I remember having attended nine lecture-meetings of Sokei-An, and after each talk he permitted just six questions. He never dodged, he never equivocated, he went straight to the point, and I know of no occasion on which anybody ever went away confused or dissatisfied. (This has been confirmed by several of his early disciples.) Besides these, I was fortunate to have had a number of private interviews and meditations.

In common with all Zen monks, Sokei-An considered speculation as most dangerous. There is a great gap between the devotees of the First Zen Institute on Waverly Place in New York and the respectable who have attended Professor Suzuki's lectures. At the Institute, they

78

learn and practice Zen; on University Heights, the chemistry of the orange-peel is so alluring that they have no idea of the juice that quenches thirst and gives life.

Following the Rinzai pattern, Sokei-An used ko-ans and, indeed, paid more attention to them than did his "Uncle" Nyogen Senzaki. Buddha had taught that all humanity had the enlightenment and perfect wisdom but did not know it. The ko-an is one method by which we may realize we are truly "sons-of-God." Discussion only hampers.

Sokei-An explained and discussed *dharma*. The word *dharma* (philologically connected with the word *form*) may be interpreted to mean "law, essence, universal harmony, thingness," even *Tao*. It is man that has divided the dharma, the "legal" (Sanskrit, *astika*) schools now being known as Hindu, and the "illegal" (Sanskrit, *nastika*) include Buddhism. But each teaches dharma, whether as *Sanatana dharma* (eternal way or perennial philosophy), *Arya dharma* (noble truth, etc.) or *Saddharma* (perfect wisdom). In Sokei-An they were all blended—there was just dharma. It is to the nonconformists that one leaves discussions about "Zen," whatever *they* mean.

Between lectures and answers to questions, there was revealed a profound knowledge of the dharma, including the wisdom of the Upanishads, the cosmic Indian psychology (no European has touched more than the surface of what this Japanese monk knew), the basic philosophies of Mahayana and a lot more. One learned to transcend the time and space and even to "see" into the future.

My friends, do not seek such faculties. It will bring only misunderstanding and enemies. You will be misunderstood. Find your true nature first and then, if you will, look a little.

Digressing for a moment, I once visited a hospital in Japan to see a Korean patient. He had been raised as a Christian and was very devout, very ethical, but thoroughly frightened. There were three other young men in the room, all Japanese, two of them followers of Zen, and one of another school. The young men, adept in meditation, were considering the surgery just as any other event in life; the other Buddhist was slightly but not noticeably afraid. The contrast was so great that the Korean began to doubt his faith. Was it faith if it brought fear? Again, it is hoped this will lead to objectivity—and to the value of meditation. There is no reason why people of all religions—or no religion—cannot learn and practice meditation. No lectures, please, just effort.

In 1945, I returned to New York, full of anticipation, to learn that on the day of my arrival Sokei-An Sasaki had entered into Parinirvana. It was the saddest period of my life; since then it has been impossible to experience such sorrow. Devotees on Waverly Place, New York *and* Waverly Place, San Francisco will understand.

In 1956, while travelling with Kiichi Okuda in Japan, we visited Mrs. Ruth Fuller Sasaki the first thing upon our arrival in Kyoto. "What did Sokei-An teach you?" she asked. "I cannot tell," I replied. "There was nothing secret, it is simply that one cannot quantitatively tell." No, friends, there is nothing secret.

Suzukis may come and Salingers go, but friends, if you are near New York City, you should visit the First Zen Institute. Occasional visits show the remarkable development in dharma of those who are curious or sincere and who do not determine their spiritual future by leaning on anybody else.

There was at one time an artist named Sabro Hasegawa living in San Francisco who had rooms in the then-prospering American Academy of Asian Studies. I told him that Nyogen Senzaki had taught me seven forms of laughter. He said, "Come here sometime, when nobody is around, and I'll show you the *eighth form of laughter*." It turned out so, and by the Prajna—that universal impersonal communion-communication—this aspect of the dharma was awakened.

The laughter was also part of the entry to Japan. While metaphysicians lecture about "synchronicity," it is interesting that on the day of this person's arrival in Japan, the first Sesshu exhibition opened. Sesshu was one of the greatest—if not the greatest—of Japanese Zen

80

artists. Sabro had lectured interminably on him, and yet it was my fortune to be at the opening of this show, and to enjoy it to the full. Someday it may be possible to write an "Advice to Diplomats," but this is useless in a world that proclaims Christianity and confines "love"—not so much to sex as to a very narrow portion even of sex—so that instead of love (in a true sense) being much vaster than sex, sex (in any sense) has come to be much greater than the "love" proclaimed by the media. Exit love, exit life, and there can only be physical and mental debilitation.

When Kiichi Okuda and I visited Master Furukawa at Engakuji (described in the last chapter), we were sent to his successor, Roshi Sogen Asahina. This Master signaled for us to sit in meditation and immediately: the "lotus experience"—no longer any Kiichi Okuda or Sogen Asahina or Sam Lewis and yet the reality of "I am the Vine and ye are the branches thereof."

After it ended, Roshi spoke to us about God and Christ. There is no time between "here and eternity," and the Zen experience is *sudden*, but it is not a "sudden philosophy" that is presented. In mathematics, one jumps from the numbers to the infinite— suddenly— and the same in the spiritual experience.

Then we were taken through the compound behind the Engakuji Monastery and saw scenes described in L. Adams Beck's writings. And the fact that I knew about Roshi Shaku Soyen was enough to have me honored and taken to the tomb of his teacher. When there is no ego-self, there are no walls, no barriers—this is true the world over.

As we left the monastery, I said to Okuda-san: "This was an omen." Though just arrived in Japan, the doors had already been opened. And it was so, for over the next month and a half, we penetrated places not usually open to either tourists or Japanese. But as Edna St. Vincent Millay has beautifully put it: "The world stands out on every side/ No wider than the heart is wide" ("Renascence").

On the next day, we took the bus and stopped at Akusaka. There was a smoke-baptism at the temple of Kwannon, and the police must have taken notes. Soon a most favorable dossier and a glorious tour.

We next visited the Nishi Honganji Temple in Tokyo, and when they learned that their visitor knew about Pure Land (too seldom taught to us in America), we received all kinds of invitations: a free Noh-drama performance, free flower arrangement exhibitions, real tea-ceremonies. Just where does Zen begin and where does it end?

Later on, Mrs. Sasaki sent us to Phillip Karl Eidman, then staying in Kyoto—a living Bodhisattva if I have ever met one. He explained the relation of the different schools and sects to one another. I am only hoping that he is selected, if he has not been already, to instruct Americans about Buddhism.

The Nishi Hongwanji Temple at Kyoto, where Professor Eidman resided in 1956, contains one of the most beautiful gardens I have ever seen and some of the most exemplary art work. There also was a form of sudden-Prajna experience. When the self ceases as a discrete being, the whole universe may be opened before us. This was a teaching of Lord Buddha. This is inherent in the actual dharma. True, Buddhism is based on the experiences of life, and perhaps pure religion in every form is experience—from very simple, emotional types to union-with-the-All wherein oneself is not.

I remember on the first day in Japan, stopping at Tsurumi at the great Sojiji Zen Temple where Okuda-san asked me, "How do you feel?"

"I feel very strange," I replied.

"Well, you are in a strange country."

"But that is not why I feel strange. I feel strange because I do not feel strange. I feel I have come home. I know these trees, this landscape, the surroundings. I know the people, the ceremonies, the robes. The only thing I do not know is the language."

When we later visited Sojiji, we met the Roshi, who immediately gave instructions in Zen. Instructions? The Pagoda-communication —or communion—is not a dualism between one and another. Theosophists, who affirm that there are seven planes of existence, are liable to treat them like a chessboard of the "Alice-Through-the-Looking-Glass" experience. Neither are they like the Hanging Gardens of ancient Babylon, which symbolized them. Each phase transcends the previous one, and the six lower planes belong to the wheel-of-life (not necessarily the wheels ordinarily depicted). The finite in consciousness does not grasp the infinite any more than school arithmetic grasps the infinite of multiple integration.

It was my privilege in Japan to be introduced to the Kegon, Kobo Daishi Shingon and Shingi Shingon teachings; to have visited the Royal Cemetery and, ultimately, the Imperial Grounds and Imperial Botanical Gardens, the outer semblances of inner union. When a biography or autobiography is written, the details may be supplied. We have set up too many barriers, or rather we have permitted exotics to set up too many barriers before us, to enter into proper communication with Asians. The Viet Nam complex is only one phase of it.

CHAPTER SEVENTEEN

Excerpt from Papers:

Dharma-Transmission

GRANDPA ROSHI (THE VENERABLE SHAKU SOYEN) RETURNED TO San Francisco in 1906. On his first trip to the U.S. in 1893 (to the Columbia Exposition in Chicago to speak at the World Congress of Faiths), he had met a Mrs. Russell of San Francisco. She had invited him to return and stay at her home in a sort of village near the city called Oceanside. It has long since disappeared along with her home, so it is impossible to make a pilgrimage to the first Zen shrine in America.

* * *

Grandpa Roshi brought two of his sons: Daisetz and Nyogen. To Daisetz he said, "You are my skin, my flesh, my bones." To Nyogen he said, "You are my marrow, my heart." Then he returned to Japan. From Daisetz, we get Zen Philosophy, not to be confused with what is called "Zennism." From Nyogen we have the Dharma-Transmission, no relation to Zennism.

* * *

Great-grandpa Roshi lies buried in a grotto at Kamakura, Japan. Grandpa Roshi had two daughters. One of them, L. Adams Beck, has described this grotto in her *The Garden of Vision*. The other, Beatrice Lane, married her brother-in-Dharma, Daisetz. She wrote, she collaborated and she left the world. Her husband became famous.

* * *

Three ladies have had the Dharma-Transmission in this line: L.

Adams Beck, Beatrice Lane and Ruth Fuller Sasaki. This has nothing to do with Zennism.

* * *

The Reverend M. T. Kirby had been a Roman Catholic monk. He did not obtain enlightenment. He went to Japan and studied under Grandpa Roshi. He became enlightened and received the name of Sagaku Shaku.

He Kwang met Kirby the first month of 1920. At that time, there were no laws by Zennists about the behavior of Zen monks. Sagaku Shaku told the story of his enlightenment. He told it plainly, openly and like a child—or a scientist [ed. note—see chapter "In Search of Satori"].

* * *

Sagaku Shaku gave instructions in Pali Scriptures and in Zen meditation. He told about the historical Buddha. He did not see any Buddhism apart from Buddha. He did not see any Buddha apart from Buddhism. There were no rules in those days by scholars or metaphysicians. Only that which was connected with Buddha Sakya Muni was Buddhism; but Buddhism was connected with both Lord Buddha and Amida, the Infinite Light.

Sagaku Shaku was so successful he was promoted. He went to the Hawaiian Islands and deposited the Dharma with the Reverend Hunt. In San Francisco, he turned things over to his brother-in-Dharma, Nyogen Senzaki.

* * *

Nyogen Senzaki was a homeless monk. He worked as a menial. He had been a professor. He knew many languages and much literature. He regarded this learning as a jockey regards extra weight in a race. This was before the days of Zennism.

* * *

We had the "Mentorgarten." It was an open forum. Anybody who had been to Asia could speak. We sat around the fire and listened. We had short meditations. If there was no speaker, we had longer meditations. Everything was informal. Any knowledge was accepted. Only one thing was barred—speculation. Speculation was the one evil. We had many great Buddhists come and go. They all said the same thing: speculation was the one evil. This was before the days of Zennism.

* * *

The prophet Mohammed said, "I am an ordinary man like you." Nyogen always acted as if he were an ordinary man like others. He had greater scholastic learning than most of us and hid it; he had greater wit than most of us and did not hide that.

The Mentorgarten was a place of learning, of entertainment, of comraderie and of meditations. We meditated according to the teachings of Shaku Soyen.

* * *

Shaku Soyen had written *Sermons of a Buddhist Abbot*. We did not study it. We did not reverence Shaku Soyen. Nyogen treated him as if he had been his father. Nyogen was an orphan and his early history reminded us of King Arthur. We regarded him as a sort of spiritual King Arthur. His meditative prowess was his sword.

* * *

Nyogen did not tell us much about himself or much about Shaku Soyen, excepting on rare occasions. He had us become acquainted with his atmosphere.

* * *

In 1926, the twenty year's probation put on Nyogen by Shaku Soyen ended. The first Zendo was opened. No more entertainment, excepting on special holidays. No more discussion excepting on special holidays. We learned to meditate. We jumped from 15-minute periods to half an hour to an hour, sometimes two hours. We had theoretical breaks every 15 minutes.

At first 15 minutes seemed like an aeon; after awhile 15 minutes seemed like a breath.

* * *

We did not waste any time trying postures. We kept the back straight. We learned the Zen breathing. We then went out to battle with our egos. After awhile one of us attained enlightenment and was named "Zoso." As soon as this happened, we were sure Nyogen had the Dharma-Transmission.

* * *

After Nyogen went to Los Angeles, this one said to Zoso, "Nyogen is not a homeless monk, Nyogen is a Master, he is more than a Master, he has the Dharma-Transmission." "Of course." We vowed to silence until one of us was left. Zoso is gone, Nyogen is gone, and when Nyogen was gone it was discovered—or rather uncovered— that he was the Dharma-Master of the Age.

Zoso and this one did not take our disciplines from Zennists. Our speech was our speech, silence our silence.

Nyogen was of the Rinzai School and used harsh methods. The Reverend Gido Ishida was of the Soto School and used soft methods. We did not learn anything about the differences of schools, we only studied the methods toward enlightenment. Ishida seemed all heart, Nyogen seemed little heart, but this was our illusion.

* * *

One tells a story for the record. All the lovers of Dharma used to celebrate Buddha's Birthday, Buddha's Enlightenment and Buddha's Parinirvana. We regarded them as historical realities and as spiritual realities.

There was a lady living in this region at the time named Elsie Nor-

wood. She had known this person since childhood. She was clairvoyant. She could "see" and told what she saw, and this one wrote
what he regarded as a poem. He gave this to Master Ishida (the vision
took place in Fairfax, California, in that part called "Deer Park"):

Thus have I heard:
In Deer Park they celebrated Parinirvana Day.
Hosts of Bodhisattvas gathered from afar,
Kotis of Bodhisattvas from the Pure Land of the West,
Bodhisattvas of the dim and distant past,
Bodhisattvas known and unknown to men today—
And in their midst the Tathagata,
Unmoved, serene, compassionate.

Thus have I witnessed:
In Deer Park we celebrated Parinirvana Day:
With the multitude of Bodhisattvas came Catholic priests,
Around the Catholic priests were Jewish rabbis,
Sufi dervishes, Hindu gurus,
Teachers and preachers from every race,
Holy men, sages, sramanas and prophets—
The cosmic parliament of religious leaders,
Countless as the sands, yet all enlightened—
And in their midst the Tathagata,
Unmoved, serene, compassionate.

Thus have I beheld:
In Deer Park I celebrated Parinirvana Day:
Radiant in light, and light upon light;
With that diamond glorious to behold,
That diamond most brilliant shining in his forehead,
Magnificent, incomprehensible, the sun of suns.
Unmoved, serene, compassionate,
In their midst sat the Tathagata.

Thus have I heard,
Thus have I witnessed,
Thus have I beheld,

Salutation To The Perfect One, The Wholly Enlightened One,
The Most Supreme Buddha.

* * *

This formulation of an experience was the first of many efforts in life. When the Reverend Gido Ishida came, he demonstrated the Tea Ceremony. Then one showed him the above. He gave this person a private Tea Ceremony. It was like a communion. It was a communion. It was a communion in the sense that those who have or have been "given" the Dharma find the One Mind.

The teacher (sensei) did not have to explain anything. He accepted.

* * *

This was the first of many experiences in the life of a person born in the West. He meets a teacher, perhaps on common ground. The teacher accepts. Then generations pass. The pupils of the pupils of that teacher reject. Whether they teach that the ego is real or unreal, they reject. Their "teacher" is always a special case. Then the children of the enlightened keep the world in more darkness than the children of the dark. Nyogen used to say, "There is no such person as *Nyogen Senzaki.*" Now that we have the Zennists, there are persons, there are people and there are differences.

* * *

If Gido Ishida offered "The Taste of Honey," soon the *Pot of Honey* came and transformed Nyogen Senzaki. This man, both exceedingly fair and exceedingly stern, was transformed in a moment and never returned to his Fudo pattern.

* * *

Master Tai Hsu could change an atmosphere and an audience. He did not have to preach "Joy," he did not have to say a single word about "Enlightenment." He took all the weight of the Zendo.

* * *

Master Tai Hsu behaved like some of us thought a Master should behave. We always went away lightened and happy. Meditation became a joy, not a chore.

* * *

Not long after Master Tai Hsu departed, Roshi Furukawa came from Engakuji Temple in Kamakura. Too late. You cannot bring Fudo back after Samantabhadra has taken over.

* * *

It is folly to think in dualistic terms. Roshi Furukawa appeared as Fudo in San Francisco. Years later, when myself as Kiichi Okuda and my appearance as He Kwang came to the temple in Kamakura, we were turned away by the attendant: "Roshi was very aged, Roshi was in retirement, Roshi would see nobody." We sent him our cards.

We could hear footsteps running rapidly down the hill. Roshi welcomed us with joy and the lightheartedness of a child. We were not Master and pupils, we were not even Sanga-members. We were boys on a picnic.

The first meeting with Roshi Furukawa was to experience the hard sternness of the traditional Rinzai monk. The last meeting was to experience: "Unless you be as little children, yours is not the kingdom of heaven." Let it remain that way.

* * *

Dr. Trebitsch-Lincoln came to the Mentorgarten thundering fire and brimstone. He was a dualistic Buddhist, even a dualistic Zen. He had changed his faith many times, but not his fire, not his prowess. He finally went to Omei-Shan, the sacred mountain of Szechuan in

Central China and center of esoteric Buddhism. He continued to thunder fire and brimstone. The celebrated Boake Carter prophesied and the world applauded. The uncelebrated Dr. Trebitsch-Lincoln, known as "Dr. Ruh," prophesied the opposite and the world sneered. Then World War II came. Boake Carter had been wrong on every point and committed suicide. Dr. Ruh had been right on every point and was quickly forgotten.

Thus has been the history of the world. Christ comes and defies the scribes and Pharisees. After his death, the scribes and Pharisees take over and hang out a sign, "Galilean, thou hast conquered." But the Galilean has not conquered, the scribes and Pharisees control — but only on the surface. They never get below the surface.

Trebitsch-Lincoln was the Jeremiah of his age.

* * *

Professor Perlham Nahl used to come occasionally to Mentorgarten. He had been an art teacher at the University of California where one had studied drawing with him. A friendship has been established.

Professor Nahl went to Japan to study and returned a convert to Zen Buddhism. He introduced the principle of immediacy. He practiced the One Mind. He illustrated the teaching both in his own work and by introducing both Chinese and Japanese instructors. He became responsible for bringing Professor Obata to Berkeley. The doors were opened.

* * *

When the doors were opened, there was a great increase of interest in the Orient.

Professor Nahl introduced the real and hidden values in the Zero and in the Infinite. One still remembers them.

* * *

In 1915, Professor Cassius Keyser of the Mathematics Department of Columbia University came to Berkeley to lecture on Fourth Dimensional and Non-Euclidian Geometries and on Hyperspace. He introduced us into what he later called, "The Pastures of Wonder."

The more one studied Keyser, the more one learned about Zero and Infinity and Hyperspace and non-Euclidian Geometry and Psychology and everything else. Among his pupils was the late Count Alfred Korzybski.

One could discuss the Zero and the Infinity and Trans-space of Keyser with Professor Nahl and the relation of these projections with actual satori and samadhi experiences. There were no social bars, there were no institutional bars.

Some mathematicians threw out their own George Cantor for presuming the Infinite might be real. We had no ecclesiasts then to throw out social peasants who found the Infinite to be real.

Long before Einstein became too popular (or notorious), we learned about the Relative in Buddhism and in the Dharma as a whole from Professor Tscherbatski.

* * *

Years later one gave a public lecture on "Infinity and Space in Mathematics, Art and Spiritual Awakening." An elderly lady arose: "Where did you learn this?" It was Miss Katherine Ball, longtime art teacher in San Francisco and specialist in Korean and Buddhist Art.

"I have taught thousands of people, and I think three understood me," she said. "You are one of them."

One learned much about Oriental Art from her. This was one form of Dharma-Transmission.

* * *

Sagaku Shaku (the Reverend M. T. Kirby) left Hawaii for Japan. He gave an introduction to Dr. Kenneth Saunders, who wrote books and lectured on Buddhist Art. The subject has never been exhausted.

One became friend to the Chinese Chingwah Lee and the Japanese Shibata San (owner of "Daibutsu" in Chinatown); later owner of a small shop on Fillmore Street in San Francisco.

* * *

Hierarchical Zen stands out as the greatest contribution from Uncle Nyogen. He told us the stories of Mahakasyapa and Ananda. Ananda was the cousin and friend of Lord Buddha but never received the enlightenment during the Tathagata's span of life. And when he tried to get the "secret" from Mahakasyapa, the latter turned on him and cried, "Ananda!" Then he was enlightened.

* * *

Tathagata Sakya Muni never presented any "Buddhism." He came to restore *Arya Dharma*. All he discussed was "Arya Dharma" (noble truth or essence). For our purposes it is not different from *Sanatana Dharma* (eternal way), which Aldous Huxley has loosely interpreted as "Perennial Philosophy." It also inspired Nietzsche and other great savants of the West.

* * *

We are taught that if we become enlightened, we could write sutras ourselves. But nobody expects others to accept that! Yet Sagaku Shaku introduced us into "The Sutra of the Sixth Patriarch." This poor beggar chap Hui Neng was not very welcome among the elite. The story of the transmission of Dharma, Robe and Bowl has become an idyll. But let any beggar monk come into our respectable places and the whole thing would be repeated.

* * *

It is very unconvincing that any Eternal God of Justice should stop His revelation at any particular point in time or with any particular people.

* * *

The Bible says that the Risen Jesus gave so many instructions that not all the books in the world could contain them. Mohammed said: "Quran was revealed in seven dialects and each has an inner and outer meaning." Human institutions will have none of that. So there is a great gap between "Buddhism" and "Dharma-Transmission." The Christian people do not accept that Jesus gave all those teachings; the Muslims do not accept that Quran has so many meanings; and the speculators, taking over the vocabulary, do not relish Dharma-Transmission.

* * *

Jesus started out with the Beatitudes. The great Brihadaranyaka Upanishad explains the importance and immensity of Ananda (bliss). People say "The Garden of Eden." He Kwang says "The Gan of Bliss." Why should the word *Gan* be translated (as "garden" or "paradise") and the word *Eden* not be translated? The Upanishads emphasize the Universal Bliss which is found in all beings from the grade of humankind (or *manas*) up through Infinity. It is Ananda which separates mankind from the animals; it is Ananda which "unites the children of men with the sons of God."

* * *

He Kwang offers the Ananda story as a ko-an. So many people write books on ko-ans who have never been under the ko-an discipline. Uncle Nyogen gave the Ananda-story and the Ananda-ko-an. Now everybody is unhappy. We say, "The Kingdom of Heaven is within you." Jesus said, "The Kingdom of Heaven is at hand." When people go on the path of Dharma-Transmission, this will be a very valuable ko-an.

* * *

In the days when the teachings of Lord Buddha were regarded as the basis of Buddhism, we used to say:
May all peoples be peaceful,

> May all peoples be blissful;
> May all peoples be happy.

So He Kwang invites everybody to the Ananda-ko-an.

Chapter II — Roshi

Uncle Nyogen was asked, "Is the Zen monk bound by Causation or is he outside of Causation?" Uncle taught, "The Zen monk is one with the Law of Causation." Unless you can understand and appreciate, you cannot grasp the incarnation of the Cat's Yawn known as Sokei-An Sasaki.

* * *

Roshi Sokei-An Sasaki was one of the most approachable men ever encountered. Not until one met Swami Ranganathananda Maharaj of the Ramakrishna Order years later did one meet someone so approachable, so simple and utterly profound that words are but the shadows of conveyance.

One heard nine lectures, but had innumerable personal and impersonal sessions.

* * *

Each lecture was followed by six questions, this being the upper limit. If you were an intellectual, you received philosophy. But if you had the Dharma-Eye, you *saw*. One of his lectures was on "Dharma-Eye." This makes a reality of *Samma-Dhrishti* (Right Views), the first principle of Lord Buddha's "Eightfold Path."

When you received this spiritual Darshan (inter-view), you received. When you were taken beyond *Maya*, you entered the realm of the Immeasurable.

* * *

Once Roshi was asked if he could see into the future. He answered, "It is too terrible." Dharma-Transmission is not intellectual, it does not stop at *manas* (mind). It includes Vijnana, Ananda and Prajna, which intellectuals do not understand.

Indian languages have no terms for "electricity" and "magnetic" and "turbine." Indians do not object to adopting our terms for these. English has no equivalent for Vijnana and Ananda and Prajna and Samadhi, and so we grasp any words — appropriate or inappropriate — and become confused. The end is likely as not psychedelism or trance-mediumship, which have no relation to these things.

* * *

Roshi opened these eyes to the whole history of the period 1930–1945, and some of these records were miraculously preserved from a fire which destroyed twenty-five year's research and a whole Oriental library. Roshi took one into Prajna *without destroying* levels between the seemingly finite and the seemingly infinite.

* * *

The painting of the Buddha's Parinirvana shows that the artist had the Dharma-Transmission. Naraka, Preta, Tirthaga-yoni, Raksha and Asura are the creatures of Darkness. They were welcomed at the bier. These are Sanskrit words. They have no European equivalents unless we accept that there are more things in Heaven and Earth than are thought of in our philosophies. We do not do that. We call what we do not know "unreal." Roshi explained these terms.

* * *

In the Grand Experience, as illustrated by the Cosmic Wheel, all the above creatures exist, within or without. The world, especially the Western world, has refused to accept what has not been experienced.

You cannot experience radioactivity and relativity and quantum mechanics without the experience of the laboratory outside. How does one know what is experienced in the laboratory within if one does not go in?

* * *

Sagaku Shaku explained the Four Stages of Meditation by lecturing. Roshi explained the Four Stages of Meditation by Meditation and Dharma-Transmission.

We sat comfortably. One is not convinced that special asanas (postures) causally produce samadhi or satori. One is not convinced that anything can causally bring samadhi or satori.

Uncle Daisetz has given long articles. Roshi brought his presence. "A single day with the Lord is worth a thousand years."

* * *

After Roshi the scriptures became open books. To the world, the scriptures are full of mysteries or contradictions or even falsehoods, but after Roshi they became clear channels of light.

* * *

Roshi gave the Cat's Yawn. "Come clothed or unclothed, with a gift or without a gift"—Roshi gave the Cat's Yawn.

Maya is the "measurable," not the "unreal." How can a sane mind consider the *unreal?* What is unreal? What is real?

* * *

Since all the scriptures cannot include all the teachings of Jesus, since the Quran teaches that if all the pens were one pen and all the seas ink, they could not present the Revelation of Allah, one does not apologize for providing more details of Roshi.

* * *

Before the days of Zennism, there were multitudes of rules called *Vinaya*. There is a Pali Vinaya, a Sanskrit Vinaya and Chinese Vinaya. There are also all sorts of protocols in books on the behavior of Zen Masters and teachers, and these can always be used by the negative persons who wish to reject somebody else: "Of course, the real Zen Master is a law unto himself, *but. . . .*"

* * *

One day a person asked Roshi if one could smoke and still have enlightenment. This was long before tobacco was honored by being accused of occupying the seat of Iblis. At another time, it was alcohol. Indeed, anybody may be accused of occupying the seat of Iblis except the ego itself, which according to real Buddhist teaching is identified with the Evil One.

Roshi said, "That is a good question and it needs consideration. Pardon me." Then he slowly withdrew a cigarette from a package, very slowly got out a lighter, very slowly took three puffs, put the package and lighter back into his pocket and asked, "Will you please remember that question?"

* * *

Ruth Fuller will go to glory, if she is not already there, by the aid she gave Roshi on all levels, even extending to marriage to protect him.

* * *

The saddest day of one's life occurred in 1945. One was going to New York again, full of anticipation and glow. One was so happy. On the day one arrived, Roshi took his last breath.

One appeared at the funeral in tears. One seldom weeps; many were in tears. One is almost in tears as one writes. This is not a good condition to be in while writing on "Dharma-Transmission."

* * *

Whatever has happened, The Cat's Yawn can still be heard.

* * *

The First Institute of Zen in New York can still be visited.

IV. JOURNEY TO THE EAST: 1956

In Japan 1956. Next to Samuel Lewis is James Kinoshita of Friends of the World.

CHAPTER EIGHTEEN

Editor's Note:

Pilgrimages

The dictionary defines pilgrimage as *"a long, weary journey, as to a shrine."* However, the Latin roots of the word carry the meaning of *"traveling or wandering through open spaces or fields."*

Samuel Lewis approached his pilgrimages at a time of life (60) when other people think about retiring. His life to that time looked like several lives, most of them unsettled and unresolved. The drama of his blood family continued as did his intense study of Eastern and Western religions, and practice as both a Sufi and Zen disciple. A writing career saw him publish, with Luther Whiteman, a book called Glory Roads on the *"states of mind"* of California as reflected in developments in science, technology, spiritual movements, economic systems and more. In 1951, he had taken a degree in horticultural science and gained the practical, *"dirty fingernails"* experience that went with his employment as a gardener. In addition, he had been decorated for work done with Army Intelligence during World War II (the nature of which is still clouded in secrecy), had helped resettle Jewish refugees during the War, and had lived as a beachcomber on the dunes near Oceano, California.

His journeys to the East introduced him to *"open fields"* large enough to allow him to integrate all of his work — spiritual, intellectual, scientific and cultural, humanitarian and human. In his diaries from the time (which were written as letters to friends and relatives), he exhibits the goal of every mystic: one's head in the heavens, one's feet on the ground. That he was able to accomplish so much in such a short period of time is staggering. Meeting the great saints and sages of the East is mixed in with practical work on land reform, desert agriculture, seed exchange and drought-resistant crops. Humor and self-parody is mixed with deadly serious warnings about coming problems in Vietnam, Afghanistan and the rest of the Third World.

How much Samuel Lewis affected the course of history during this time is unknown. Many of his political predictions turned out to be true; much of his advice on "foreign aid and foreign understanding" has now gained popularity through the works of the late E.F. Schumacher (Small is Beautiful) and others concerned with "appropriate technology" and world hunger.

What seemed to make the most difference to Samuel Lewis was that he had personally contacted, on their own ground, more Asians than almost any other American in history. This ranged from the Hindu street sweeper to the President of India. As he was fond of saying, this was "not-news" in a society where the media is oriented to sensationalism and personalities. Yet this approach may have made more difference — and still be making more difference — than all the speeches and expressions of noblesse oblige that the USA has offered to the East.

Lately, the media have been portraying the "second thoughts" of the British about their role in the Indian subcontinent (through films like "Gandhi," "A Passage to India," and "The Jewel in the Crown"). At some point, when the USA is able to look past its own role in Vietnam to the rest of Asia, it may find "little old Sam Lewis" and his "Four, Just Men."

CHAPTER NINETEEN

Book Excerpt:

"You Must Go to Japan"
(from *The Lotus and the Universe*)

ORIENTAL PHILOSOPHIES ARE NOT LEARNED FROM BOOKS. If they were, our professors could explain the Upanishads easily and clearly. All Asia, whatever be the religion or philosophy, proclaims the spiritual teacher, the guide, the one who has become liberated.

Years ago (1953) my friend and spiritual brother, Paul Reps (Saladin) said to me: "You ought to meet Swami Ramdas."

"Who is Swami Ramdas?"

"I don't know."

"Then why do you think I should meet him?"

"Because he has what you need."

"What is that?"

"Love and laughter. That's all he teaches — love and laughter."

Surprisingly, within three days, two other people said exactly the same thing. At that time, they did not even know each other. It remained an enigma, and then one day it was an enigma no longer.

At that time I was working as a gardener in San Francisco. One day, the heavens suddenly opened up and the Guru, Swami Ramdas, appeared. He gave me his blessing and a prediction that he would appear in person in exactly one year. This was presented to others, including some well-known professors. Alas, there are none harder to convince of the reality of mystical and occult experiences than those who lecture on them — and are often well paid, too.

Exactly 52 weeks after the above happened, Swami Ramdas did arrive in San Francisco with an entourage. He spoke several times and his speeches and the expected debates are recorded in the book *Ramdas Speaks*, a series covering the Guru's world travels.

Swami Ramdas and his entourage accepted this person at once. The bond was made.

Several years passed by. My father died and I received a legacy. Poor all my life, I did not know what to do when Paul Reps reappeared and said, "You should go to the Orient. They are waiting for you."

"Why?"

"You must go to Japan and teach them Zen, and to India and teach them true Yoga and to Islam and preach Sufism."

My friends, this is exactly what has happened and is happening. Only this is not an autobiography; one may come sometime. The day has not arrived when the mystic may speak on mysticism and the occultist on occultism out of his own experiences and out of the experiences of those whom he has contacted — exactly as in the sciences. The day has not yet come, but some day, *inshallah* (God willing). . . .

—1963

CHAPTER TWENTY

<u>*Newspaper Article:*</u>

Marinite Tours Orient: Leaves As A Gardener, Comes Back a Dervish

—from the San Rafael Independent Journal, May 13, 1957

Sam Lewis, 60-year-old Mill Valley bachelor, was a gardener for the state highway department a little over a year ago.

Now, back from a tour of the Orient, he is a member of the mystical dervish orders of Chisti and Nakshibandi.

The tale told by this wandering Marinite approaches the fantastic at times.

Lewis says that his father did not believe in college and as a result took him out of school and made him go to work.

"However, when I was 52," Lewis adds, "my father evidently changed his viewpoint and although it meant dropping a regular job, I went to San Francisco City College, taking courses in floriculture and chemistry. I took a degree in 1951."

After working as a gardener for the state until 1956, he received a sizeable inheritance from his father's estate, which immediately sent him flying to the Orient.

"My interest in that part of the world stemmed from my studies in Oriental philosophy and religion," he explains, adding that when he reached Japan, he immediately made contact with one James Otoichi Kinoshita, described by Lewis as secretary to "Friends of the World," an organization designed to promote world peace through the international exchange of trees and seeds.

"Actually," says Lewis, "this man Kinoshita is a front man for the emperor himself, who is quite a horticulturist."

After traveling to Hong Kong and Bangkok, Lewis flew to East Pakistan, then visited the Indian cities of Delhi, Bombay and Madras, where he conferred with horticulturists and scientists in several fields.

"In India and Japan," Lewis declared cryptically, "those who do not make religion a profession are religious and vice versa."

Lewis avers that he is the first American ever admitted to the dervish orders, contending this was done as a result of his intense study of the Orient together with his religious experience. The Chisti Order, he explains, is one using music, while the Nakshibandi can be described as "one having symbolic significance."

When he left India, Lewis flew to London to visit the famed Kew Botanical Gardens prior to his return to Mill Valley.

And now, this floriculturist and dervish from India is again devoting part of his time to gardening, while he also prepares to lecture on his experiences.

CHAPTER TWENTY-ONE

Excerpts from Letter-Diaries:
Japan, 1956

May 15   *Written at Tokyo Station Hotel*

The journey over was a surprising one. No illness but indisposition for the first week, due in part to the pressure and parties before leaving. . . . List of passengers with addresses given. Some may become good friends. To my amazement and in contradiction of past "enemies" I became a sort of leader in both entertainment and serious matters. Did some poetry writing, too, but mostly canasta.

Good old Okuda-san met me at the pier. The customs, etc., was not difficult but exciting. Did not feel as if I was in a strange country at all. Other than the language and a certain percentage of old type clothing, everything seemed familiar. The trees interested me, mostly plane and ginkgo, with pines in the parks. The azaleas are in bloom. Flower arrangements everywhere. Some planting on the highway. . . . Bought first map of Tokyo and marked out place for Friends of the World.

May 16   *Tokyo Station Hotel*

O Sabro-san [ed. note: Sabro Hasegawa]:

Today I begin my plan of writing a letter and using the carbon for my diary. I arrived in Yokohama yesterday morning and was met by my good friend Kiichi Okuda. He was manager of Daibutsu in San Francisco's Chinatown and in partnership with Shibata. We are always good friends. I hope someday that American students who are interested in Zen will come to know what "good friendship" means. Emerson said, "He is my friend in whose company I can think aloud."

But in the friendship of Zen there is generally one thought between two persons and also sometimes one silence between two persons. While many people were guessing at my reasons for coming to Japan and some had a slight appreciation of my lesser reason, Okuda-san knows my deepest reason.

It has been raining very hard. On our way to Tokyo we stopped at the Soto-Zen temple and it seemed almost like home. I cannot explain it. I did not feel as if I were in a strange country. But between the rain and the fact that hundreds of children were visiting the place, we went on.

There was an exhibition of Sesshu at the Museum in Ueno Park—of originals. Only the heart can speak of such things, and the heart prefers a kind of silence, interrupted by "Ohs" and "Ahs." There were hundreds of children there, and they were delighted that an American should enjoy their fine things.

Why does one feel happy with such things and not with European art? The inner being has a sense of space as well as of form and may regard the two as aspects of a oneness-of-nature. The line does not tell everything any more than the senses tell everything. The space was living and full, just as we know now that there are all kinds of sound and light vibrations which we pick up by instruments. But there is also an instrument within us that may pick up these things in a better fashion.

It stopped raining at sundown and tomorrow we hope to go to Kamakura. We must be back, because I have been invited several times to dinner. I have met my old friend Kaoru Nakashima who used to be vice-consul in San Francisco. It was a wonderful meeting. He learned that Okuda-san and I have the same "secret," and neither of us looks much different than fifteen years ago, while Nakashima-san has aged, just as most people do. Okuda-san is now past seventy but does not act or look as if he were even close to sixty. There are some "secrets" in Zen which seem to belong to the essence of life and even the body may relate them.

May 17

O Sabro-san:

Today the weather has cleared and we spent much time at Kamakura. We climbed inside the Daibutsu and also visited Hachiman shrine. We were very fortunate to witness a wedding ceremony there and hear the flute music first-hand, which we both enjoyed.

But most of the time was spent at Engakuji Monastery. This has been the place of my dreams for longer than a generation. My true journey has some aspects which, when I tried to explain to Mary Tabushi, she said, "One does not speak of such things." I answered, "That is correct, one does not speak of such things and that is why there are all sorts of wild dreams and rumors going around." But there is no such thing as a coin with one face.

The first thing we were told on entering Engakuji was that the old Roshi Furukawa was still alive but in retirement. We sent notice of our presence to him and in a few moments, to our surprise and delight, we were ushered into his rooms and served tea. It was a grand meeting of old friends. The old Roshi is now way into his eighties but full of life and fire. Although he has resigned himself, he still has plenty of vigor, though no doubt he could depart at will. He showed us much of the grounds himself, and then introduced us to his successor, Sogen Asahina. Sogen is a very vigorous, muscular-looking man but also has what I would call "the eye of the dharma." We were served ceremonial tea by the attendant—I took three sips to each cup and hoped this was correct.

We learned from him that Ruth Sasaki is in Kyoto, and we may see her before many days. He gave me his book on Zen and was very happy when I identified the pictures of Prof. Suzuki and my very dear friend, Robert Clifton, who is now in Thailand. He has asked me to edit the English portion of this work, which I may do later. We seemed to understand each other, speech or no speech.

After tea, he continued to show us the part of the grounds open to the public and then asked his attendant to take us to the part of the grounds not open to the public. We were led to the tomb of the teacher of Shaku Soyen and also to the tomb of Baku Zenshi (if I remember his name correctly) who founded the first temple there.

The attendant seemed to be excellently informed on both Rinzai and Soto Zen. He gave us minute details in the lives of the monks, some of whom we saw working around. I was charmed by the trees and vegetation there.

May 18

Morning and afternoon were spent in outer affairs. Some time in trying to locate held-luggage, then more time in arranging trip to Kyoto.

Late in the afternoon things began to happen. My baggage was located, things all in good order. Dried figs and perhaps part of chocolate to be sent to Roshi Furukawa. One jar coffee and copy of Netsuke book for Kaoru. Rest of books to go to Itako with rest of food. Also some fertilizer.

Balance of fertilizer given as gift to Friends of the World. We got in touch with James Otoichi Kinoshita, chairman of the board who came over with some literature. It was obvious that he, and his organization, are not only working along the horticultural lines I had planned but also more or less along the same spiritual lines. The result was a long and profitable conference. He said he would arrange meetings with the proper agricultural scientists. This was enhanced when he brought up the subject of rapid growth trees for fuel and swamp drainage. I told him of *E. globulus* and he may arrange for me to meet representatives of New Zealand and Australia.

May 21

My dear Lois and everybody:

I have sent some air mail letters to Sabro, but my correspondence is so heavy and often pressing that I actually cannot afford to keep up this form of correspondence. Postage has been running well over a dollar a day. Here a dollar goes either a long way or a short way. Last night it cost 1400Y (Yen) for a *small* Italian dinner for two. Tonight we divided sushi and a big dish containing spiced rice with all kinds of side dishes, vegetables and tea. The whole (for two) less than a dollar — 280Y to be exact — and better food. It pleased my host very much, because we leave for Kyoto shortly where I will have my initiation into Japanese inns (ryokan), and sleeping on the floor, etc. These inns throw in breakfast and supper.

I am not, however, writing about food, though I think I have gone from a B.S. to a Ph.D. in chopstickology. The same beautiful opposite-to-irony continues, as I wrote to Sabro. Yesterday morning I picked up the paper and found that there was an English celebration of Shinran Shonin at a temple not far away. We went and the next thing I knew I was meeting Californians! We had a discussion in English and I guess I was the only one who knew about Nagarjuna or Shinran. I got my 10Y worth.

The result was we were invited back today (Monday). We were admitted to a tea ceremony free, saw a big ichibana (flower arrangement) exhibition and my first Noh drama, which also included a comedy about drunks which needed no explanation. However, my friend Kiichi Okuda was kind enough to explain it to some Americans. This attracted some Japanese who knew a little English, and the next thing we knew we had some excellent introductions to Nara and Kyoto, or Kegon and Zen Buddhism. We open our mouths, and instead of putting our feet in, we stick in our thumbs and pull out the plums.

Actually, I seem to have made a hit all over although I have not been trying. But a stranger is under observation. Accepting bowing, smiling, chop sticks, Japanese foods and Japanese religion cuts down the barriers. Then when they hear me offer my explanations of ichibana and Buddhism, there are no barriers at all. Besides, my two closest men friends, Paul Reps and Robert Clifton, have been accepted in Japan. And so it goes.

May 23   *Tokyo*

My dear Harry (Nelson):

[Harry Nelson was Samuel Lewis' main horticulture teacher at City College of San Francisco.— ed. note]

I sent you either a postcard or letter by regular mail some time back, but things are happening so fast and so excellently that it is most important to get this off airmail. Sometime ago I mentioned that my past was catching up with me, that many things which I had tried and failed in were coming to life. They have not only come to life now but are coming to success.

I am keeping a fairly complete diary which must remain in the background. It covers all kinds of subjects. I came to Japan with some knowledge of Buddhism, tea ceremony, painting, ceramics, gardens and horticulture, flower arrangement, history, customs and food — in a word, a good deal outside the language. I caught on and was caught on before I recovered from "land sickness." I met my old friends and met my new friend, James Kinoshita. I have already seen many things that few, if any, Americans have seen and am gaining new acquaintances, and perhaps friends, at a rapid rate.

You may be surprised to learn that Harry Nelson also is known and respected here — in the horticulture world, in the department of plant quarantine and in some sections of the Department of Agriculture. So much is this so that people are more than ever anxious to cooperate. In turn, I expect to take out a membership in "The Friends of the World" in your name.

On the third day here I went to Kamakura and was "taken behind the scenes." This gave me the opportunity to witness natural park scenery which was here used as a backdrop to the landscaping.... Ginkgo trees are prominent all over and at Kamakura also I saw one of the old and historic trees, which was huge. Of course, there are lots of cherries, plane trees and conifers. Cryptomeria more in temple grounds than in parks....

In the evening I was guest at tea given by some VIPs, chief of which was Baron Nakashima, who seems to have played an important part in his country's history and development. While most of the discussion was around Buddhism and Semantics, it was all done by leaders of The Friends of the World and will, I understand, lead to invitations to parks, gardens, etc.

When you consider that I have taken up here just one-third of one day's accomplishments, you may get an idea of how much is experienced.

May 24   *Kyoto*

Tonight my diary is dedicated to Chris. Here I am in a Japanese Inn, Seikuro Ryokan, dressed in a kimono, typing. We arrived last night and my first night sleeping on the floor was *sleeping.*

I had ordered a Japanese breakfast with coffee. Not being sure whether I had ordered a Japanese or American breakfast, they brought both. The slogan "eat a larger breakfast" ran into almost gargantuan dimensions.

We located Ruth Sasaki by phone last night and had very little difficulty in finding her. Ruth jumped right in and asked me some pointed questions. I told her that when Sokei-An Sasaki had in my presence said, "Yes, I see the future of the world, but I will not tell you about it," I caught the whole thing and foresaw World War II and the downfall of Hitler even before his rise. I told her you could find evidences of that in my poetry and in one notebook saved for many years, but I never told before that I got this in a single glimpse from Sokei-An. I then told her of the immediate cosmic communications I got from him. As I had told her about Furukawa over the phone and then how I brought Sokei-An and Senzaki together, there were no more doors.

KO (Kiichi Okuda) places Ruth Sasaki in the same class as Abbot Asahina—among the realized souls. I see no reason to change such a stand. We did, it is true, go over some semi-mundane matters so I could visit the N.Y. headquarters in a more intelligent manner. There is now a Roshi there. We both accepted our visit to RS as a pilgrimage to a living bosatsu [one who has realized Buddha-consciousness — ed.] and of the first order.

We then went downtown and bought two sightseeing tickets; having an hour to spare, we then taxied to the Sanjusangendo Temple. This contains the Hall of the Thousand Buddhas, which is an actuality and not a symbolic term. It is incomparable. The figures are all of the same size and of the same materials but with different mudras [symbolic gestures — ed.] and details. I do not know if it were possible for a single one to have been made by anybody without some enlightenment and the huge number made examination impossible. Besides, they are in rows and I do not know how to examine or judge those in the rear. However, there are so many in the front rows that you get dizzy. Unless, of course, you practice some meditation or spiritual concentration....

On the tour, we were then taken to the grounds of the Imperial Palace, very grand with all sorts of trees, and taken to all sorts of places which made it difficult for the photographers. "You must not take here, you should not here, here it does not matter and here you must take and we will not go on until you do." It was all very difficult for them. Fortunately, I have no camera. Add to that where you must and must not walk, and the fact that we were permitted to walk where the school-children were not and it becomes complex.

One thing is illegal, and that is to stand in front of the throne. This is not only discourtesy to the emperor, it is also discourtesy to the hundreds of sightseers who also want to look at it....

We got home tired and very hungry and supper was slow coming. Then it came: first tea, then a sort of custard with a soupy base which had to be eaten warm — some fish in it. Then the heaven-man-earth dishes with fish (raw) on the "heaven" side with onions, a kind of anchovy with some kind of bark or vegetable product on the "man" dish, and pickled vegetables on the "earth" dish. Arrangements, size and shapes according to symbols.

It is now the morning of the 25th; got up at 5:30 to type and be ready to go to Nara as early as possible.

May 25   *Post Cards to Stanton Delaplane*
[Ed. note: Stanton Delaplane is a columnist for the daily *San Francisco Chronicle*.]

Dear S.D.:

I am in Kyoto. I am not going to write to you about Kyoto. I am going to write to you about JTB. This is supposed to mean "Japan Travel Bureau." But as I am behind the scenes and using the "smile-with-chopstick" instead of the "cloak-mit-dagger" technique, in the interests of our country I should tell all.

The JTB uses a weapon we call the "abacus." It came from China. It does calculations. Once they set up a Japanese with an abacus against the adding machine. The latter got stuck at the post. Then we invited the calculating machine, but put your bets on the tortoise, gents, the hare hasn't got a hair of a chance. Then came the lightning calculator, but even Einstein didn't give that the speed of infinity. Finally, the electronic robot, but the abacus just laughed.

When MacArthur got unconditional surrender on the Missouri, he did not invite the abacus. That was the hidden weapon that even the kamikaze forgot. The General said (I ought to know, because my travelling companion is Kiichi Okuda, late of Daibutsu in Chinatown, who was Doug's interpreter): "You Japanese bad people. I fine you one billion yen." That looked like a lot. Well, they inflated and deflated and flated the yen until there are supposed to be 360 to the dollar.

The JTB got busy. The hotels raised their rates just 100 yen a day. 100,000 tourists came, paid 100 yen a day extra and that meant already 10 million a day. They stayed 10 days and that meant 100 million Yen. The restaurants just gave a slight revisal and the stores got busy, and pretty soon, before the season was over, the Americans raised the one billion to pay the debts we put on Japan. When we got a little soft, the abacus went to work.

There is another thing I notice in Kyoto—the national game called basebaru, which is played on every lot. I understand this game is popular in Brooklyn and Milwaukee. But as every American boy aspires to be President, he learns to play golf instead.

Of course, I am in difficulty. I have been a Braves rooter and was delighted to find Milwaukee ahead—maybe they use the abacus. But after one quaff of Asahi (beer), goodbye Schlitz, goodbye Blatz and we'll bury Anheuser-Busch by the old pine tree.

May 25

We took the 9:15 to Nara and arrived before 10. We went to the Shoso-in Treasure House containing almost the oldest art works outside of Horyuji. Almost cried before the Buddha there and chanted. The skill and inward calm of the artists was terrific.

We then went to the Daibutsu [Great hall of the Buddha—ed.], which is the largest wooden building in the world. The Buddha was stupendous and we saw the guardians and attendant Bodhisattvas flanked by many children. Before leaving, Okuda-san explained that I was interested in Kegon. This had been said before and brought most friendly greetings, but here we were invited to climb up and around the Buddha. We saw the details, where there had been gold inlay and the wonderful carvings in pictures and Chinese characters, some of which survived fire and what-not through the ages. This Daibutsu was originally financed by the Emperor and in some sense continues to be imperial property, although now part of the national treasure.

The monk said that Kegon was Buddhism par excellence and not sectarianism. That came later. We were united in a spirit of devotion. We were then taken through a courtyard (restricted) and saw the Bo-tree which was brought in, I believe, from Ceylon. It does not grow so tall and massive here as in India, but still is a large tree.

We were then introduced to Kainu Kemitsukasa, secretary-general of the Kegon Order and abbot of this temple-monastery. We were served ceremonial tea and met a professor who lectures on Kegon. . . .

116

All the beauty of the day, the seeing of the oldest treasures, the Daibutsu and the men have gone to my head. Now my introductory work for Japan is to all extent and purposes closed and my real work may begin.

May 28

After Horyuji, it did not seem possible to have another banner day, but yesterday was something again, for we are sure we have met a bosatsu. Philip Eidman is an invalid, confined to a wheelchair and with twisted fingers. Yet his knowledge of Buddhism seems second to none; he has karuna as well and perhaps better than wisdom, and he has plenty of intellect. . . .

Eidman gave us some knowledge of the weaknesses and strength of present day Buddhism.

Zen is in a deplorable state due to the legal anarchy concerning ownership and operation of the monasteries. It is neither congregational nor episcopalian but has resulted in either "abbotism"—the head monk controlling all without recourse — or the "museum attendants" holding the property and letting the monks get along as best as they can.

I told Eidman that so far I had seen two types of temples: the wealthy and the collectionists. At Nishi Hongwanji, which is wealthy, they have one collection box per temple. At the Kwannon temples and Horyuji you are reminded every moment to contribute (the Roman Catholics are pikers to what I have seen). Kwannon temples cut across sects and everybody seems to accept Kwannon. But instead of divinity helping humanity, the poor are giving and giving and with the number of statues abounding and the temples, the collection must be something, only it is not collected. It is just piled up, and I wonder what would happen if a typhoon came along and blew all that paper money around.

Buddhism is also divided between the intellectuals and the devotees, and there are several self-imposed philosophers who know all the book-Buddhism, but who are utterly lacking in compassion and humanity. Eidman has met many real awakened saints in Japanese country districts and in Burma. He is confident that their inner power will be strong enough to overthrow the self-imposers and the dilettante politicians who are making a cause of Buddhism.

May 28

The greatest pleasures of the Japanese seem to be bowing, being on wheels and becoming Westernized. That is all right for me. The first Father I met was in Kamakura, and I greeted him like a brother and he so greeted me, but the only priests I have seen since have had sour faces. This Father was beating the Japanese at their own game, while the others were refusing to play it. For there is something missing in Japanese religion. I have enjoyed Shinto music and weddings, but I see nothing deep or moving in folk religion as religion. Thus I am very far away from Judaism and from a large part of Christianity. In Catholicism and in temple Buddhism, one can step from folk-religion to cosmic-religion without too much difficulty. However, even I prefer the art and devotion to delineating philosophy. The look on eyes, faces and hearts is more striking than mouth-words.

May 29

The work with Kinoshita covers many facets, and we prepare to work together closely. The idea of an international tree-and-seed exchange and of building up the greenhouse, nursery, etc. at City College goes ahead. I mailed a cut-out from one of the papers on rose growing in Japan. I also took out a membership for Harry Nelson (City College) in the Friends of the World. This will enable Harry and JK to correspond and cooperate while I am off in other lands keeping separate contact with each. We settled visits to other experimental farms and gardens and actual visits to gardens on June 1 and 2. Then, after I go to Itako and spend some time writing,

118

to return to Tokyo and meet VIPs who are interested in the same subject.

May 30   *Sojiji, Tsurumi*

So far cost has been somewhat above even the highest estimation while the results far overbalance that, being beyond the wildest dreams and fulfilling down to the letter what Paul Reps and Hugo Selig predicted.

After our experiences at Engakuji, Daikokuji, Nishi Hongwanji-Tokyo, Nishi Hongwanji-Kyoto and especially Nara, we could not expect any more climaxes, but one came just the same. If I cannot pay Okuda-san in money as I hoped (which will be made up later anyhow), he is the living witness to experiences which we share together marvellously. This has led to the conclusion to start studying Japanese.

We were hosted by the Senior Monk Thizen Saito and offered tea — at least three times and given cakes for souvenirs. We were taken all around with changes from shoes to sandals to stocking feet — which I do not mind at all, in fact I enjoy. He explained to us the position of Amida and Buddha in Soto, which is exactly the same as that of Allah and Mohammed in most of Sufism — this down to details. The position of Manjusri makes it very clear and accounts more for the differentiation between Soto and Rinzai teachings than all the discussion which followed.

We talked about the need of English-speaking masters-of-meditation going to the States. The monk in San Francisco does not know much English and, ironically, he has been more successful in attracting Americans than Japanese. I have been asked to write at least one paper, to come and speak and even to live. The paper came to me inspirationally on the spot: "How To Be A Buddhist — How To Be A Buddha." This I may write at Itako for I have a full program the rest of the week. But at night the inspirations continued for my poem: "The Ascent of Mt. Fuji"....

I am not fooled by weaknesses or mistakes, but I do not let them cloud the vast areas of agreement. The whole nation must be lifted out of a miasma. Industrialization, followed by militarism and then defeat are three terrific shocks to these people.

June 8-9: Itako

I am living in a village, northwest of Tokyo, which is the home of my friend Kiichi Okuda, Japanese style. This place has been known for its iris, geisha, pretty girls and folk songs. I have been told they are no more. So I came to Itako and what do you think I have found? Right! However, my maid (and me a perennial bachelor) is much prettier than the geisha and a lot of the girls sing better. I guess they thought I was a G.I. I am the first American here since the G.I.s left. But we'll have to skip the girls here and go to the irises. . . .

Not far away from my ryokan was the Rinzai Zen temple, and we stayed so long that KO became hungry, but I was so interested I did not think about eating. Some of the original trees of this temple are still standing; they have preserved the actual trees which were admired by Basho long ago. This, to me, is one of the great wonders of Japan. Although the Bible teaches that "God does not dwell in temples built by human hands," here I realized it more than at any other place. These people simply would not cut down any imposing tree to build any house of worship. Not only that, but they give trees — not men — memorials. They put all the human memorials on a huge tablet and let it go at that. Tomorrow morning I shall be catapulted into a series of events which will climax my visit socially and scientifically, as it has already been climaxed spiritually. The receipt of the letter from J. Kinoshita, outlining the program for the coming week ends all of my past rejection forever. To be guest of a peer of the realm and later on to be invited to the Imperial Gardens, an honor restricted to high diplomats, climaxing a number of honors, makes this diary look like a fairy-book. What Inayat Khan proposed to me in 1923 is coming true and coming true rapidly.

June 10-14
(To Harry Nelson):

Yesterday we went to the Kitori shrine, which is northwest from here (Itako). I notice that whenever there is an old or majestic tree someone starts a shrine. The word *kami*, often translated "god," seems to be rather "nature spirit," and more related to the Grecian ideas than anything of the Indo-Germanic peoples. . . .

I had to continue something of my program of reading, singing and telling stories and games to children. When I became tired, we went to the iris show with the intention of voting and were begged to do so upon entering. We had no particular basis upon which to vote, but I selected one with a unique (to me) color combination. . . .

Unfortunately, at this date (6/14) I have heard neither from Hong Kong or Thailand, and if I do not hear soon will go to Thailand Embassy for advice. This becomes important because Baron Nakashima wants me to call on the P.M. of Thailand with his ideas; also Radhakrishnan, to whom I must write. We discussed, all rather melanged, Buddhism, Friends of the World and Universal Love. My later discussions with the Baron show an anti-Christian feeling, and I have proposed that instead of his Buddhist-Confucian front he work with all the Bandung nations. So far as Christianity is concerned, I defend Christ, but see no room for any "God" which excludes trees, flowers, mountains, atoms and light. It is not Christianity that is to be feared, but ignorance that goes by the name of enlightenment.

June 15
(To James Michener):

I once wrote you after reading "Sayonara" and now I write again. . . . I have come here to feel from the top of my hairs to the soles of my feet "Sayonara." I have come, perhaps, to write later, "The True Philosophy of Travel," to show the difference between a spirit rising in America as against a spirit sinking in Europe. I purchased new spectacles for this journey and, in a sense, am using them.

Samuel L. Lewis, a totally unknown simple American citizen, is guest of honor at the Imperial Gardens this afternoon. Coming here after studying Buddhism, Japanese spiritual and folk-art, history, horticulture, the first day of my arrival, I said, upon being taken to Sojiji Monastery at Tsurumi, Yokohama: "I feel strange that I do not feel strange. I do not feel as if I were in a foreign land, I feel at home." Since that hour I have been received as perhaps no American has been received.

I have seen Kwannon staring out of the eyes of millions of women. I see all the longing, hope, sadness and futility, deep passion and compassion, and these smothered by a strange combination of total exploitation and masterful spirituality which does not seem to belong to this world. The conversations with leaders have been at the highest level with requests to carry messages to other countries, or with introductions. Hongwanji and Zen, Kegon and Nichiren have treated me as a friend. I have been invited into homes, slept in ryokan, eaten their foods, enjoyed their baths and been here only a month.

The highest talks have everywhere centered around universal love, of a quality and type and degree one would hardly expect.... But all in all, where does Kwannon end and your "Sayonara" begin? Where does "Sayonara" end and Kwannon begin? The hearts of all lovers beat in unison, but the world, while saying it, does not know it—yet.

June 17

My visit to the Seicho movement this morning causes me to write now what may be a terrible warning, being superseded by something, which in the name of love and brotherhood, can do more to destroy the power of Uncle Sam than all the arms and weapons in the world. This is especially true if we continue to develop such scientific weapons of destruction as endanger all civilization. The simple answer of Jesus Christ is now being used and used effectively by all non-Christian peoples, i.e., the predominance of love.

The Seicho foundation is a fusion between synthesis and eclecticism of Shinto, Buddhism and Christianity. It emphasizes the practical side and admires Unity. It believes that ultimately we come to spiritual realization. Steps between manifest in healing and other phenomena which can be demonstrated in daily life. The people had more sense of humanity than any other group that I have yet met and women were permitted the same privileges as men.

We could easily forestall these movements, but I doubt whether we shall until it is almost too late. Ambassador Mehta came to San Francisco and pleaded for us to send Whitmans to the Orient. Instead we sent that glorious trinity—hip! hip! hurrah! and plenty of newspaper space: Richard Nixon, Glenn Clark and Billy Graham. . . .

Japan, in the name of anti-communism armed against China, with the U.S. and Great Britain leaving Russia alone. We, in the same name, backed the landlords of Korea and Indo-China, and backed the missionaries against anything which in any way resembles democracy. We backed the landlords and missionaries in Thailand and have won, so far. We backed them in Burma and Ceylon and got beaten at the elections. We backed the missionaries but *not* the landlords in India; we backed the landlords but *not* the missionaries in Pakistan. We have an organization called "brotherhood" in San Francisco headed by a man with a most suitable name: Just-Us. Against Just-Us is Pearl Buck's memorial translation of the Chinese counterpart of the Arabian Nights: "All Men Are Brothers."

June 27   *Tokugawa Biological Foundation*
(To Harry Nelson):

The basic purpose of this laboratory is to study from both the scientific and economical points of view the adaptation of the Algae Chlorella for food. Ford Foundation put up $300,000 in 1954 and the Japanese government an equal amount. . . .

I called attention to the work being done on microbiology and its value in plant feeding and questioned the use of inorganic fertilizers. They have come to the same conclusion—even for Algae, the inorganics are "dead" and are really forcing rather than feeding. They have come to the conclusion from their experiments that plants need many of the trace elements which have been shunned alike by the medical profession and the larger producers of fertilizers (inorganic).

Chlorella has the tremendous advantage of being a relatively cheap nitrogenous food, which is also replete with vitamins and trace elements, and if added to unpolished rice should be a perfect meal. Besides, there would be and could be no objection to it in India excepting taste. I ate some with Tendon (shrimp and rice) immediately afterwards, and with vegetable curry rice today, and to me, they made harmonious tasting meals. The taste is somewhat like seaweed, which I happen to like.

Japan 1956 (holding placard is Kiichi Okuda).

CHAPTER TWENTY-TWO

Magazine Article:

How to be a Buddhist?
How to be a Buddha!

—Written for Roshi Taizen Saito, Sojiji, Tsurumi, Japan
[Ed. note: first printed in The Western Buddhist, Autumn 1959.]

THERE ARE MANY PEOPLE IN ALL PARTS OF THE WORLD WHO claim to be Buddhists and some say there are 500 million followers of this form of Dharma. Yet although they accept this huge figure, many of them have been speaking in derisive terms of others and one is not always sure as to what they mean by "Buddhism" and "Buddhist."

Lord Buddha never actually taught "Buddhism." He sought to revive *Arya Dharma*, which means "noble wisdom" or even "ageless wisdom." He said that all people had perfect enlightenment but did not know about it. He laid down certain fundamental principles but these are fundamentals only insofar as they are expressed in words. They cannot be called absolute. For words are creations of minds at certain stages of cosmic evolution. It may be difficult if not impossible to express in words what belongs to other stages of evolution.

Buddha Sakya Muni tried to express his experiences in current terms. These were memorized by disciples, some of whom, according to the records, did not experience enlightenment. Still, the words were remembered and recorded. Many of these words have been accepted with reverence even by those who would not be called Buddhists or included in the 500 million.

Among these words are *anatta, anicca* and *dukha*. These belong to the Pali language, which was employed as the literary vehicle of the time. Anatta means that there is no inherent self in things. Anicca means that every thing (not everything) is subject to change and decay. Dukha means that pain is an essential ingredient in life. In this every follower of Dharma should show compassion and respect to the Theravadins, for they are Buddhists, and they have both respected and preserved fundamental teachings.

We have from the same source the very celebrated Pali formula:
Buddham Saranam Gacchami. . .I put my trust in the Buddha.
Dharmam Saranam Gacchami. . .I put my trust in the Dharma.
Sangham Saranam Gacchami. . .I put my trust in the Sangha.

Their repetition in some form may qualify what is a Buddhist, as apart from one who may be known as a non-Buddhist.

Here one may ask: If there is no "self," no "ego," who is it that says: "gacchami"—"I put my trust"? How can this first person personal pronoun be used if there is no self? Who is it and what is it that becomes enlightened?

From a certain point of view, this Pali formula of the "Three Jewels" constitutes the essence of the Dharma. Not the essence of Buddha or Sangha, but of Dharma. And this acceptance of Dharma, in this form, constitutes the essence of Buddhism, or the Arya Dharma of Lord Buddha.

Those who accept this formula without realizing Buddhahood may be called Hinayanists or Theravadins, which is to say, followers of the old or traditional teaching. In a sense, they have the Dharma, but have they the Buddha-jewel and the Sangha-jewel? Do they really know the Eightfold Path?

One must comment on the usual interpretation of the Eightfold Path as offered by the Southern Buddhists:

(A) The interpretation is not given from the standpoint of the experience of enlightenment.

(B) The whole Tripitaka literature is presented as if it were a supreme revelation offered by a unique personality appearing in the midst of total savagery.

This may be far from the truth. The India of Sakya Muni was of a very high order socially, intellectually and theologically. There was, if anything, too much prosperity; but the easy acquisition of wealth did not bring peace of mind. Much time was given to disputations and one mission of Lord Buddha was to end useless disputations. The very fact of these disputations proves it was not an era of idiots. Buddha did not come to destroy anything but ignorance. Consequently it is a mistake to ignore the Indian culture of the time and of preceding times.

Naturally there have grown up interpretations of the Eightfold Path quite diverse from the experience of enlightenment, and even showing verbal contradictions. The word *samma* which appears in each of the elements of the Eightfold Path really means "highest" (correlated to our "summit") or "universal," not "right." True Buddhism does not propose any "right" way of life as against any "wrong" way or ways, but a superlative, universal, supreme Way; an all-embracing anatta view, terminating in samma-samadhi consciousness of totality.

In the Pali literature it would appear that one of the first missions of Buddha Sakya Muni was to elevate humanity to perfection so that all who joined his brotherhood became *Arhats*, that is, perfect, enlightened beings. Yet this universal point of view seems to have become lost and while Buddhism spread both as a religion and philosophy, it did not always carry with it this experience of samadhi, or satori—as it is now called. This led to a break between those who had the experience and those who did not. It was something like a break between those who could write cookbooks and those who could cook. Humanity cannot live off cookbooks: it must have food.

The same diversion may be seen in the interpretation of "sangham saranam gacchami." Was this sangha—or brotherhood—composed of monks only, or did it include lay devotees (*sravakas*) or was it confined to those who experienced enlightenment? Could it not also be that many monks—i.e., bhikkus or bhikshus—may not have achieved spiritual emancipation and that many lay devotees did? As the power and authority rested with the monks, theology and institutionalism were fostered. All Buddhists did not achieve enlightenment; many non-Buddhists did.

There is also the formula *Namatasa Bhagavato Arhato Samma-Sambhodasa*, which is translated: "Salutation to the Perfect One, the Wholly Enlightened One, the Most Supreme Buddha." This formula identifies the Arhat-experience with the Buddha-experience. It does not leave large gaps between one stage and the other. But in Mahayana literature there are such gaps. One may sometimes wonder if, having become freed from one set of recipe-writers one has not fallen into the hands of another set without finding any real cooks and so obtaining bread.

From another point of view, the Dharma-tradition is not a Dharma-transmission. That is to say, it cannot be limited to doctrines. The Three Jewels emphasize Buddha, Dharma, Sangha. Satori also emphasizes Buddha, Dharma, Sangha. But this is not a verbal experience, it is not a limiting of truth to words; it signifies the truth of Buddha-enlightenment passing from person to person and it also means a Sangha-transmission of truth-in-the-while-of-manifestation.

Here we have something more than philosophical truth. We have living truth. Buddha-transmission goes from enlightened person to enlightened person and this has been from the time of Sakya Muni to now. This is also called "transmission of Dharma."

And what does the experience of enlightenment bring? Not some philosophical explanation of ten kingdoms which may exist in theory or in actuality, but the conscious realization of them both within one's "self" and in the universe. Then there is no difference between self and the universe. Then there is no difference between self and self, between self and totality. We are everything we comprehend or apprehend. What we understand is — or becomes — us; separations are in words and illusions.

Thus there is much more in universal Buddhism than in becoming a Buddhist. One becomes Bosatsu, the Bodhisattva who sees all beings, enlightened and ignorant, with the same compassion. He does not frown upon the multitudes who do not know the Dharma or who have incomplete notions of Dharma. He treats all from the standpoint that nothing is true except enlightenment and yet this enlightenment belongs to all. Thus he is able to help others though he does not consider his actions as help-to-others. In other words, the supreme end of Buddhism is that every one is a Bodhisattva and comes to realize that he has always been a Bodhisattva — or Buddha.

May 1958: "Mill Valley, California, horticulturist enthusiast Samuel L. Lewis, right, last Thursday presented to Los Angeles City Recreation and Park Commission a supply of Gingko tree seeds from Japan for planting at municipal parks and play grounds. Lewis made the presentation as a member of 'The Friends of the World,' an organization which seeks to promote world peace through the exchange of trees and seeds" (Los Angeles City Recreation and Parks Department photo and release).

CHAPTER TWENTY-THREE

Excerpts from Letter-Diaries:

Hong Kong, Thailand, 1956

I have been writing seriously and funny, and doggone it if a syndicate did not approach me, and I am not ready yet. . . .

June 30   *Hong Kong*
(To Stanton Delaplane:)

Hong Kong is a British Colony. It is not English—good heavens, no! It is largely Chinese. The loyal subjects of the Crown are divided into three groups: (a) Veddy; (b) Semi-veddy; (C) Right Joes—who are in the vast majority. The Veddy people are few in number and won't let anybody join them until one departs from this land by any and all means. They include some who were incarcerated by the Japanese; anyhow you have to be here a long time to join their ranks.

They include school-teachers, clergy and any remote relatives of clergy, retired civil servants and such. They teach the children to sing "God Save the Queen," but not very successfully. The children have some remote idea that this refers to Queen Elizabeth II, but the Veddy are always thinking of Victoria or at least Queen Mary. This has produced a serious impediment in getting the children—who are of all races, but mainly Chinese—to take anything too seriously.

The Semi-veddy form yacht clubs and drink. They have money. Their motto is, of course, "We have not been introduced." They want it that way except that it keeps them out of the Veddy group and they would like to be Veddy and are thus self-excluded.

I must not write about the "Right Joes," because I could never get in, ever. The "Right Joes" are often in trade and to be "in trade"....
Yes, I actually once had a grand uncle of the Uncle Bim Gump type, Australian citizen, of course, and I still have one loaded cousin down there. The rest all died off and let her struggle with the collector of internal revenues. They told me what it means to be "in trade." Let the Chinese be "in trade."

July 1

Ever since Stoddard wrote "The Rising Tide of Color," there has been an undercurrent in Asia of "Asia for the Asiatics." No matter what appears on the surface, it is my belief that underneath the Bandung nations will support Japan and take every advantage of the American-Russian impasse to see that both are gradually put in their places.

As I see it today, both Russia and the U.S. have stuck their necks out, both are imperialistic, both are working in their own ways for a kind of white supremacy, which both will deny. And both contain large sectors of people who will be more against the Africaans (Boers) in South Africa than the British or Hindus are. In other words, that same strange psychology that gave us both prohibition and liquor is in operation....

I must confirm my suggestions that non-Christian religions will become anti-U.S. in a way that communism has never been anti-U.S. and we can lose our tempers and howl and that is all. My host says I am one of the few people who knows how to perceive and wants to take me to the Press Club to tell your colleagues how to really get information in the Orient. He is very pessimistic after living here a long time. He insists that the newsmen are lazy and exceedingly subjective, that they do not know where or how to find real information. Certainly my methods are different.

In the past I learned about communists by going to communist meetings or meetings where they spoke and not by interviewing them or their enemies privately. I have learned ways of infiltration—which have been reported to the FBI—ways too subtle for the press.

What does the Fourth Estate stand for: Christianity, staying away from church themselves, liquor and plenty of it, whoring—high class if possible, low class if not—and disdain for humanity, humanism and humanitarianism. It is so far away from realities that I find less difference between high industrialists and leftist unskilled labor than between either and the press. The press simply will not stand for reforms. The press follow the Senator from Formosa and concentrate on "anti-ism" without facing or realizing what the problems of the world are.

When I went to the Embassy of X in Japan, more to test where I really stood after being so well received by the Japanese, I presented the following:

A. Introduction of trees for swamp drainage and for arid areas.

B. Introduction of economically valuable cacti in desert regions.

C. Introduction of fertilizers which will not leech out with rains and which will cooperate with micro-organisms (this may invoke enmity of certain large businesses and goodwill of others).

D. Methods of getting fresh water from the ocean at low-cost.

E. Introduction of algae as a source of low-cost proteins with natural minerals and vitamins, obviating the need of medicinal expenses to supplement foods.

F. Respectful visits to shrines and holy places of any and all faiths.

First I was refused audience on the ground that I was too important (a new one for me). Then, after 1½ hours, I was asked to terminate the interview and meet the ambassador.

I represent the opposition of reality to realism. I represent views based on actual historical and cultural knowledge against superficialities. I represent direct observation, as insolence, against indirect methods. The rise of Buddhism, Confucianism, etc. will not be reported. The ways these will be used against the U.S. will be bypassed. The possible alliance of Nasser and Nehru with these forces will cause both the U.S. and Russia to retreat. And our confounded trust in super-power with the superficial claims to religious beliefs will cause us to be distrusted even by some of the most anti-communist groups in the world.

I have been to more places where the supreme teaching was love and compassion. And this "love" has nothing whatsoever to do with the four-letter-word covering the behavior of cats (and their human counterparts) in the daily press. I can only repeat my warnings: in the Orient, one reporter is worth four communist agents; and what is more, the U.S. pays for the reporters and thus saves China and Russia money.

Of course the actual *teachings* of Christ could counterbalance all this. But not even Schweitzer and certainly not Stanley Jones—a thousand times less Billy Graham and a million times less the playboy from Orange County. I am well prepared to meet any Indian or neutralist in debate, but know this is difficult. I shall carry Whitman and Emerson and Jefferson, and above all Bobby Burns's "A man's a man for a' that."

July 3

Dr. Leung Tit San belongs in the same class with the Buddhist abbots met in Japan. We were together for 2½ hours, and it was nothing but a symphony of close harmony. It was another glorious occasion where I found myself in complete accord with an Oriental on Oriental matters where in some instances Occidentals have refused to accord, or have given downright different interpretations of Oriental "wisdom.". . .

The Human Body: We proposed two points which are entirely out of accord with present day Western teachings: (A) The human body and human personality is essentially a cosmos. (B) There is something more fundamental than even blood which he says roughly speaking means "air" or "breath" and yet is not either. I found absolutely nothing which was essentially different from Kaballah and the highest aspects of Sufism and Hindu teachings, which things have seldom if ever been given to the Western world.... The immediate conclusion is that the human body reflects everything in the universe. He says that the bladder is more important than the heart. His further explanation threw, for me, more light upon the "chakra" in the gonadal region than anything I have gained from Indian or Tantric writing. It is both cosmic and down-to-earth and none of the hyperbolic "psychic" stuff thrown out to the West by the pseudo-enlightened. I could follow his nerve tracings and believe he could knock all the neurologists over....

Chinese Wisdom: Truth is universal. It was mutual recognition that brought Taoism, Buddhism and Confucianism together. They are still together on Mt. Omei-Shan which he assures me is the repository of the greatest living wisdom. By this he means the greatest living sages, illuminated men. It is also a region of great beauty and if it be possible I should go there some day....

American Medical Association: He is utterly uncompromising on this point. To me there is no such thing as "medical logic," just a huge trial-and-error society with a monopoly on drugs and practices....I called his attention to "Gestalt Psychology," and to the crazy pattern that in America if you don't accept "Gestalt" you may be regarded with suspicion, but if you want to apply "Gestalt" to Physiology, you are ruined. The AMA simply won't let it....

Breath: It is about time to take a lot of fake mystery away and put the true mystery there. The relationships between breath, consciousness, time-and-space functioning, etc. have been sealed off....

In order to understand Chinese medicine, as well as all herbologies stemming from ancient wisdom, it is necessary to change our entire concept of space. Can we prove that space is not living? We have a glorified vacuum, or void *psychology* of space which has only a negative satisfaction. European science, up to and including Paracelsus was based on the existence of vital forces in bodies — human, animal and plant....Christianity has done incalculable harm by making use of words like "pneuma," and 'psyche" and clothing them with entirely different meanings than that of the Greeks. *Pneuma* (as used in the

Greek New Testament and elsewhere) in particular seems to come very close to the Chinese conception of fundamental-wind (or air). And thus Galen and Hippocrates may have some contents not too far from Chinese science.

July 11   *Bangkok*
(To Rudolph Schaeffer:)

Here I am in the land of the "free" or Thai. I arrived after a comedy of errors, but somehow or other located the house of Princess Poon Diskul. She was not at home but presiding over a big Buddhist meeting. The Vice-President greeted me and to my surprise, I learned that my very dear friend Robert Clifton—now Bhikku Sumangalo—was in a house nearby (monastery). We met and spent 2 hours together and then I was directed to my friend K. Patel. Mail on both sides had not come through.

Patel seems to know everybody in Southeast Asia and could be of greatest assistance to the United States. Actually all power is in the hands of the monks. I met the Chief Abbot through him and found that he is the Chief Abbot's chief lay assistant. So I can meet anybody in Burma or Thailand.

Yesterday I was with Princess Poon about 2½ hours. We spent a good deal of time at the National Museum. I regret to say that both there and while with the Senior Monk of the Chief Abbot, while they both extended all kindness, they walked too fast for me. Now I am one of these guys who is a rabbit at climbing mountains but a snail in art galleries. This is confusing, and I don't blame anybody, but that is the way it is. . . .

Now, for the record I am going to give you the nasty news. All Buddhists and pseudo-Buddhists theoretically believe in karma—that we reap what we sow; then they make many, many exceptions. That puts the stock of certain schools of Asian studies in the U.S. pretty much below zero. . . .When I mentioned my own criticism of certain Buddhist intellectuals in the U.S., I was all but thrown out on my ear, only to hear these same people criticized in Japan. When I told Princess Poon I had done this she all but embraced me. Religion and devotion are not elaborate forms of metaphysics without beginning and without end. The devotion of the heart, the expression of calm compassion, the extension of love, the actual growth of wisdom which is reflected in one's daily deeds—these matter. I have met so many leaders now, wise men, realized people, and they all tend toward universality and the experience of cosmic illumination. Some are engrossed in deep translations and interpretations and some in esthetic movements. But there is no real difference.

There is a coming together of hearts which neither politicians nor Roerichs can understand. My host, K. Patel, understands and he is one of the leaders. Neither materialistic Russia nor materialistic America will dominate the world. But the United States has to make some changes, and I hope you will, at least, see my point of view: *if the United States wishes to further either capitalism or democracy in the Orient, she must stop supporting Christian missionary movements*. It is that simple.

However, the U.S. is full of Professors-Suez-Canalas who think they link the East and the West and whose influence does not extend beyond their campus and not always there. I tell you, Rudolph, if you admire a single Buddha figure here it goes as far as if you have read all the Pali Scriptures—and sometimes further.

July 13

Today I went to Mahatato Temple where people come from long distances to practice Dhyana (meditation). It is a samadhi-dhyana— I don't care what the books say. . . .

Bhikkus (monks) seem either to smile or scowl, and my bet is that the smiling ones are the realized ones. I saw a boy go into samadhi-dhyana and the monk first explained why and how the boy was strong and I tested it. I also realized more fully the source of my own strength. There is more attention to breath than text-books suppose. . . .

July 14

The next visit was one of the high points of my life. It was to the Annamese Temple which is called War Samanamboriharn. I was told that these people have no use for Americans and one would be unwelcome. I experienced no such difficulty.

In the first place, on entering, I pointed to a scroll on the wall (rough outline painting) and said, "That is Tamo." It was correct. I saw an altar which is very elaborate. Again the Omito figure dominated with a comparatively small Buddha. But there were many kinds of Buddhas, including the Burmese type. . . .

I was told that the Abbot, Bao-rung, was an illuminated soul. I must say that he looked very much like Roshi Asahina in Japan. In fact, the whole resemblance was remarkable. Later, he looked over to me and this confirmed it in so far as one can judge outwardly. The chief difference is that Bao-rung gives up all his time to help humanity and to heal people. He seems to understand the nervous system, and prods the vital spots with an instrument which seems pointed, but did not puncture any tissues. It was like a sort of "chiropractic" on finer bodies, or based on the physiology of the traditional Chinese system.

July 20

I did not receive other mail at Bangkok, nor were my own letters received, nor did I get letters written by some people. I left with the information that my flights have been okayed onto Calcutta. When I got to Rangoon, it was not so. I found I could not book passage. Then I located Pakistani Air Lines and was told there was a plane which would take me to Chittagong and a hotel room would be provided. . . .

The Hotel Strand in Rangoon is the scene of mystery, cloak and dagger intrigue. I was watched from the beginning. I began to talk softly about Buddhism and increased the amplitude so people did not have to eavesdrop. As there were Czechs and Chinese of doubtful backgrounds and others around, it was as well. No one dares to handle a good Buddhist. But when I took a taxi I learned to be a Muslim. The Hindus overcharge; the Muslims have a fixed rate, and when I greeted them they shaved this down.

Hyderabad, India, 1956: At home of M. Fayazuddin Nizami Chisti (second from right). Next to Samuel Lewis is Usman Solehani, Minister of Parliament.

CHAPTER TWENTY-FOUR

Excerpts from Letter-Diaries:

East Pakistan, 1956

[*Ed. note: The selections from letter-diaries for Dacca are supplemented with material from* The Lotus and the Universe, *Chapter 15,* "In Search of Sufis."]

July 20   *Dacca*

I got off to Dacca bright and early and all bound with red tape and arrived to find that my host friend had just left Dacca for Chittagong. I was left a message which led me to the Shah Bagh Hotel. Hardly had I signed the blotter when I found myself talking to a University of California student from Berkeley who knew the first reference I gave him and also knew Muin Khan, who had invited me here in the first place.

I completed a letter to Vilayat (son of my first teacher in Sufism) and went out on what is to me one of the most remarkable of all my adventures so far (and they are crowding in on me thick and fast). Through a chance meeting in the hotel lobby, I met one after another the family of my friend Muin Khan. This included Sophia Kamal who is the leading poetess of East Pakistan. Her husband asked me if I wanted anything and I said I would like to meet Sufis.

In half an hour I was in a courtyard filled with men of all sorts and I was about to sit down when the gentleman next to me demanded: "Who is your Murshid?"

"Pir-O-Murshid Sufi Inayat Khan."

"Just a moment . . ." He turned away from me quite abruptly, stood up and said: "Brothers, there has just arrived in our midst a man from whose speech I judge is an American. He is a disciple of the late Pir-O-Murshid Hazrat Inayat Khan whose works you know I am now translating into Bengali. I think we should meet this American brother."

Maulana Abdul Ghaffour was the Chisti Pir-O-Murshid in Dacca. He had been a professional athlete, a champion football player, adept at other games and had been manager of a stadium in Calcutta prior to partition. He had been suspected of being mixed up in politics and had to flee, leaving members of his family behind. Here again one was struck with the very "unsaintlike" behavior of the Murshid. When I came into the courtyard he was showing one of his disciples how to cast, what flies to use and when. Perhaps there was something in it vaguely resembling "Zen and the Art of Archery." Hazrat Inayat Khan's invocation: "Toward the One. . ." is equally Sufic and Zen.

I asked the Maulana a very deep question and he came up with appropriate deep answers. He gave me my new Ryazat, or spiritual practice, and predicted my future for a limited period. I shall not go into details, but despite the deprecations of some of the followers of Hazrat Inayat Khan in Europe and America, he more than confirmed what Murshid said to me in 1923 and 1926, and added to them. I no longer have any choice. It is the same as foretold at birth: either world fame or ignominy, no middle path here.

I read my "Sand and Glass," a tribute to the Prophet Mohammed on his birthday two years ago. . . .This has come quickly on my first day. All the things of my life are clearing. I am with friends of Murshid and even before I knew it had the spiritual directions for my next stages. Everything I have felt or thought or said has been confirmed, and this by an illuminated soul. It was foretold I would get guidance, but this has come with suddenness and swiftness. I cannot turn back. The work that God has given me will, inshallah, be fulfilled.

(further entry on the 20th July:)

One thing I cannot overestimate is the kindness and hospitality already received. It is the finest yet. I met the Japanese as if we loved each other, but I meet these people as if we were part of one family, very close indeed.

July 24

The visit to Dacca is like an elongated comic opera. Each day the Sufis give me a big feast, then the Vedantists give me a larger one. . . .

When you meet real saints, real qawwalis, real sages and real Sufis and feel that marvelous spirit, you can ask for no more. But neither can you surrender to less. . . . I was strongly challenged last night but reached this agreement: either Islam or universal religion. Either Islam proves its superiority or it must join with other religions as one of several ways. It will not bow down to other religions, but it must either take its place alongside of them or prove its prowess. It does not prove its prowess by argument and force, still less by rage and anger.

I admitted it was possible for sages of other faiths to reach the higher stages and perhaps even the highest. But I had to add I have not yet myself met any non-Muslim superior to my own teacher and I have met the greatest in Buddhism and Christianity. The real test will be with the Hindus. If they have love and insight, I shall have to admit it. . . .

Therefore I am not against Nehru as some people are. I speak here of his philosophy. My stand on Kashmir is that if we surrender to God, this will straighten out the problem. But the Muslims are going to lose Kashmir because they have made the thought about Kashmir a partner to the thought about God and sometimes they think more about Kashmir. This is not Islam and can only have the same results as happened in other lands. Seek wealth, property and empire and you will lose both them and God. Seek Allah and you may gain wealth, property and empire. At least this is my stand now.

July 27

Last night I went to an Islamic wedding. The place was packed. The scene stepped right out of the Bible and offered what our Christian missionary friends have seldom displayed. Perhaps it would not be fair to say I was overfed. Guests were limited to one helping, then the servants, then the poor relations, then the poor from near and far until all the food was gone. I understand that about 700 persons partook thereof. Not only did we not see the bride, but the groom proved to be quite an unimportant person, a sort of manikin on display. All the people came to see the Sufi teachers. I sat between the Chisti and Kadri Pir-O-Murshids so it happened I was not only greeted more than the groom, but even more than the respective fathers-in-law, who bore the brunt of the proceedings. . . .

I must now state once and for all that this nonsense in San Francisco about there being no Sufis or that they are unimportant must stop. Pir Maulana is the most perfect *ordinary* man I have ever heard about, but his father was extraordinary (about that later). Through the Pir I have met leader after leader here — civil, military, professional, educational. There is hardly an important man in East Pakistan that I have not met.

I did not have a chance to rest when my friends took me to the tomb of Pir Shah Ali. Dervishes came to East Bengal around 856 A.H. and began converting the peasants and established the first mosque in a wooded country. A century later the Pir came and really established Islam, this long before the Mogul conquest. . . .

My name has been changed from A. Murad to Ahmed Murad by Pir Maulana. My initials will be S.A.M., which stands both for Sufi Ahmed Murad and also for SAM, my usual name, short for Samuel.

July 29

There was a grand send-off dinner. I was feted and had the most loving embrace from a large number of men, some saintly, many officials and intellectuals, but all loving. I was advised to visit the tomb of Pir Maulana's father Dadajan in Calcutta. He is reputed to have been *Qtub* or head of the Spiritual Hierarchy recognized by all the Dervish Orders and is popularly known as "The Murshid." The symbol of Atlas holding the world on his shoulders gives a faint idea of the Qtub, who feels the responsibility for all the sorrows of the world; in other words, he is also Bodhisattva, but in another terminology.

The departure from Dacca was most notable. I was accompanied by the army chief, Brigadier Ghulam Mohammed Khan; his aide Captain Mohammed Sadiq, Ansar Nasri of Radio Pakistan, Abdul Wahab who was translating Inayat Khan's works and who brought many associates, a delegation from Dacca University and the whole income tax department.

I also found fellow Sufis on the plane. I came directly to Mr. Haidar's house in Calcutta. After a short supper, we went to the Murshid's shrine and I started to chant *zikr*, but soon the Murshid was using my body to chant through. He then told me that I need not wait to go to Ajmir. He confirmed the "flute music" which plays through me and said that I was to use this gift immediately. Also, he gave me the blessing of the crescent and star at the top of my forehead above where Murshid Inayat Khan had made his sign. He said he would guide my footsteps in India, certainly 'till I went to Delhi and visited the Dargahs (tombs). . . .

Now I have been nominated as a candidate for the Waliyat. My directions with regard to the disciples of Pir-O-Murshid Inayat Khan are simple: I am to be the Shams-i-Tabriz and Vilayat the Maulana Rumi. . . .

The whole trip has been stupendous but the Pir Maulana said it will be more so. "Food for India" and "Water for Pakistan" still stand out. There is much to be done, but I must take one thing at a time. Pir Maulana says, "This breath is the one that counts." At the same time, there is an all-abiding, all-pervading Divine Breath.

CHAPTER TWENTY-FIVE

Excerpts from Letter-Diaries:

India, 1956

July 29   *Calcutta*

I have just returned from Dakshineswar, the temple compound famous for its association with Ramakrishna, Vivekananda and the Tagores....I am not to be taken as an authority. I can only see according to my own light and training. I differed somewhat from the Hindus on the subject of awe. I differ from them very, very strongly upon returning from the temple. I entered the place with more interest in architecture than in religion or sculpture. I left with the same feeling. There is a distinct flavor of the buildings which is akin to frozen music....

I admit that I have a tremendous respect for Ramakrishna, Vivekananda and the Tagores. The Swami Maharaj of Dacca (of the Ramakrishna Order) who gave me an introduction is a saint; there is no doubt about that in my mind. But there is an almost impassable gulf between Indian scriptures and Indian worship, only part of which is bridged by the architecture....

There are several temples in the compound, and I liked better than those the meditative place under the banyan trees. Saints build up atmospheres, and ignorant people have enough *savoir faire* to know they can benefit by breathing in those places. There is a possibility that someday I shall write on "Real Saints, Real Sages, Real Shrines." I stand between those who deny their existence and those who clothe them with awe, imagination, fantasy and hyperbole....

August 1   *New Delhi*

The diary is getting full. I spent two days in Calcutta, chiefly in the company of disciples of Maulana Ghaffour. In addition to twice visiting the shrine of Pir Maulana's father, we also went to the tomb of a Syed saint and I felt the atmosphere very strongly. I then sought some healing power to help my friends.

Ansar Nasri had given me an introduction to Hussein Nizami (son of the late Pir Hassan Nizami of Delhi), which I had showed to many people and had somehow misplaced. So upon arriving in Delhi, I hailed a taxi to take me to Hussein, only to discover this. By a "fluke" the taxi stopped right in front of Pir-O-Murshid Inayat Khan's tomb. Went in and cried copiously.

Then I met Hussein, who is a fine, spiritual young man, and had a long talk about Sufi publications in English and an international Sufi alliance. Together we visited the tomb of Nizam-ud-din Auliya and Princess Jayonara. Once again one was greatly impressed and chanted Zikr.

August 5

(To Harry Nelson:) I am in a land made famous by Kipling. My actual life is much more like that of an actual strange character of some of his stories. I want here to restrict the communication to horticultural notes. My host here in India, Rajenda Singh Parmar, has risen in the world since we last parted company and has told me that he can introduce me to almost everybody in horticulture and farming....

East Pakistan is having a famine. There is plenty of meat to eat, so I did not starve and was actually given a feast every night. The land is rather barren and I have written to Washington on the need to have more people from the South come and advise. The country has had only three products: rice, jute and tea—the last of which you can't eat. I came out boldly for diversified crops. I also

145

learned more of the failure of chemical fertilizers and the need for organics.

August 19   *Dehra Dun*
(To Harry Nelson:)

I came to Dehra Dun, because I heard from all sources that it had the best Forestry Station in Asia. I agree. I have already purchased three books: "Forty Trees Common in India," "The Afforestation of Dry and Arid Areas" and "A List of Plants, etc." I shall try to mail them in Delhi. My time here is taken up in writing, forestry men and personal contacts, the most important of which so far threw me right back into your lines. . . .

August 19

After having a most satisfactory meeting with representatives of the Arya and Brahmo Samajes, I reached an impasse with the leader of Sanatana Dharma in Simla. My point was that equality in size of statues of Kali and Krishna and equality of ceremonials did not result in the same spiritual elevation. Finding he could not satisfy me, he sent me to one Swami Baskrananda.

I called on the Swami the next day, after finding he was head of a Parliament of Religions in India. Their methods are very straightforward. If you went to a nuclear physics colloquium, you would have to present a paper or some evidence of your laboratory research. In a similar way at these parliaments, you must have had some religious experiences to be permitted to speak. Otherwise you would be ruled out; opinions and documentaries regarded as wasting time and also showing lack of consideration for others.

I felt very distinctly that the Swami wanted me to attend such colloquiums at some future time and also to present his ideas abroad. We then went into the discussion of the day before and on the whole he was getting the best of me. I then asked for a recess and chanted

146

my "Flute of Krishna." He never said a word but sat and stared me straight in the face with an expression almost of amazement. To him I had proved my point.

Stopped at the Anandamayee Ashram. I had been told of the place twice. I went in and most immediately felt an elevating atmosphere, the nature of which is hard to explain and which I intend to write up in their magazine. . . . I told someone there my criticism of the magazine. It was short: Mother says, "I want to be honey." The disciples say, "I want to taste honey." I told her that was the destruction of the work of every divine personality in the history of the world. But as I have received a blessing at least 10,000 times that of Dakshineswar, I have been asked to write that, too.

August 24   *Delhi*

Returned to Delhi and saw Hussein Nizami as soon as possible. He gave me a book which I have asked him to send to the Pakistani Consulate in San Francisco. This book has the picture of Rabia Martin in it and I am going to have it translated from Urdu to English as it contains some material about Murshid. I am to have a special photo taken at Murshid's tomb. . . .

I have gone to the Jama Masjid, which looks better in photos than fact, the opposite of the one in Calcutta. But when I was shown the hair of the Prophet, I broke into a loud cry; it was a cry neither of joy nor sorrow but like that of a madzub.

August 29

At night I went to the Tara Singh testimony. It was remarkable. The meeting was opened by a descendant of Nizam-ud-din Auliya. Hussein told me that Guru Nanak (the founding Sikh teacher) was originally a Sufi. There were other Muslims also, one speaking passionately for the Kashmiris. He did not think much of the politico-religious state. There were also several Indians. One of the main speakers was the Sikh in opposition to Tara. When it was nearly over Nehru came in, and he was the only one who did not speak like a politician. In the end Tara and Punditji (Nehru) went out together, and the next day news came of a political alliance. It is hard to tell what it means—Sikhs accusing each other of not wanting to line up with Hindus and pro- and con-communalism—quite confusing to a foreigner....

Later visited Hussein and we visited the tomb of Humayun, which impressed me very much. Next we circumambulated the grave of Dara Shikoh with "Ya Allah" 7 times and then repeated "Allah Hu" 21 times. Then visited the ruins of the khankah of Nizam-ud-din Auliya. Wish to meditate where he did, to spread out a carpet and also give spiritual help to humanity therefrom. This should be possible on my next visit.

That evening at dinner I was introduced as an American Sufi.

"What does Sufism mean?" someone asked.

"God alone exists."

"That is the same as Vedanta."

"Yes."

September 3   *Agra*

I went to Jaipur on August 31, because it is a "must." Everything is a "must" here. You "must" visit places which the other fellow hasn't seen, and you are free to give whatever contribution you want to men who cannot read, and there is a sign on the wall to report to the Government all efforts at beggary. If you did that it would take up 24 hours of each day. Jaipur is the cleanest city in India; they have laws there that you can only build in pink or white, and you have to keep it clean. So it is called the Paris of India....

I didn't see any slave girls, and if I dreamed of them at night I would charge others admission to come in. But the Maharajah of Jaipur is still functioning, and when I was in his palace they were getting out the red carpet for Earl Warren. I mean just that—and no figure of speech. They were also getting out the blue, green and a lot of other Persian carpets. Because nowadays Maharajahs cannot buy slave girls, only carpets. . . .

Then I came to Agra, and at the Imperial Hotel I met a woman who had to leave to be hostess to the Warrens. But she introduced me to a temporary guest—ah! young, beautiful and costumes. Well, I have given pictures and two addresses, and she not only does all the ancient Indian dances but is said to be the best rhumba artist in the country. She is divorced, but don't get any ideas, because there are several girls back home who have. Anyhow, I am going south and she north. Think nothing of it. But we are both going around in circles. . . .

I am not going to write on the Taj. A book has been written on it. If I come again, I may write on the landscaping of it. Most of the writers are filled with such enthusiasm—and ignorance—that no matter if they turn out bestsellers, they are often wrong. The Taj is, was and ever will be the acme of *Persian Art*. The whole thing is essentially Persian from one end to another. The use of columnar cypresses and the employment of squares and fountains is a continuation of a traditional art.

I don't know the names of many of the trees. You find long-needled pines in Agra and evidently the choice of materials is due to uncertain rains, often drought. There are two kinds of lawns, one of which is watered by flooding, or control of the water table. The other depends on rain and is kept mowed. Several species of *Impatiens* serve as central plants and the border seems to be a kind of *Boracaea*. Everything is kept clean. Fountains only run once a week. There are faucets for emergency watering. They use two-inch hoses mostly. The trees are filled with birds and the park with chipmunks. Dawn is musically noisy. A large portion of the gardeners are women.

September 3

This is the 15th letter of the day. One was a sarcastic letter pointing out a serious defect in the Hindu religion: first God, then Paragod, then Mahaparagod, then Mahaparagodnarayan, then Mahaparagod-narayaneshwara who is small stuff before Shri who quails before Shri Shri who is nobody before Shri Shri Shri. . . .

I will not say this for the Ramakrishna Mission which claims it is now very strong in India. If it is strong, it is because they have better Swamis than those they send to the U.S. . . .

My final visit to the Anandamayee Ashram was short and most important. I definitely felt her instructions which were like this:

All these swamis, true and false, establish sanghas and in turn these sanghas tend to perpetuate the names of their founders. This has the two questionable results of establishing rival sanghas— which is ridiculous—and producing mental idolatry in place of the physical ones at the temple. In either case, instead of finding God, you find something or someone else. Real instruction comes from self to self.

September 17   *Nasik*

I went out for a walk early and ran into a real Swami. Then in the evening I thought I would speak to a stranger in the hotel. I had just written some poetry which I hope to be able to present to the Nizam of Hyderabad—at least I can hope—and pushed it in front of the stranger. He proved to be a Chisti Sufi. You see, the unconscious, when God-guided, is more successful than anything. . . .

Every 12 years there is a great pilgrimage to Nasik where Rama is supposed to have stayed 11 months. People go there and bathe in the river. Yesterday was the climax and the crowds were in tremendous multitudes. . . .We got to the river and I baptized myself. There were all kinds of ceremonials going on and I can say the sideshows out-distanced the circus. After a lot of walking— which I enjoyed—we visited the "Fruit Swami." He began immediately to talk about God and self in ways I think one ought to talk about God and self. A Mrs. Kabali makes it her business to collect funds to give to him and this is used to distribute fruit to the people. Another lady was distributing bread free. She gave to multitudes sitting quietly against a wall. But a crowd began to follow her and make demands. She called the whole thing off. In this you see the best and worst in India. There is an extreme lack of human consideration, with an intense devotion.

Evidently the fruit swami has his own disciplinary methods. But he impressed me both inwardly and outwardly and gave me "spiritual" instruction, by which I do not necessarily mean intellectual dissertations. He explained to me the two methods of spiritual training, called the "monkey method" and the "cat method." In the monkey method, the baby holds onto the mother and wherever the mother goes the mother carries the baby. In the cat method, the cat picks up the kitten and teaches it to walk. So the cat tries to make its offspring an adult as soon as it can, and the monkey tries to keep its offspring an infant as long as it can. So you have two types of spiritual training: those who lean on the teacher to do everything and those who teach their disciples how to become adults. He told me I was on the cat path, that Ramdas would take care of me, and that he had nothing more to tell me. In the end, I chanted for him and he has invited me to Brindaban. Brindaban is one place where Krishna lived just as Nasik is one place where Rama lived. I accept these places much more than I do Benares, which has become a pilgrimage-center built up largely by priestcraft, I think. The Ganges was not originally the "sacred" river it became. What makes a river sacred?

September 19   *Hyderabad*
(To Harry Nelson:)

Noting a quarantine station and a park nearby I visited each of these in turn. I have written to Dow Chemical with attention to Raynor telling them of my experiences in the Central Provinces and Bombay in regard to Disease and Pest Problems, which are far underrated. . . .They are well aware of the problems, and there is another problem—to convince the people of the need of a spray and dust control, and then to establish a valid program. I learned here as I had been led by the hand of the Indian Commercial Co. in Bombay that

151

there is need for good stickers. As one goes south, rain is uncertain and sudden and may follow any spraying operations. . . . I ran into some other problems. One is bat control, especially fruit bats. They said that Oregon has this problem and they want literature.

I see that I am going to be very busy. It is evident that my ideas of flooding this country with farm literature is having a fine response. It is all the more important because Indian magazines and also stores lean heavily toward Russia. Russia is well able to give them cyclotrons and tractors but not simple machines that can go out into the fields. It is impossible to take any but the lightest two-man equipment into the paddy fields.

Another thing was brought up. There are many pharmaceutical factories and after they take the vitamins and hormones out of livers, etc., the leftover animal matter contains a good deal of nitrogen. They do not seem to know how to powder or dry it. It cannot be applied directly for it not only acidifies the soil, it partly sterilizes it, and the labor to put it down deep is too costly. They know nothing about Milorganite, sewer sludge transformation, etc. here in Hyderabad and there is certainly a cry for nitrogen fertilizers. I'll try to follow this up.

I then went to the City Park. They are doing here what I have been belly-aching all over India about. The trees are pruned—and well pruned. The leaves are taken off and put in composts (and they have large compost piles). The wood is divided into twigs and fagots and heavy wood, which is then used for fuel. No wastage. . . .

October 1   *Pondicherry*

It is indeed a strange experience to find oneself in a realized "Shangri-La" or Shambhalla—to find in fact what has appeared in books or legends. Talbot Mundy's "Shambhalla" or Hilton's "Shangri-La" may have excited many. The Roerichs wrote long tales of fancy and fantasy and considered the "truth" of them more important than the facts of life. One stands constantly between the surrealists who vainly consider themselves realists (and in no case will examine the world as it is), and those metaphysical people who are only interested in hyperboles which they also call "truth."

The Sri Aurobindo Ashram belongs in all three classes—it is fact, yet it is full of fancies; most of the people here want to be realists with regard to their own accomplishments and skeptics or downright scoffers with regard to others'. The worship is directed to Sri Aurobindo and the Mother, which obviates a good deal of prejudice, sectarianism and nonsense, but equally veils the Cosmic God so that He becomes a sort of backstage hand who obeys orders. This is a terrible indictment of what is undoubtedly one of the most serious and also marvelous places in the world. . . .

This place seems to be organized much like the human body is organized, with its cells, systems, organs in one grand whole. I think this has always been the "ideal" society and one finds it in Swedenborg also. I myself lean very much toward the same view. My objection is that the integration, while sometimes real and valid, is also accompanied by views that it is an extension of Hindu spirituality and rather offhand attitudes are taken toward other faiths. . . .

I have not seen all of this place. I recognize transformations in human nature here. Men like Billy Graham and Glen Clark would be compelled to bypass this place. Yet for all that, I do not see any Universal God here who created all humanity, sinners and virtuous alike, and Who controls the destinies of the universe, *not* under any rules and regulations of anybody.

In a sense, it is a shame to say this. One is very well treated. The place is being constantly visited by pilgrims, many from India, and some from all parts of the world. Nehru and Prasad have recognized it. There is no idolatry and little of superstition. Yet it does retain some Indian customs and, alas, a lot of Indian chauvinism masquerading as integrated spirituality. And also despite its literature and word-usage, *very, very little YOGA*. . . .

The Mother is a sort of saint and to me her darshan seems effective. She has a kind of real motherly love, the magnetism of which is too strong to be a mere affectation. I think most of the devotees are sincere.....

October 6 *Kanhangad*

This is written at Anandashram, Kanhangad, which is some miles below Mangalore on the South Indian-Arabian sea coast....I am with Swami Ramdas who is my guru. He is the embodiment of love. It rather surprised the people here that I came as a disciple, not as a visiting tourist.

The events that I experience have little to do with the "news." You can be sure that when there are large strikes and boycotts in the U.S., the press will exaggerate the Muslim-Indian outbreaks; and when there is a great internal language problem, the Indian press will be full of disturbances over "integration" in the U.S. The American weeklies we get here will over-exaggerate trivialities and water down real troubles. There is a gradually awakening social consciousness and many are becoming "just like us"....

We have 5:30 a.m. singing, then 15 minutes meditation until 6. At 10:30 we have another meeting, and there are no more spiritual gatherings until 7. From 7 on there are music, instructions, meditations and conversations until not later than 9:30. Lights out at 10. This is fine for me. In the afternoon one can see "Papa," i.e., Swami Ramdas. He is an all-embracing love who uses love first, foremost and always without discarding intellect.

October 14 *Bombay*

This finds me in Bombay with a diary sadly neglected. On October 1, I made a mistake in trying to leave Pondicherry and by this mistake met Mirza, which was a God-send. I met Mirza at his brother's house in Madras. Before that I went to the U.S. Consulate and told them of my Pondicherry visit—the pilgrimage to Margaret Wilson's grave, the tip-off first and the contact second with the Communists and how they are using the Ashram. This was not only confirmed by the Mirzas, but their position is so strong that it leaves me in a delicate situation regarding some colleagues in San Francisco who idolize the Ashram. These angelic souls simply do not see or do not know what is going on.

Mirza of Madras is a Sufi. We found ourselves looking eye-to-eye on many things. He is also a friend of Nehru, Prasad and Radhakrishnan, just like Fayazuddin of Hyderabad (the present exoteric head of the Nizam-ud-din Chistis).

The week at Kanhangad was very different. Swami Ramdas is a real guru and gives spiritual unfoldment through music, meditation and love. Very little intellectuality. My plan is to come to India next by Bombay and then I could visit him at either Ashram and conduct my researches accordingly.

India 1956: To left of Lewis is Fayazuddin Chisti; at far right is Neellam Nizami, the young esoteric head, son of Hasan Nizami.

CHAPTER TWENTY-SIX

Book Excerpt:

Papa Ramdas & Mother Krishnabai: The Real Yogis Meet the Real Commissar
(from *The Lotus and the Universe*)

Q. What have you to say about communism?
Ramdas: Communism without violence is true religion.

THE LIFE IN THE BODY OF PAPA RAMDAS IS NO MORE. HIS physical work in this incarnation has been completed. Many will be mourning his departure, and many more will rejoice that he manifested the love-life (*Ananda*) that he preached. There is a relation between *guru* and *chela*, between master and disciple (and also between Pir and mureed in Sufism) which is based on the principles already enunciated and not on the persistence of ego-individualism where this ego-individualism cannot be.

Brother Arthur (Koestler), to write books is one thing. To meet a real man is something else. To find a Yogi facing, if not a commissar, then a strongly-organized communist movement is something else. But we of the West are so sure that "God" is on *our* side that we cannot always appreciate a God Who has no sides, no limitations.

Swami Ramdas was never a student of semantics in our sense. He did not stop where Mary Pickford did in her book: "Why Not *Try*

God?" In a true scientific and yet noble spirit, he sought and—even after finding—continued to seek as if the living God were a mine of ceaseless treasure, a fountain of truly living waters. That God is the Reality, the Life, the Love, the Bliss is neither new nor original. Papa Ramdas was not the first, nor will he be the last of such a stream.

The Scriptures say: "Prove all things; hold fast to that which is good" (1 Thess. 5:21). But instead of trying to prove, religion has often become dogmatic, asserting and assuming. Churches opposed the scientific evolution of the 19th century—both the doctrine of evolution and the manifest evolution of the sciences. They have as well ignored the spiritual evolution of the day.

The lover of God is the lover of humanity. He does not have to hide in forsaken caves and monasteries. Jesus has told us, "Let your light shine before men." This can be a reality even here, even now— and not just a symbol.

Go down the Malabar coast and not far from the town of Kasaragod, there is a little railway station called Kanhangad. A taxi or a man may be sent to take you to Anandashram, the "Abode of Bliss." It is like stepping into a Marie Corelli novel: someone will shortly appear and whatever has been your thought or wish will be provided. This is due to the living Grace operating through Krishnabai, the Mataji or Mother about whom we shall write later.

Like all conformations, Anandashram has been subject to change. Its early history is recorded in the writings of Swami Ramdas and in the records which have been scrupulously maintained. The Divine Grace which it proclaims manifests in all its operations.

Anandashram is Sanskrit for *Gan Eden,* which we translate as "Garden of Eden." Both mean, "The Abode of Bliss." All religions proclaim the primordial and the ultimate bliss; some insist that bliss and everyday life are not separate. This is the teaching of scriptures, unfortunately not the teaching of men, for men proclaim (they do not *teach*) what they themselves have not experienced. Bliss is operational. God can be and is known.

Swami Ramdas, whom many of us called "Papa," *was* what he

preached. His writings and his personality alike were vibrant. He has given us his life down to little details. He has been both a man of the world and a Sadhu (recluse). He has known both society and solitude; pain and pleasure have been his wont and his limitations. He lived in God, for God, with God.

One need not write at length about Swami Ramdas. One can obtain his books. He explained his Yoga as being *Bhakti* in the beginning, then *Jnana* and finally *Bhakti* again. These words have no exact equivalents in English and are made more confusing because so much literature is offered from and by those who are neither Jnanis nor Bhaktis. Jnana is said to be the path-of-wisdom and Bhakti the path-of-love-and-devotion. The terms are not exact. Even the most sober—and incidentally the greatest—of Jnana Yogis, Sri Sankaracharya has given us beautiful love poetry.

Yet to this writer, Papa was the finest of the Mantra Yogis. He affirmed the Name, he taught the Name, he used the Name, he manifested the Name. Someday, it is hoped, the Christian world will look beyond "Hallowed be Thy Name" to the Name (or Word) which Jesus used. Sometime, it is hoped, the people of the synagogue will turn from *shemy rabbo* (the "name of the Lord") to the Word (or Name) Moses used.

Practical people may wonder whether this has any meaning in the everyday life. We hear all over both from Zennists and others who seek emancipation that Truth and everyday life cannot be separated, that Nirvana and Samsara are indentifiable. Some people are sure that God must be against the communists; others are equally sure He must be against others. But is God *against*? Even the most bigoted Muslims must sooner or later recognize that Allah has permitted non-believers to discover and to invent improvements in the conditions on earth.

The communists in the province of Travancore-Cochin in India have plenty of votes. India has abolished caste somewhat like we abolished alcohol consumption in the U.S. (though ultimately caste cannot persist in India nor segregation anywhere.)

There are many Brahmans in Travancore-Cochin, and there are many Brahmans who have had trouble with their parents or in-laws or the government there, just as in the United States. So among these well-born are plenty of crusaders who, through humanitarian zeal or through frustration or dissatisfaction, have become leaders in "working class movements." And in India, as elsewhere, this consists mostly of hating those in power. Personal observations indicate that politicians in Travancore-Cochin are more concerned with hating each other than in promoting justice.

Elections in Travancore-Cochin are hard-fought and close. The Congress Party wanted Papa's support. Logically, this seemed obvious. But God-conscious people, and even Vijnanavadis, do not see the distinctions that analysts and dualists make. All of God's children have stomachs.

Papa loves everybody. From one point of view, I am a Muslim being a Sufi; from another point of view one could call me a Buddhist, for the whole life has been commingled with the intellectual and spiritual pursuit of the Buddhadharma. With Papa, I was his child, and in the last visit my closest companion was an Englishman who had the same sort of background and foreground.

India has many problems complicated by the predicament that Indians know everything. They know everything and do next to nothing. There is no difficulty in convincing these people: whatever one affirms is in their tradition. It is only that Papa *does* (or did).

If Papa had met Friedrich Engels, they would have probably gotten along fine. Actually at Anandashram, Papa concentrated on feeding the poor and not on treatises on the subject.

Anandashram lies at the foot of a mountain. There are some hillocks on the grounds and the barn has been located on the summit of one of these. The barn is kept scrupulously clean and the washings gravitated into a surrounding foss. All available animal droppings are also thrown into the foss along with vegetable wastes. In other words, it is an organic gardening farm.

Springs have been found at two points where geological formations indicated they should be, and so a complete irrigation system has been provided. There is absolute regulation of water supply with the addition of the manure run-off, so together they are used to fertilize the soil. This is in accord with current practices in greenhouses: better a constant supply of weak fertilizers than periodical feedings. All this in a district where there is ample rainfall.

A sort of three-story farm has been established. Coconut palms are the foundation plants and the giants. There are two programs which operate under them and these go on simultaneously:

A.) There is the continuous harvesting of protein crops. Besides the coconut, one finds cashews, peanuts and other legumes. It is also hoped that pecans and avocados may be added someday. And, of course, there is a perpetual supply of milk and usage of milk products.

B.) There is proper spacing so that smaller trees like papaya, cashew and banana can grow to full size. Below them are herbaceous foods including vegetables and legumes. Some leguminous plants are plowed under to provide further nitrogenous manure.

I did not see any rice growing at the Ashram nor did I make inquiries. Rice, milk and milk products are the basic foods served. There is also an endless supply of delicious "Brahma Coffee" which is supplied from a neighboring region. One can have all one wants— at breakfast, at least. No one starves and there are always guests— visiting sadhus and the poor of the surrounding region.

The economy has helped bring about an unplanned prosperity. There has been a slow increment in the purchase of land. This means the settlement of more farmers, who are selected for skill. The latest group included many Muslims. There was a vast diversity of class, religion and aptitude among the newcomers and this in turn redounded to the good of the community.

Here we find poverty is faced—not by dialectic, not by ethereal planning, but by substantial effort. While the Congress and Communist Party people stood glaring at each other, the expanding Ashram has been caring for more and more of the poor of the region.

Theologists may dispute as to whether Jesus said, "The kingdom of heaven is *within* you" or "The kingdom of heaven is *among* you." The newly-recovered Gospel of St. Thomas gives both versions. Anandashram manifests both versions.

The Ashram also has a hospital and clinic; attention is now being paid to having a suitable staff at all times. The "garden" is dominated by a kind of cotton bush which functions horticulturally like an ornamental rose. It supplies bolls continuously and keeps one man busy full-time through the year attending them, harvesting, spinning and weaving.

The real Yogi has met the real Commissar—and without hatred, without malice, without fear. Truly, God alone is great (Allaho Akbar)!

Mother Krishnabai

Papa has declared himself to be a little child, and he was remarkably childlike, only without ceasing to be a sage, a philosopher, a seer, a saint and a mystic. And like a little child, he was most fortunate to have had a loving mother in the person of Krishnabai.

Howard Williams, who coined the title "The Mother of Us All," calls Mother Krishnabai a living miracle. Her heart and being comprehend everything and everyone. She has assumed responsibility for the operations of the Ashram at all levels.

The Ashram is farm and hospital, hotel and retreat. She supervises every facet, down to the slightest detail, and she does this naturally. In the dining hall, in the kitchen, in the offices, in the chancel, in Papa's rooms, she flits like a stream of light. The guests are holy devotees, God-seekers—so received, so treated. The guests are her little children, needing food, needing comfort, needing solace and so treated. The poor of the neighborhood are her charges, everyone needs love and protection. Mother Krishnabai is the servant of the servants and yet. . . .

The first meeting with Mataji Krishnabai came in San Francisco.

There one learned again that karma yoga does not consist of lectures. In San Francisco, Mataji helped prepare a dinner for Swami Ramdas and one could observe her manners. It was like preparing for the communion service. Later I saw her both supervise in the kitchen at Anandashram and prepare the meals. She is the heart-blood of the Sangha which brings all the vitality and takes away all the poisons.

Anandashram, Kanhangad, India.

CHAPTER TWENTY-SEVEN

Excerpts from Letters-Diaries:

India, Pakistan, 1956

October 22-25   *Ajmir*

My coming to Ajmir was nothing but a series of miracles. Before I had put my baggage down, my room was invaded by Chisti Sufis. How they found out about me, I don't know. I was with them constantly for two days and am now officially Ahmed Murad Chisti.

The impetus to study Indian music reached its height here. I have heard nothing like the Sufi Qawwalis. They make Chaliapin and Marian Anderson look like amateurs. It is beyond belief what happens to the human voice actually in love with an actual God (as Murshid taught).

I spent many hours at the Dargah of Khwajah Moineddin Chisti, the most celebrated Islamic shrine this side of Iran. There are a number of ceremonies which take place around the Dargah. One has to kiss the steps, the cloth, the railing. Here I was given a strange blessing in vision, with two types of tassels put around me, and later a robe and shirt with the instruction that I was henceforth to represent Chisti Sufism in all non-Islamic lands. This was confirmed by Syed Faruk, my Hadim (guide), before I could report it verbally. I had an inner initiation from Moineddin Chisti and an outer initiation from Syed Faruq Hussein Chisti. Similar things happened in vision and outer form. . . .

I also saw what I had seen in pre-vision: great iron pots which were used to feed the poor. There are many beggars around— too many, in fact—but no starvation and there has been little starvation in India, only malnutrition.

I saw many tombs and places of saints; I was taken up on a holy mountain—not an advertised "Mt. Abu" but one in which you have to get "Masonic permission" to visit. That spiritual masonry which got me "in" at Hyderabad overwhelmed. I visited the shrine of Pir Wali Bakhtiar Kaki twice; he was the successor to Khwajah Sahib Moineddin Chisti. The first meditation, I heard all around me: "What do you want? What do you want?" I answered: "Divine Guidance." "Go, you have it." The next time I received a supernal instruction in the love and compassion side of Islam with a stern warning for the Pakistanis, who are 90% politics, 10% religion and that religion in turn 90% smokescreen.

This visit, which was to have been the supreme goal of my trip, justified itself, and I left Ajmir feeling wonderful . . . excepting for too much food. Each group there seemed intent on showing that they could give me a bigger feast than the next. . . . I learned a little of the connection between these Chistis and the Nizami-Chistis of Delhi. With this combined backing of all the official Chistis of India (five branches) and the U.S. government, there will be no repetition of the former nonsense in San Francisco with the "Professors Oxford." We are bringing peoples and countries together. Far from my greatest expectations, I have been in a series of whirls since reaching Japan.

October 25

After all the feasting given me in Ajmir, I became ill from dysentery upon leaving. I arrived in New Delhi, got the same rooms as previously and was about to collapse, being quite weak. But Pir-O-Murshid Inayat Khan appeared and said I should go to the Egyptian Embassy. So I went. There was virtually no one there, but there was one gentleman.

"What do you want?" he asked.

Out of me came, "I am interested in Moineddin Ibn'l Arabi and Islamic Art before the Turkish conquest."

His jaw dropped. "How did you find me? I am the world's greatest authority on those two subjects! This is the first time that I have ever left Egypt and have just arrived here — and you found me." I told him how, and we became excellent friends. It was Dr. Mohammed Kemal Hussein. I came back from the embassy healed....

I visited Murshid's tomb as if for the last time. He told me he was everywhere, and as he had already manifested elsewhere, it was not necessary to pay spatial obeisance....

The worst side of Indian politics is that when a Russian and American, or for that matter a Czech and a German, say "Boo!" to each other, all the papers yell: "World War III!" Riots here — real riots — are not reported. Real strife is not mentioned. There is not much of it, but I have been in circumstances where very little has actually happened, yet by the time *Time* and *Newsweek* got ahold of it, it was terrible. All the anti-Islamic riots here are a combination of school-boy rowdyism, gangsterism and Pakistani pressures and amount to almost nothing. And all my reports from Burma — although they are much more above board than India, indicate that the fighting there has been at least on a level with North Africa. News is where you *read* it, not where you *find* it.

I leave this Saturday for Lahore. I have failed in my astrological and ayurvedic efforts. The former has little promise; the latter became too big, plus the fact that my hosts were compelled to change their posts without notice. The ayurvedic investigation will be resumed later. From Lahore I go into the Northwest.

October 28   *Lahore*

The entrance in West Pakistan bears some resemblance to that into East Pakistan: hotel reservations not received. While this was being straightened out, I was able to contact the Ahmaddiyas....
Ahmaddiyas differ from Sunni Muslims on: A.) Death, etc. of Jesus (having about the same view as Roerich); B.) Selection of a reformer; C.) Modernization of customs; D.) Liberal versus rigid interpretation of Quran. Yet I find rigidity here and suspicion of each other among Muslims who are divided also into Sunni, Shia (strong) and Ismaili

(weak). I shall try to follow this up. I am as yet unsatisfied with the way they write their books, using whitewash instead of ink.

November 4   *Rawalpindi*

Went to dinner on November 3 to meet a lot of VIPs. Spoke a few moments, and when I said I would introduce Sufism to Harvard was given an ovation, followed by questions and discussion with a few. One young man wants to introduce me to a saint.

I have since spoken on the influence of the Prophet on human destiny and on November 6 at the Forestry Experimental Station on "Forests I Have Dwelt in and Visited." Well-attended and met some fine scientists. I am awaiting tree lists from both the Conservationist and Director of the Forestry Station at this writing.

November 6   *Abbottabad*

I came to Lahore and was treated royally by the staff of the *Civil & Military Gazette,* the paper Kipling once worked for. I also made friends with the Chief of Security Police and later with the Public Prosecutor (Boy—you'd better!). Then my geography got weak. In India, I had to use a railroad, highway and airlines map to get any idea of where and how I was to go. Here I have a railway map only and it is partial: little villages and big cities get the same consideration. . . .

Abbottabad is not on the rail map and is much larger than many places that are. I am somewhere between Kashmir and the Indus Valley. The hill people are Pathans, where men are men and the hunting season is all year around. I saw the Rock Edicts of Asoka. Many centuries ago, he forbade the killing of birds, so the Pathans did not kill birds, only "Mad Dogs and Englishmen that went out in the noon-day sun." Now it is very quiet, especially the Pathans. The "civilized" Urdu people are busy doing nothing but having sit-down strikes to yell at Englishmen and favoring Egypt, and most of them do not know where England or Egypt are, much less the Suez Canal, and anything is better than working hard. . . .

The Forestry Dept. has done a lot of work on medicinal trees and shrubs, which is out of my line, and a little — too little from my point of view — on mycology. The above leaves a lot of room to follow up. They have worked out an ecological map based on acacias for Western Pakistan. I once worked out the same thing for oaks in South Carolina. . . .

November 12   *Rawalpindi*

I have before me "Great Men of India" edited by L. Rushbrook Williams. The article on Aurangzeb is by Elizabeth D'Oyley and on page 184 I found the prayer which I have searched for for years, having lost my copy:

"Less wise than Akbar his greatgrandfather, he (Aurangzeb) could not see that no power on earth can make men think alike, and that God is to be reached by many ways. Wrote Abul-Fazl, friend of Akbar:

O God, in every temple I see people that see thee, and in every language I hear spoken, people praise thee.
Polytheism and Islam feel after thee.
Each religion says, "Thou art one, without equal."
If it be a mosque, people murmur the holy prayer; and if it be a Christian Church, people ring the bell from love of thee.
Sometimes I frequent the Christian cloister, sometimes the mosque.
But it is thou whom I seek from temple to temple.
The elect have no dealings with heresy or with orthodoxy; for neither of them stand behind the screen of thy truth.
Heresy to the heretic, and religion to the orthodox.
But the dust of the rose-petal belongs to the heart of the perfume-seller."

November 18   *Lahore*

On my return to Lahore I was challenged by a German "expert" on Oriental philosophy, a graduate of Heidelberg, Leyden, Cambridge and Columbia. He thought that I was a great humorist or crazy, because I told him I had been speaking in the Northwest and was asked to return. The next day I learned that the staff of the hotel thought he was crazy, and I have become a kind of hero. The attitude towards the "experts" of this kind here is quite different from that in the States.

Following this incident, a tonga-wallah took me to a wrong shop, and there I learned that the brother of the owner was in Brooklyn seeking to start a Sufi order. Returning later, a merchant hailed me and explained that I could not buy anything more as God had put a limit on my purchases. I told him my name was "Murad," meaning I was under grace and therefore different from a "mureed" who was under the guidance of a spiritual teacher. A man standing nearby overheard me and identified himself as a mureed. As a result of that "chance" meeting, I have been to the assemblage of Nakshibandi Sufis, witnessed their ceremonials, took part in their zikr and was given a cap and beads. We also had a long conversation as several of them spoke good English, and at least two had been to the U.S.

The khalifa in charge was very handsome with beautiful eyes showing love and spiritual light. After the experience of the meeting, I told one of the mureeds that I had never seen a man more like Jesus Christ than their khalifa. "You should meet our Murshid" was his reply. As he lives near Rawalpindi I hope to meet him. I had to bless them all and embraced nearly all the older men (an experience which left me "high" for two days afterwards.) Everybody was happy and they chanted loudly and joyfully "Allahu" as I was leaving. There is a great possibility that I shall become a recognized saint . . . a joke to the Western world and a very serious matter here. . . .

The *Pakistani Times* is the most bigoted paper I have ever read, and as dishonest as the Communist press, although possibly subsidized by them. I say they have lost Kashmir on account of it. I have said I did not know God made so many mistakes until I came to Pakistan. Yet strange to say, there are more saintly people here also. Thank God they generally do not read English. As I left Ashraf Publishers, I visited a mosque and paid a few rupees. When I left and sat down in the tonga, I heard a voice saying, "You have completed payment of your Zakat" and saw a scroll with all the small payments I have made from Dacca on, and they added up to more than I had figured. It was a wonderful vision and I am released from doing anything more at Karachi.

November 23 *Multan*

It is gratifying to learn that I am fully accepted here as a Sufi both by the actual Sufis and the professors of Sufi philosophy.... I have been with the Chief Engineer at the town hall here and learned about the problems of flies, soil fertilization, etc. They are doing compost work here, and I could come back and do a big job. We shall learn more when I get through the ropes at Karachi. But success is now beginning to tire me; I feel as if I have done enough, and more than enough. I will now go to the biggest people in the U.S. without compunction. I have learned not to be afraid of anybody.

These things were foretold again and again by Murshid. But I never was successful in communicating what Murshid told me, excepting to five people, four of whom—thank God—are still alive. One of them, in turn, added to Murshid's predictions and these have also come true. It is now done. The question will be what it means.

December 3 *Karachi*

There is the moral side of Sufism and the esoteric side. The one you learn by following the precepts and practices of others; the second, though you are given directions, you must perform for yourself. The moral emphasis is much greater than in Hinduism; the esoteric certainly less than in Tantra. But Sufis never give long discourses on the wonders of wisdom. Discourses on the wonders of wisdom are only veils over truth. They often do not even awaken the intuitive qualities in us.

I am satisfied today with what I have accomplished. The immediate result is a bigger outlook before me. Sometimes I shudder at it. All the people I have seen for so long take me seriously, listen and talk so I get along wonderfully. Let those who talkie-talk about God continue to prate. The stirring events within men's lives or men's minds doesn't tell of the phenomena on the surface of the earth, outside their skins. . . .

December 3

I am winding up, I hope, my Asiatic tour. It has been somewhat more successful than my brightest hopes. The only disturbing factor is that either my mail has not gone through or I have failed utterly to convince my S.F. pals of what is being accomplished. That some mail has gone through is assured, but that mail has stopped is also evident because invariably my reservations do not go through. . . .

I have entirely changed my point of view. I have converted myself to my own philosophy. This was one of integration, having an all-over view. It is very hand to understand, but once understood it goes over. Man is one. This knocks out with one blow all the dualistic views of those Pakistanis and Israelis and Chinese and Muscovites. What is a class? The Negroes contend there is only one race, the human race. If "race," which is biological is untrue, how much more untrue is the artificial class?

In practice, in S.E. Asia, if you are a great landlord or capitalist and pay lip-service to Marx and tribute to Mao, you are a "worker," and if you are a peasant and do not like forced collectives, you are a fascist enemy of the "working classes." Just take the stories of Alice by Lewis Carroll, treat them as realities, and you get some idea of Asia. . . .

December 3

I have the fly problem in my lap, and I am communicating this in person to Dupont. I have the pest control problem and shall see Dow. I have a big fertilizer problem I may handle in person. . . . I have gotten hold of more than I can chew, but I won't let go the lion's tail. And Sam Lewis is a small fry, but Ahmed Murad Chisti . . . !

December 5

It is with some difficulty that I pen my closing words on leaving Pakistan and the continent of Asia. The recent events of my life and the future plans, such as they have been made, seem to stem from the instructions and advice of Pir-O-Murshid Ghaffour. The events that led me to the brethren in Dacca and the subsequent events seem all part of a sort of drama, an act of which is closing. . . . As a man, and as an American, I have my personal ideas as to India and Pakistan. But as a servant of God and one who may be on the path of Ansar and Abdal and even Wali, I am supposed to help Pakistan. . . .

December 17   *London*

Despite "Joy to the World," despite "Nirvana," despite "Islam," there is almost universal gloom here and I am running around calling myself "Puck of Pukhtunistan" and laughing. Jon says I look younger than 12 years ago, which may be true. I am Alice at the finish of the two books, finding all those great characters to be mere pawns or cards.

Papa Ramdas and Mother Krishnabai. Inscription gives their principal practice, the mantra Om Sri Ram Jai Ram Jai Jai Ram (To God—both personal and impersonal, both truth and power—victory, always victory).

V. JOURNEY TO THE EAST: 1960–62

Samuel Lewis, wearing robe of investiture as a Sufi Murshid given by Pir Barket Ali of Pakistan in 1962. For the photo Lewis exhibits the Sufi practice of tawwajeh, *or sharing magnetism through the glance.*

CHAPTER TWENTY-EIGHT

Excerpts from Letters-Diaries:

By Sea to Cairo, 1960

August 11, 1960   *New York*

My dear Margaret:

My war against the press goes merrily on. The other night there was a brawl at a party in which my roommate and a newspaper man actually came to blows and a professor, the putative guest of honor, brained the newsman. It had been the professor's party. The newsman was a fill-in guest for an absentee—which did not bother him, he just took over. This was symbolic.

Last night was really more serious. I have been to India and seen riots not reported and noted brawls extended to fast fracases. I was on a pilgrimage with 100,000 people in India—not a word in the press. We went to Central Park to attend a Shakespeare presentation of "Measure for Measure." This is neither one of the best nor best-known of the plays, yet we had a long walk to get to the end of the line; we never did reach the theater. The press had been printing that the plays would be stopped—no public interest. Two days back, 300 or so athletes raced across Manhattan. There was a policeman at every corner. Here there were so many thousands, you could get no idea, yet—no policeman. Despite that the lines were orderly, everybody kept their places. And I could read nothing in the papers today. Some interests *say* there is no interest in Shakespeare or art. We may have seen 20,000 people; we may have seen 50,000. By comparison, despite the many millions who live here, the attendance at the ball grounds is small—and the Yankees have often been in first place.

The attendance was far more wonderful than the show. I guess there were representatives of almost all New York groups. As we stood in line, the conversation was on modern art and modern poetry. I told them that where I came from Frank Lloyd Wright was God-the-Father and he had the angels San Rafael and San Gabriel on his side. You would soon see his temple called "San Rafael Courthouse" or something. You can put that in the books. The general opinion was that the art museums are vast expensive buildings for contractors, architects, Boards of Directors and great names of the past.

It was a pleasant evening and we decided to go to the Village. At the moment my pockets are rather full and the days for spending few. There I met Anca V. Brovska and her protege John Duffy. He objected to something I said, and I returned, "But I am a quarter-leprechaun." From then on it was one of the best evenings of my life.

Sean O'Casey occupies much space in the press, and we started there. John is a lover of Masefield and Whitman. He is very much opposed to Ferlinghetti and Kerouac (where have I heard those names before?). Our ideas of poetry and poets covered much common ground. Anca is primarily a teacher and editor rather than a writer per se. We agreed that I might send her some of my shorter things, and what I write on shipboard.

My aesthetic studies have given me a picture which is between painting and poetry, very suggestive of what I might write on board. I am scheduled to leave now on the 16th.

August 18   *Mid-Atlantic*

Dear Bill,

This is long diary, and I am not sure of continuity or anything else. There are only four men passengers, the rest women, and the men are either harmonious, alike or tamed—this includes myself. The women not so.

Sam is not having too good a time. The weather is very stormy and there is almost a continuous headache, but not so far, thank goodness, any trouble with the stomach. This makes for listlessness, and I am taking refuge at the typewriter, but there is no eagerness. I did a few moments calligraphy this a.m. and have my language books out, but no campaign figured as yet.…

I have had no dreams and can't think, ideate or get in any mood—creative, literary or otherwise—at the moment, 14:40 o'clock watchtime, which is neither authentic or anything but quasi- (or crazy) New York time.

August 27

[Leonora Ponti was one of Samuel Lewis' folk dance club partners—ed. note]

Dear Leonora,

I have not kept a diary. In crossing the Pacific, my stomach was bad and my head good; in crossing the Atlantic, my stomach was good and my head bad. Still I prefer the latter. We ran into hurricanes and billows until we neared the Azores. After that, things calmed down, head got better and I have been feeling fine since.

I found that many of the officers seem to like folk music. One man specializes in Polish dances and on American things which we use in square dancing. Purchased a small transistor from Japan just before I left New York. Got it at an inside price. Around the Azores, we began picking up Portuguese stations and more and more of them, and then Moorish stations. We had a near collision last night, and the whistles woke me up—just in time. For we were passing Gibraltar, and I thought the whistles were signaling that. I found nearly everybody was up to see the lights on either side.

Have I had a castanet session! Have I? D'unt ask. Boy, was it great. We had flamenco and all kinds of la musicas, and I got excited and came back and finished my writing so I could record this. I may be out on deck more, so I can try out the stations and castanets and all. There is a woman from Puerto Rico who is hoping we can still pick up Spain tonight, so she can put on a floor show. The dining room is wired for records, but we may go on deck or have some other arrangements.

Have written a few other letters, but again don't know where I shall post them. We do not land until Beirut, which means a quick trip, but after that . . . ! Only I get off at Alexandria. Some may fly immediately to India, and others will not get off until Karachi, thinking they can "see" India in a few days and pick up the boat at Bombay. I am afraid there will be awakenings for these. My writing is on "Saladin," the guy who gave the Crusaders the good ol' one-two.

September 2

It is with extreme delicacy that the diary entry for today should be written in the name of Puck or another than Samuel. We reached Beirut on the night of September 1st, and the captain summoned us to his quarters to meet three Lebanese doctors and all that. "Assalaam aleikum (peace be with you)," I said, "I am darveesh." The captain then challenged me and we gave a lot of answers that he could not understand. Then when the customs men came around— "You have nothing to declare, no contraband"— holding their heads in the opposite direction and saying, "Glad to meet you, Ahmed Murad." Neither the captain nor anyone else was around. This adds another chapter to innocents abroad, or something.

By 6 a.m., we docked and a grand rush of men came up the gangplank. Were they customs men? Money-changers? Merchants? Travel agents? How wrong can you be? They were barbers, and they followed everyone around, making all business on board impossible. We could not organize, we could not eat, the cargo could not be unloaded and they could go in and out of a crowd like nobody. Then they went around and knocked on everybody's door, waking up those who had just come off watch.

Then the barbers surrounded us, and I said, "I have plenty of business."

"What kind of business?"

"I am Ahmed Murad, and I am dar-veeesh."

Barber No. 2 looked at me, dropping his jaw, his tools and his hat. Then he said:

"I am Ahmed Murad and I am dar-veeesh!!! Come! I give you a free hair-cut!"

We visited the American University and had a fine time. Almost every country in the Near East sends students to the American University. They are successful in everything but religion; indeed, the trend is toward weakening the Americans in their faith, and the theological section is far behind Harvard. They are most successful in medicine and veterinary science. It was in summer session and the place was empty of Syrians, Lebanese and Americans. This was fine for Puck, who ran into Pakistanis about every three inches, and finally settled for two from Dacca. "You know Shatinangar St.?"

"Of course, of course."

"You know Maulana Abdul Ghafoor?"

"Of course, of course."

"He is my murshid, I am darveesh."

More jaw-dropping, etc. They also know Sophia Khan, the poet and all that. They introduced me to a man from Iran.

"Where do you come from," I asked.

"Shiraz."

"O city of beautiful poetry, O land of Hafiz and running streams and holy places. . . ."

The Iranian began to drop his jaw more than the Pakistanis. Anyhow, we gave them all chocolate and distributed chocolate all over campus— even to the profs.

CHAPTER TWENTY-NINE

Excerpts from Letters-Diaries:

Egypt, Fall 1960

September 8   *Cairo*

I am now in Cairo, and I find things totally different from most reports. The first thing I ran into is that for all practical purposes, the United States has gone "underground" and is doing very well indeed.

The countryside, coming down from Alexandria, looked far more prosperous and energetic than anything I have seen in India or Pakistan, or for that matter, Mexico. It may be that I have come during the "bright" season. The Nile impressed me far more than the Indus or Ganges — all of these are different from the rivers of the "Far East" where many people live on boats and fish or trade therefrom.

I am both going slow and yet not losing time, trying to fall in with the local rhythm. As Monday was Labor Day, I could do nothing with Americans and called at Al-Azhar, the famous Egyptian University. I may be going there again.

My main Egyptian host is now in the United States, but I shall be a guest of the Government Agricultural Department Saturday. Another host is also away, and I shall wait until he returns. He is head of one of the banks and also the Chamber of Commerce here. Make no mistake about it, this country is not "neutralist" economically. It is definitely ahead of any Asian nation except Japan. I shall not compare it to Israel, which was heavily subsidized from abroad.

One of the outstanding features is the willingness and the policy to "begin at the beginning." Our old homestead idea of "40 acres and a mule," slightly modified, is the basic feature here. The U.S. is helping this become established, both in the older lands already cultivated and in new lands being opened up. The water research is going ahead full speed. Americans are working with Egyptians at their level and pace. There is no published material; it is all done slowly and quietly.

The banking and business sections indicate a nation quite bourgeois in outlook, but with strong doses of humanism and humanitarianism. After all, there is plenty of land. American engineers are undertaking hydrological surveys and on a grand scale. This land used to be rich, and water is underground at many places. It has strange physical and chemical properties which are being studied. This will lead to indications as to what crops may be sown. There are, fortunately for me, many University of California graduates in high places in both American groups and in the UAR government itself. In other words, here is a land running on essentially capitalistic bases, modified by monetary power, and the enormous tracts of lands which have become deserts. On the other hand, the people are more strictly Muslim in a certain sense than elsewhere, and this keeps them from following the United States with its strange mixture of Christianity and libertinism— which become confused in the eyes of foreigners.

Recognition of folly in the past, such as cutting down trees, is quite evident. The planting of eucalyptus trees, which I tried to "sell" in India, is operative here on exactly the basis I wished to see: fast growing trees, giving firewood and enabling the peasant to return dung to the soil.

September 7

My dear Harry:

I feel like a person who has asked for permission to visit a playground and while he is waiting has been given free tickets to the World Series. When I visited the Soils Section of Cairo University, I was told that a new government regulation had gone into effect requiring permits for visits. This was undoubtedly true for I was fortunate enough even to get into the high echelon offices, and most of the time was spent trying to get through crowds who were being held back. It was not that way before.

Mr. Paul Keim of ERIS, which is the Reclamation-Irrigation Service cooperative between the UAR and the US has given me a stack of names, and I can't visit them all. In fact, I have not gotten very far down the list and am busy every day. He sent me to Dr. Turki, who is head of the National Research Bureau. This is a coordinating *functional* department of all the top scientists of this region. It is divided into five sections: Chemical, Physical, Agricultural, Medicinal and Coordinating-Publications. Dr. Turki turned me over to one Dr. Kabash and the big parade is on for me. . . .

I was particularly interested in the soil science, because I have been argued down by "brand names" people *not* in horticulture on this point and equally commended by brand names *in* horticulture for the same thing. . . .

Plant Physiology: They are conducting a number of experiments on light and heat exposures with wheat and datura. There is absolute control. They are under no illusions and are very objective.

Wheat: It is interesting to find that wheat can be grown at high temperatures. There is not enough moisture for rice, and it is too warm for rye. If they flood during early stages, they get a maximum of protein; if they flood later, they get a good hay crop with a maximum of starch, so they are now flooding early. They regard this as an important discovery.

Sugar: They are having trouble finding the maximum sucrose yield analogous to the maximum protein for wheat. There will have to be, in my estimation, not only light and heat tests but also potassium control. What the Russians miss is that potassium may be present in large quantities yet not available for use. That is true here. Anyhow, I have copied my Louisiana materials for them and will turn over some more stuff tomorrow.

Soils: I took this matter up here, because they asked me whether we had any sugar cane in the dry areas of Arizona and California. I told them that because of the high salt content in various places, we plant sugar beets instead. I shall bring them the farm bulletin on desert agriculture tomorrow. I do not think they have given enough attention to sugar beets; on the other hand, they have not industrialized cane by-products and waste. . . .

After all these USIS burnings and Vice Presidents being mobbed, we have come to realize that nations which are 85% agricultural are just that. In Egypt, we have appealed to the farmers and farm workers and we are working with them.

There are no signs of Russians, the city is typically commercial, the banks seem to be thriving and the anti-Ugly American work is gaining many friends. Mr. Keim is a man, coming from the campus which authored *The Ugly American* and doing everything the opposite, with official sanction. But no publicity, no newsmen, no press releases. Neither Mr. Keim nor I am optimistic about the Russians being able to build the Aswan Dam. Not only that, I have my material on salt-water conversion and the Americans are making the badly-needed hydrological survey.

September 10

I have not been in Egypt one week and my troubles have begun. No, not that kind. Things happen so fast that there is not enough time to record it in my diary or it is too hot — and then more things happen.

There are, however, two passwords. The first password is *"Assalaam aleikum"* which means "pax vobiscum" in Arabic. By means of it, I got a courtesy visa and entered this country as a V.I.P. All they looked at was my radio and typewriter (and to think what I might have done with Luckies and Chesterfields!).

After the way Mr. Nixon and Mr. Haggerty got treated, the government has awakened to the truth: get rid of the commentators, newspapermen, analysts, radio swashbucklers and get down to work. But first I will give you the awful news and the second password. Deep breath — it is *"Oski-wow-wow!"* Oh yes, "Yankee go home" worked. All

the Harvard, Yale and Dartmouth men resigned and in their place —
UC, Arkansas and Tulane. No more Yankees, just other Americans.
The top banana is Cal. '23. The top agricultural men in the UAR
government — supposed to be infiltrated by Hruskies — went to the
Muscovite university at Davis, California.

September 20

My Dear Harry:

I have been doing some thinking. Before you challenge, I recall
the very first lecture I heard you give on this subject, and even
though you did not exactly say, "Go and do thou likewise," it might
be a good idea sometimes.

The subject is the problem of the Nile. Now I am not so vain as
to presume I can offer a "solution" to a large problem. I came to a conclusion which may have merits and demerits but have been terrifically stimulated by two books borrowed from the American Library
near here. The first is *Out of the Earth* by Louis Bromfield. The second is *Theory and Dynamics of Grassland Agriculture*. Both these
works emphasize the need of restoration of organic matter to the soil.

Turning to the Nile, I have been opposed to the Aswan Dam for
many reasons. One is that the cost is too much for the nation, and
the same money, used in salt water conversion plants and in a more
complete hydrological survey including chemical analyses of soils
and water would be more effective.

In one respect, the Nile resembles the Indus. India and Pakistan
have just signed an agreement with regard to the waters. On the
other hand, it resembles the Colorado, where a number of states have
entered into a pact almost like an international agreement. But there
is no such pact concerning the Nile. And it is always possible that
Ethiopia may indulge in engineering projects like Colorado, carrying
water over a shed into another region where feasible, to open up large
tracts. Ethiopia is a land of extreme contrasts between wet and dry
regions, and she may do something about it.

In the southern part of Sudan, there is a region called the *Sudd*. It is filled with papyrus plants, often called "worthless." Sudan also has vast deserts, though there is some rain in parts. Presumably these deserts, like those of Egypt, have a high pH. It came to mind that it might—just might—be possible to dredge the region, making channels and taking the muck and organic matter and putting it on the land. Simple grinders might do the work (or there may be other methods) and this would benefit both the river and the land.

Today I visited the Vegetable Experimental Station and took up the soil problem briefly. They told me that manure was plentiful and cheap. Granted, but the pH of manure is certainly higher than that of most or maybe all leaf-molds. And with a high pH in the soil already, this is only a partial corrective. Next Sunday, I am scheduled to go to the Soils Department and will report to you what I find out there.

September 18

Many factors are working for me here. The two outstanding are my interest in Islam and my being a life member of the University of California Alumni Association. The third element in my position is the type of integral thinking I indulge in. Today's venture was my second to Al-Azhar. They understand pretty well the situation in the United States, and I told them that I was in no hurry for a plan of action.

I took a note over to Al-Azhar Mosque, but the attendant speaks English and welcomed me. This made me feel very happy. There are actually two mosques, one being a grand courtyard, surrounded by alcoves. There were many classes in these alcoves; so far as I could see, they have co-education with the boys and girls, not particularly different than in our country. The inner mosque is, I presume, the famous one. There were a few classes going on, entirely of older people. The place was not a congregation of beggars and "bums" which one finds in India and Pakistan. Some of the staff at Al-Azhar said they did not like what they saw there, especially around the shrines.

As I belong to the Chisti tarikat, they told me some of their objections. I admit ceremonially and outwardly there is "saint worship," but inwardly there is something else, and there are only two ways to convey that "something else." One is by a visit and the other is by disciplinary instruction.

The tone here is of high intellectual approach, and I am thoroughly in favor of it. I am not looking for saints. I am not looking for noble moral outlooks in others which are not reflected in my own life. So far as I can see, President Nasser did work out a grand revolution in so many directions that we in America, who have never bothered to study Egypt, may never really discover it.

My "undiplomatic" ways of life constantly open new doors for me, and I am seeing all kinds of things, but mostly in the technical fields to date. Tomorrow I shall try to find an Egyptian versed in both modern science and Sufism. So I am having a grand time, despite my grumps.

September 21

I spent some time with George Scanlon at the American University. He is the contact man on Islamic culture, especially art. By agreement I am to wait for one Dr. George Creswell, who is considered by all hands to be the art and literature expert. I then called on the head of the University Library, one Mahmud Sheneeti.

I told Scanlon I differed from the "experts" on Sufism, because despite their statements, I had met Sufis in high places. He conceded that this might be true of further Asia, but was not true here. Later, however, when I was talking with Sheneeti, he brought up the name of Abdul Kadir-i-Gilani, and we found ourselves in complete agreement.

I also met a Sufi yesterday at the Vegetable Experimental Station. He is Mohammed M. Billah. I am going to take some of my poetry and perhaps other writings when I go there again on Saturday. Actually, the politicians seem to be cool toward Sufism, the scientists quite warm. . . .

Mohammed M. Billah is a member of the Shadhili Order. He told me that there are lots of Sufis around, chiefly Shadhilis and Rufais. The latter are the "Howling Dervishes" and they perform all the phenomena which we attach with the term *fakir* (piercing themselves with knives, swords, etc.). The word *fakir* has been wrongly thrown at the Hindus, who are not so adept, I believe, in either mysticism or magic, though they get the name for it.

October 2

Two weeks ago I was told I would be in for a grand surprise and met one M. M. Billah, who is a leading scientist here and a member of the Shadhili Order. It was love at first sight, and has been ever since. Actually it is very difficult to delineate between "orthodoxy" and "Sufism" in the lives — not of the poor, ignorant and superstitious — but in the lives of the most educated and enlightened people here. Yesterday, Mr. Billah said he that he would like me to accompany him on the birthday of the original Syed Hussein, the Prophet's grandson. His tomb is here in a mosque which I have visited. There will be a gathering of dervishes from all over the Near East. And praise to Allah, our birthdays fall on the same date. I am looking forward to this occasion like a child to a great party.

Last week I visited most of the historic mosques. It is difficult to write much at the first visit, because some of them are architectural monuments, some quite artistic and others must be distinguished by their inner atmosphere of (what to me is) sanctity. I have heard some chanting almost up to the level I heard in Ajmir. I called my companion's attention to the difference between the singing of the devotee and that heard on the radio. He had not noticed it before. Sometimes I wish I had a tape recorder with me, but one must not interfere with the connection between the devotee and Allah.

My visa calls for a temporary 4-year period in Pakistan, subject to the authorities. Inasmuch as I should be speaking in many universities, I cannot gauge the time, and I want to visit the farm of Mr.

Jamshid Khan at Mardan also; we have much to discuss. Today I feel much more self-assured and even capable of performance.

October 4

After I left Al-Azhar yesterday morning, I met Mr. Pande, cultural attache at the Indian Consulate. He invited me to meet Prof. Chandrasekar, who is perhaps the best demographer on earth and who specializes in population problems and *their solution* — more in their solution than their problems. Last night he gave one of the most rousing talks I have ever heard and was well-received by the intellectual elite. He was very pleased that I remembered his talk in Berkeley. He is one of the men that I definitely respect and, in a sense, follow.

October 15

I have been going around in deep waters, and what happens is that I generally get in deeper and deeper water in about everything. I am scheduled to meet the head of the Pan-Arab League and I can turn over to him the research I did in Cleveland, Ohio. . . . I have been going around trying to find out whether the food supply may or may not be augmented by algae research and will write that below. Then my friend Mr. Kinoshita (of Friends of the World) in Tokyo wrote that he is going to send soy and garlic seeds here. After I mail this I go to the Vegetable Experimental Station, only now with a long list of stuff. . . .

October 18

The plans worked out by Mr. Harry Nelson and myself have brought about excellent response. The other day, two federal government experts looked up my work and have commended it, so much so that it will be much easier for me when I get to Pakistan.

Then today I was questioned closely about agricultural information. Mr. Nelson collected bulletins from all over the country for me, and I shall take them and have them reviewed first at the Vegetable Experimental Station, and then perhaps elsewhere. Mr. George Kenyon, Jr., who has an office in New York and who may be the largest magazine distributor in the country, said he would cooperate fully in the plan to distribute all agricultural literature to Asian countries. All he wanted was the depots, and there are certainly a number of willing depots here.

If the press would only face the fact that the people of the world are much more interested in food than sex (from our point of view), we would be gaining friends instead of losing them in the U.N.

October 19

Yesterday was my birthday, but here it was the birthday of Hussein, the grandson of Prophet Mohammed, who is said to have obtained the divine wisdom and to have died a martyr. Although the people are not Shias, the day was a holy holiday, and the nighttime was the climax of a festival which began Monday.

I do not know whether the American public has been shocked by the closeness of the vote on admitting China to the U.N. I know these two things do not seem related. But Americans continue to harbor huge blind spots about the cultures, religions, outlooks of Asians and are either cynical or look to these damned European "experts" who tell us what is *not* or else throw out the term *fanatic*.

The same is true of the Arabs as with all other Asian peoples I have met: it is very difficult to delineate between Islam and Sufism until you get deeper into what is called *tarik* (the esoteric school). The first nonsense that has to be cleared away is that there are not many Sufis nor persons interested in Sufism and that they are a lot of fanatics and superstitious humbugs who are lazy or worse. My immediate introduction has been through Mohammed Murtaz Billah. I do not know whether he was converted to Sufism or not, but if so it was *by his wife.* And who is his wife? She is a top graduate, who is now train-ing for her Ph.D. by doing research on ice cream....

The Khan-i-Khalili is a bazaar district near Al-Azhar. It is full of narrow streets and lanes and has many small mosques and still more khankahs where Sufis meet. One needs a guide at night unless one has a compass. Last night was something like a mixture of Chinese New Year's and a Summer Fair at the same time. Tremendous crowds surged down alleys, lanes and what not. Progress was made difficult by boys using a sort of football formation to surge forward, endangering the blind. There was considerable lack of human con-sideration. There were many women in the more open places, but the narrow spots had only men. There are women dervishes who meet separately, I found, but so far only the Chistis have had the men and women do Zikrs (chanting remembrance) together.

It took us quite a while to find the Shadhili khankah. Each group meets separately in the same building. My friend's Sheikh is no more, but two or three Khalifs led the ceremonies. There was some reading of Quran and chanting, then the Zikrs—singing the name of Allah—which I could join.

The first thing noticeable was that these Zikr groups perform functions like both antiphonal and choir singing in the Christian churches (but to me with a rather purer sound). Later on, there were melodious songs—beautiful arias, not just chants, in which others, including the younger men, repeated a phrase of Zikr as a sort of rhythm-background. Then we held hands and performed Zikr stand-ing close together and later on in a sort of jump movement with some swinging their heads. This was heightened in speed and loudness for awhile and touched the depths of my being. Then they varied the Zikr phrasing. I notice all Sufi schools do this somewhat, passing from the intelligible to the semi-intelligible or non-intelligible *intellec-tually*. On this point, Alan Watts has been entirely correct. I find when one says *Elah* instead of *Allah*, it is much easier to sing and feel. I noticed also that these men tended to pronounce the name of God, i.e., Allah, as I have been wont to do. I have been corrected in parts of India, but stubbornly refused to withdraw. Whatever impetus I have had for my pronunciation, it accorded with the Shadhili chanting and must have made me more welcome.

The ceremony was long and involved; after it, we had some discussion, food, more discussion and finally tea. The one thing I objected to was the insistence that I must learn Arabic. And so far as Sufism is concerned, the "mantric" modification of words makes the argument seem weaker than ever.

On the other hand, in conversation with those who speak English, I find surprisingly great agreement. Orthodoxy is needed for the beginners. It is best to be trained in some form of ceremony, law and custom, but that is introduction only. The men explained "spiritual liberty" exactly the same as my first Pir-O-Murshid Inayat Khan did, and they had the same attitude toward religion and religions. The educated ones were far from dogmatic and were all universal. There was agreement that Mohammed was the *Seal of the Prophets,* which meant recognition of all prophets and their teachings. This was far from the Arabism of some of them.

Around 10 o'clock we went to the Syed Hussein Mosque, where three groups of dervishes were holding forth, but the place was too crowded. Then we visited some other khankahs where the groups were completing their sessions. Most of these were "wild," but the largest one seemed to be made of intellectuals, who were sober and far more numerous. The Rufais were more ecstatic than the Shadhilis, but some of the latter were also very wild. I did not meet the Nakshibandis. The first and most obvious impression is the fact that there are many thousands of Sufis here.

I find that not only do the Zikr sessions take the place of hymn and other singing, but there is undoubtedly a lot of blowing off of steam and even transmutation of sexual and lower faculties. This is obvious when one sees so many hundreds of young men. We have not looked into the psychological advantages of these processes, and I do not intend to do so now. But there is a moral advantage, and more. A single experience on almost any level is worth thousands of lectures. . . .

191

The dervishes as a whole are more on the occult than the mystical side, but this is no doubt due to the fact that mystical experiences per se come from divine grace. If you don't have some clairvoyant experiences here, you just don't get it. I do not know how far this is so. The books on Sufism are all wrong. Sufism did not develop in Persia. Yes, you had mystical poets there. But the atmosphere of Egypt is thousands upon thousands of years old and electrified and magnified esoterically.

I condemned a young Christian severely until he was pale, and then said, "Wait. I am only half done. Now I am going to answer every one of my objections." He knew nothing of Gnosticism or the early Christian yogis who lived in Egypt or even of the Gospel of Thomas. I sent him back to his church. Fortunately, as the engineers clear land here and dig for water, they also combine archaeological digging and may bring to light much of the Christian Gnosticism and Hermetism which has been covered by the sands. This is more interesting to me than ancient Egypt—and there is a big gap here. But the atmosphere is the same.

October 25

I am now waging a war and a peace. The war is against all European professors of Asian teachings in the length and breadth of the U.S. who are not on good terms with at least one Asian nation. The harm done by them is incalculable. Some are quite unaware of it, some do not care. We cannot have communication between East and West until all intermediaries are removed, and there is honest conversation between us.

On the constructive side, there are no intermediaries in the scientific field. The U.A.R. has problems, sometimes we have the answers. They can go direct to get the answers. I am working now on two agricultural problems in this way, finding out what American research stations or chemical firms can bring the answers.

Today I visited Dr. Hasan Bagdadi. He is also a graduate of the

University of California. He is in charge of the Ministry of Agricultural Reform, and so has a big job. We discussed water problems at length, and I think I have some answers for him right on the Berkeley campus. This is the work I like to do: you bring people together, they make exchanges directly. Not only are there no European professors acting as intermediaries, but no Moores, no Northrups and in the end no Sam Lewises either. Man can meet with man, and man can help man; that is why I am here. I don't care if none of the self-esteemed Orientalists in the U.S. don't recognize this. I feel this is working as Allah wants man to work.

October 26

I am overworked largely because my plans are being taken seriously. There are two definite themes here, and they are in some ways similar. Egypt, after 2500 years of domination by foreigners, is coming into its own. We do not realize the amount of energy awakened by this. And in my own life, every plan I ever had thwarted by selfish persons has been accepted; if there is a single thing of my earlier life not accepted here, I do not know what it is. It keeps me busy as all business must be done in the morning, and then I have to write, do research, run errands and what not the rest of the day—and this is limited by the warm weather.

I have written some strong letters to the State Department on account of our ignoring the Sufis. Damn it, Bill, there must be at least 50 million people under Sufi training and we pay no attention; instead, a lot of professors who get their education God knows where deny their existence and give out as Islamic philosophy whatever they choose to.

My plans for introducing American poetry are being completed, to accompany talks on American philosophy. Behind it all we have nothing to fear if we can love people. This is the spirit of Sufism, too. But those who were interested in Inayat Khan became involved in personality. Not many accept this world as it is, and so we have international misunderstandings. The President makes wonderful speeches and the talks dead-end. Whom is he kidding?

October 30

Yesterday I had the first "day off" since I have been here. It is easy to get a bus to the pyramids as the terminus is at the square nearby. I used a guide who knows many languages and says he reads hieroglyphics. It does not matter. I visited Mina (which we call Giza), Memphis and Sakkara in one day. What I am reporting is not exactly in line with what I have read. There is no change regarding the esoteric transmission, but the places are different.

Somehow or other I was not interested in the Great Pyramids. I may climb the big one later, and I have been inside. I did not get the impression conveyed by the books; it was psychic, a la Paul Brunton, and not deeply esoteric. I was more interested in the Sphinx, and I came away feeling that Marjory Hansen and Edgar Cayce were right, that there is a lot of excavation to be done. I get no sense of finality; as the Sakkara pyramids are much older, there could easily be old buildings in the region of the Great Pyramids. I saw nothing like bottom ground, such as I saw at Taxila (in Pakistan), where only after at least six levels of digging were completed was there any conclusion that there were not cultures below. Even where there are 200- and 400-foot shafts here, there is no indication that rock bottom has been reached. My feeling is that the Sahara regions have lots to reveal, perhaps close by where the diggings are only along the green belt.

It is about Sakkara I wish to write. When I studied Shuré I felt very sure I had at one time been an initiate in Ancient Egypt. I have psychically repeated the process, and at certain times this was repeated in my own life. I see nothing to support the Rosicrucian theory that any Amen Hotep IV or Akhnaton developed the ancient mysteries. I have seen no evidence that the ancient mysteries were not very ancient, just as H.P. Blavatsky said. And it was at Sakkara that I got it right in the face — and beautifully.

To begin with, despite all books, there is one pyramid we entered which showed rooms; I understand there is at least one more which was also used. Thirty-three pyramids have been uncovered and 20 more in a state of ruin. The very number is much larger than was taught at an earlier date.

There is no question in my mind that I have been in this pyramid before. It is exactly what I have seen in vision during my Shuré days, down to small details. It also validates the saying of Jesus: "Straight is the gate and narrow is the way and few there be that find it." As in Shuré you have to climb on your hands and knees; as in Shuré, there are the decorations, which I did not see in the Great Pyramid. These decorations were hieroglyphic, esoteric and initiatory. The whole time I was at Sakkara, I was in such an ecstatic mood, I could neither take notes nor follow my guide, because things were constantly attracting my attention. I am quite willing, even anxious, to spend a full day at Sakkara with no Memphis or Mina. To me this was it and is it.

Blanche loaned me some books written by a person who seems to have memories of former lives in Egypt, which also indicates a high degree of spirituality and esotericism at an early period. I feel sure of it. Sydney Corrine used to say that the Dendera Circle showed a civilization covering two complete cycles of the equinox, that is, going back 50,000 years or more. I have not been to Dendera, and I am not going to Luxor until the weather calms down, which will be in December. I may or may not have the Paul Brunton experience with adepts down there.

Here I am meeting the dervishes, whom as I have said before, are the esotericists. When I told my close brother here of my experience with the pyramids, he said it was the same with him and that he is sure that Sakkara was the center of initiatory rites. I am not so much slapping the Great Pyramid as elevating earlier ones in the point of occult history. The Great Pyramids seem to have been for the dead and some at Sakkara for the living.

October 31

My dear Harry:

I am now going ahead full blast on our plan, writing to different states and universities for specific agricultural bulletins. I know pretty well what they want here and have a fairly full program when I return. I have three alternatives in life: a) to work on an estate as a nursery man; b) to return to college, do more plant study and some research and also a language or two; c) travel both for lecturing and research.

November 5

I was very much surprised today to find an official car waiting for me, and henceforth I shall be an official visitor. The work I am doing in using horticulture to bring nations together has been highly commended. I am consulted even on matters for which I have not much knowledge. But between training and prayer, which stimulates the intuitions, I have a facility and a faculty for finding things practically in books. Either the intense scientific training or the awakened intelligence might work, but the combination works much more rapidly.

After I learned that my work in horticultural exchange is highly favored by the U.A.R. government, we found Dr. Kemal Hussein at the Faculty of Arts, Cairo. We had met before in Pakistan and are very close. He is an authority on the real Moineddin Ibn'l Arabi.

November 12

The news from South Viet Nam does not surprise me. A number of years ago, my dear friend Robert Clifton was in San Francisco and gave me a lengthy, objective report on South Viet Nam. I placed this before Alan Watts and the State Department, and they both brushed it aside. I later visited that part of the world, saw Clifton again and had my own direct experience. He visited me in S.F. in 1959. The establishment of a Christian government on Buddhist people does not go well with those people and then when that government is corrupt as well, we — the U.S. — get the blame. I am not surprised at the revolt, but we cannot predict the denouement. It is certain that we have not regarded the Vietnamese as equals in anything and they don't like it.

On another plane, something like that is going on here. The masses in Tunisia stormed the U.S. Embassy, and now the Algerians are doing the same. We give them food, culture, morality, kindliness but we do not give them reciprocity. We do not take old civilizations and cultures seriously, and we ought to take them very seriously.

The other evening I was with Professor M. Kemal Hussein and he gave it to me strongly about the Americans who are permitted to offer their culture here, but the opposite is not true. He considers his nation as an intellectual equal and literary superior, but scientifically and technologically much inferior. He wants reciprocity, but reciprocity is about the last thing that seems to be offered.

The next day I visited the Egyptian Library and picked up a book on the Sudan. What the writer said about the Sufis and dervishes in every way contradicts the "textbook" the American Information Service here uses on the subject. This writer had the audacity to go and visit the Sufis instead of writing his pipe-dream about them. He found them, of course. Because of the multiple memberships in Sufi orders, one can "deduce" that there are more Sufis in Sudan than inhabitants.

November 13

Allah is no doubt Merciful, Compassionate, Beneficent, but that does not prevent the acceptance of truth. So long as we accept personalities, we either cannot accept truth or we are putting bars before somebody or before ourselves.

Last night after I wrote the preceding page I went for a walk. Before long I was engaged in a three-way debate over religion. A Christian attacked me from one side and a "Mohammedan" from another. In such moments I have more wisdom than knowledge and more wit than wisdom, as if Iblis and Allah were both with me. I asked the Christian, "What name did Jesus use when he prayed to God?" "Jesus was the Son of God." "I am not arguing that, I have asked you a question." I kept on repeating it, and he finally said, "It is a secret." "Oh, so you have a secret religion. I am glad to know that. Tell me, what is going to happen tomorrow?" "I bet you would not come to my church." "I will come to your church anytime you wish except tomorrow, because I have an engagement." "My priest will convert you." "No, I will convert your priest." By that time the crowd was laughing so loud at him that he withdrew.

The other man denied everything I said and then asked, "Are you a Mohammedan?" I yelled out very loud, so everybody around could hear me: "No, I am not and never was a Mohammedan. But if you are a Mohammedan, I am pleased to meet you, because I welcome followers of all religions." "What is your religion?" "To submit to Allah. I submit to Allah at all times and try to do His will. This may make me a Muslim. I hope so. But I am *not* a Mohammedan." By this time the crowd was laughing at him, too. He became meeker. "What is your opinion of Mohammed?" "That he was Rassul-lillah (Messenger), that he was a perfect man, and that his body cast no shadow in the noon-day sun." "I am sorry. I apologize. I agree with you." So we shook hands. That made me a hero.

November 18

This week I went to the reception of Ambassador M. Husain, who used to be in San Francisco. He was very much surprised to see me here. The evening was the same as all such diplomatic events: the guests rush to the cocktails and knickknacks and nobody pays any attention to the guest of honor. The only difference this time for me was that I knew the ambassador. On other occasions, I did not know the ambassador or prime minister, but just went over to the lonely man in the corner and invariably that was he. I was introduced as an

American Sufi. Wow! There being no important Sufis in the world (according to Landau) and there being no Sufis in politics (according to Gruenebaum), I was besieged by more ghosts than at any time in my life—intelligent ghosts from all kinds of countries who rushed up and greeted me in English. I had the time of my life and an easy entry into more embassies than you can imagine.

November 19

Damn it, Harry, or praise the Lord and alhamdulillah, but I have a good angel looking after me. I think I wrote that the Vegetable Station gave me six problems, and one day I found the answers to five of them in their own library. The scientists know how to conduct experiments, but they don't always know how to use American literature. One of the best things I did was to take that course on Chemical Literature, because it also covered the whole field of agricultural literature. . . .

Yesterday, I got took and am laughing. I was taken to Al-Azhar Mosque where I prayed with 3000 people and then had a shish-kabob dinner free. I asked what business my host was in, and he makes an essence which can be used for perfumes. He has all kinds of secret formulas and mixtures. I am not going to try to wrangle any, but I would like to get the lists of plants used. Some are garden varieties and some desert varieties. Whatever I find out, I'll let you know.

November 26

I learned that it is very difficult to get rooms in Luxor after December 1st, so I went down and spent two days there. It was delightful that I found Californians all over the place, including family friends who are on guided tours covering the whole world—there seems to be a lot of that sort of thing. The Luxor-Karnak area seems to be highly "civilized" and advanced, and I did not get much spiritual feeling. But I got even less that the fine art work was done by slaves. . . .

Upon entering the hotel there, I was met by a registering clerk who would accept no tip, nothing, except when he saw my tasbih (prayer beads), he said, "I want those." "Nothing doing," I replied, as they were very expensive. The clerk kept insisting. When we got to my room, I explained that I could not let him have the beads, because not only was I already a teacher and was using the tasbih, but I could only give them to a Sheikh. "I am the Sheikh," the clerk said. He was, too. Naturally, I gave him the tasbih.

(To Harry Nelson:)

The east (Luxor-Karnak) side of the river has been called the "living side," which had temples and apparently homes. The west side (Thebes) had the tombs and funeral temples. This includes the celebrated Tut-ankh-amen and the now being excavated tombs of Seti I and Seti II. On the Luxor side, I stayed at the Winter Palace Hotel, which has excellent meals, and I may come again for two reasons not connected with gardening: a) I met dervishes, and b) the headquarters of the American Oriental Institute is nearby with an excellent library.

The garden at the Winter Palace is full of the same kind of annuals and perennials which you have around you. The chief difference is the use of phoenix and ficus as foundation plants. The lay out is geometrical and formal, but one is surprised to find even here, where the summer temperature runs to 100 degrees and more, that roses thrive. Evidently some strains must be able to take the heat.

More important is the Queen's Temple itself. It seems she was quite a horticulturist herself, and sent to Punt (which is perhaps Eritrea) for all kinds of shrubs. Chief among these is henna, which grows in that region both as an ornamental and commercial plant. The police came up when they saw I was taking notes. I did not know that jotting down the names of flowers was a subversive activity, but you never can tell....

CHAPTER THIRTY

Excerpts from Letters-Diaries:

Egypt, Winter 1961

December 5   *Cairo*

Friday night I went to two gatherings of Sufis and have been invited to several more this week. The Tuesday invitation came from a Sheikh, and I have not had time to telephone other people for appointments—kept too busy. The difference between the real-Asia that I have been seeking and the phant-Asia presented in S.F. grows greater and greater.

December 13

The last week has resulted in my name appearing in the newspapers here several times and a request for a detailed account of my doings for my hometown paper in San Rafael, California, as well as by my old friend, the now-famous Chet Huntley of NBC. Mr. Huntley is very broad-minded in his religious and spiritual views, and we have never been far apart on other subjects either.

December 13

My dear Florie:

This afternoon I visited at least six mosques. We went to Bab-i-Zuela, which has two mighty minarets and a wonderful gate. I was struck by the colored glass work, different from that of the Christian churches. The one I cared for least was the grand Mohammed Ali Mosque—very huge, ornate with all grand ornaments, lighting and art work, but no fine feeling. This is built on the top of the citadel near the gates and wall of Saladin, which interested me. But today was Mosque Day, and I did not bother too much about the other remains.

The two mosques which interested me most were those of Sultan Hasan and the Rufai, which are opposite each other, just below the Citadel and are Sufi mosques. I was told Sufism is taught there. It is certain that the Rufai Mosque gave me the grandest of spiritual uplifts I have had since reaching this land. In general these mosques preserved fine wood carving also, and the Sultan Hasan Mosque is a grand example of Islamic architecture. Nevertheless, if I go to the Sultan Hasan and Rufai Mosques in the future it will be to meditate and pray, rather than to examine art and architecture.

December 19

Last week I went to three dervish groups. I visited Sheikh Abu Salem Amria twice. They meet in a very new and clean mosque which is said to have been the property of the late unlamented Farouk. Now it is kept exceedingly clean and bright; there were about 400 people — or rather, men — last night. How many women meet upstairs I don't know.

Each authority on Sufism gives his bosh about it being "derived" from Brahmanism, Buddhism, Christianity, Neo-Platonism, Zoroastrianism, Shiism and what not. None offer evidence and none consult the Sufis themselves. The Sufis say, and I believe them, that some of the methods are of ancient lineage and the chief difference is the substitution of Arabic and Quranic materials for those in existence prior to the time of Muhammed.

But there is a scientific way to test that nobody has looked into at all, and I have never seen in any books excepting those of my own Pir-O-Murshid Inayat Khan. His works are available in English, but with the exception of the World Congress of Faiths in England, not a single "authority" refers to them. He was especially trained in music and his original intention had been to make a voluminous work called "The Mysticism of Sound." This was never done, and instead he wrote a short book on the subject.

The use of music by dervishes is far, far greater than even I had dreamed. I had thought, and I found quite different, that only the Mevlevis made much use of music. That order is weak here and has become decadent. The Rufais at the Sidi Sharani had responses and antiphonies, and they even sat in a way that makes me feel there might be Christian predecessors (certainly the Gnostics, who have long since disappeared). It is certain that the two kinds of singing which I heard at the Shadhili and Rufai gatherings are not at all like the usual Arabic and far different from the Quranic chants.

December 31

I am closing a most edifying year. Everything has turned around and I think every upset of almost every earlier part of my life has been reversed. . . . I again went to mosques Thursday and Friday and expect to tomorrow also, inshallah. The atmosphere alone is feeding. The loving and lovable people here are far more numerous than one meets in many parts of the world. . . . Had a wonderful Christmas dinner, taking two young Americans as guests and go out with another one tonight.

It is morning, and the year has greeted me with a great inspiration.

January 4

Yesterday I visited a mosque and dargah (tomb) which very few Americans see and saw more dervishes. The teacher in one place was giving a lesson somewhere between the teachings in esotericism on *wazifa* and *amaliat* (psychology). In the mosque where the dervishes met, there was a sign: "God is love," or as we should say: "Mahbud lillah." You can see the difference in these people in their eyes.

I go as often as possible to Sheikh Abu Salem Amria of the Rufai school. I had experiences in accordance with this school before I met

203

the Sheikh, so I was quite ready when they appointed me as their representative for America.

The main difficulty here is not language so much as their efforts to convince me of what now appear as elementary teachings. There is nothing wrong in this, excepting the wasting of time. The meetings regarding Islamic teachings in the U.S. are very complicated. Some groups here, under the guise of religion, seem more concerned in politics. What is wrong here is that in religion, we are supposed to becalm the *nafs* or ego, and the spirit of agitation is the very thing that stands in the way of God-realization. I am trying to avoid any form of correction, but when one sees vibrations rise and fall, and agitation and disturbance, that cannot be the *right path*.

A paper I gave to Dr. Hussein concerns "Surrender Consciousness" and "Identity Consciousness." This may be long and involved, but it is an important teaching. My purpose, inshallah, is to draw heavily on the books at the Library when I return and try to "push" those who can be pushed and guide the others at a suitable rate. However, I am still cautious about any sort of division.

I do know that the karma which befalls those who essay the position of teachers and do not fulfill their functions is pretty awful. Many of Pir-O-Murshid's early works on this are just by-passed, for instance, "The Confessions of a Sufi Teacher." There he lays down the pattern of the true and false teacher. As he said later, one must not disregard a single word, and at the same time we must not emotionalize the statement "One must not disregard a single word." We must come to evaluate the words, one by one and altogether. Not that the words are any more than shadows-of-truth, as he taught, but they are at least shadows-of-truth, not shadows of imagination and falsehood.

January 4

Yesterday I went on a different errand in the Muski district, which is just on this side of the Khan-i-Khalili bazaars near Al-Azhar. The purpose was to visit the Franciscan Fathers. I suppose I have two prejudices here. One is that I was not only born in San Francisco very close to the Mission, but socially I have been on the "side of the poor" and consider this Order very noble. The other is Puck's protest against the clerical collar, which he considers the worst atrocity — or like the Pushtus, a masochistic device.

The Franciscan monastery is for study and research only. Students come from various countries and are supposed to know Latin, French and English; Greek is presumed but not so compulsory. Arabic and Coptic are the main language courses, and no one can leave until he has a working knowledge of them. Studies are made in early Christianity, not only the Church Fathers, but all aspects. There is still a big gap between the very early Christianity and the literary periods which developed before the time of the Islamic conquest. I am not interested in theological differences and schismatic quarrels. I am interested in liturgies, music, ceremonies, monastic disciplines and spiritual experiences. . . . I consider these Fathers clear and clean; while I do not wish to use the term *saint* in the earlier Hebrew sense of "holy ones" or pure ones (as in Hassidism), it would fit very well.

My trip so far has been successful far beyond hopes and dreams. It is easy to bring East and West together. Only nobody does it. Everybody is trying to remake the other like himself. It is true that I think they need dancing and some gymnastics and sports here to release tensions and energies. Outside of that, I see no basic need for alterations which are not taking place. There is some departure of morality with the loosening of religious ties. They do not see that if there is anything wrong with the U.S., it comes from just those mis-habits they are beginning to adopt. I don't think a man is a fanatic if he prays five times a day or gets up before dawn for God.

I am told there is a place where the Holy Family rested. I am not interested in testing the historicity of it. I am interested in the feeling behind it.

January 5

I have had a most busy and profitable two days. Because I have a certain élan and exuberance, many overlook the fact of my age and that I have accumulated a certain quantity of knowledge and perhaps experience, if not wisdom. The shoeshine boys used to charge me 5 ps. or more, although 2 ps. is considered high and 1 piastre normal. Now they fight to shine my shoes, not for the money but for the baraka (blessing). This, you will please note, is my diary entry, and I am not in the slightest concerned with the reactions of anybody in faraway places.

January 8

Sheikh Abu Salem Amria has in part accepted this person. Many of the Ulema from Al-Azhar were there last night also to hear him. He gave lessons, mostly moral and spiritual — not the humbug words of lecturers. This was the real stuff. The Mosque was packed to the doors. There was also present Sheikh Mohammed of Sidi Sharani. I cannot explain this man. There is such tremendous love between us that is real and the manifestation of it astounded even the Ulema, and many of the devotees. It is Sheikh Mohammed who is taking me out today.

January 13

My visit to En-Shams University was something. Sa'ad Kemal used to be Professor of Horticulture, but now handles Genetics and Statistics. He took me around the grounds and later to his place. He also took me to a farm where he does cotton research as well as work with grasses and ground covers to ascertain their value and usefulness. He says that the goat has been the enemy of Egypt and that it destroyed all the ground covers but *C. Dactylon* and even much of that. He says that economists, historians and others have overlooked this and tend to blame dynasties and political groups. He says that the goat eats so close that it does not permit plants to revive, especially the Egyptian ground covers, and that this is the prime factor in the centuries-long downhill slide of the soil.

I told Sa'ad Kemal that what the U.A.R. needs from the U.S. is neither money nor advanced technology, but the tourism of farmers who have grown cotton, cane and rice. I once wrote Senator Ellender on this subject: ignored. Some of those "lowly" whites from the South, with all their weaknesses, could make better suggestions than the non-contacting diplomats and experts who visit neither people nor villages.

January 18

My plan for Palestine has never been refuted. Everyone accepted it before, and I am resurrecting it step by step. . . .

Sunday we visited a Sufi khankah (group dwelling/school). I got kicked out of a school in California for using the term *khankah*; the professor didn't believe there were such things. I was urged to make this a "cause celebre" as it is called, and I probably shall. I went and greeted everybody there.

This week I also met Sheikh Sharabasi of the Rufai Dervishes. I had already been to the Rufai Mosque and had the most wonderful experience there. The sheikh had me stand up in a public meeting and get an ovation—this is becoming commonplace. In fact, I am supposed today to have lots of *baraka* and some people call me "sheikh."

I have been going to "The Garden of Allah" in the Khan-i-Khalil bazaar for purchases. I was introduced to a shoemaker downstairs who fitted me out. Somehow or other, the story got round that I am a dervish. Yesterday, when I was in this shop, the shoemaker came up breathlessly and took me by the hand downstairs. This was surprising, since my shoes were not to be fitted until next week. There was an old blind man there, a sheikh. We sat silently, and I gave him my beads: "Nakshibandi!" He gleamed all over—he is the Nakshibandi teacher here. We embraced, and then one experienced baraka—not just blessing but the warm fire of love and magnetism and joy penetrating all through one's personality. It was a tender moment of happiness. There are things beyond words and language....

Roughly speaking, the people here are Conservative Muslims, Progressive Muslims, Islamic Sufis and Universal Sufis. It is hard to draw the lines; there are no fixed rules and most are Muslims, but the top men are universal as I have written before and underneath a lot of other people are universal, too....

I had to criticize the American habit of raising funds which never reach here. Only the American Friends of the Middle East, the Y.M.C.A. and C.A.R.E. do anything here—or for that matter, wherever else I have been.

January 24

To Pir-O-Murshid Maulana Abdul Ghafoor, Dacca, East Pakistan
Beloved Teacher:
Alhamdulillahi Rabbil-alamin, Ar-rahman Ar-rahim.
[Praise to God, Lord of the Worlds, The Compassionate, The Merciful]

In pursuance of the duties set before me first by Pir-O-Murshid Sufi Inayat Khan and then by your gracious person in the capacity of Khalandar, I have come to this land with many purposes and little external assistance. Nevertheless, Allah is Great and though a man walk alone, whether through strife or ease, it is possible that heavy burdens or light may come to successful fulfillments.

This week two reports are to be submitted, one to the State Department of the United States Government and one to Sheikh Abu Salem Amria of the Rufai Order of Dervishes, each in its way marking the culmination, inshallah [God willing], of my external reasons for being in this land.

On the external side, the purposes were to bring horticultural information first to the U.A.R. and then to Pakistan to assist in the opening and cultivation of desert and salt-encrusted lands. Also to open things up for an international exchange of agricultural information. No one seems to have been doing this, although vast sums have been collected for such purposes.

One day, in pursuance of these tasks, I was introduced to a brother in *tarik*, one Murtaz Billah of the Shadhili Order of Dervishes. Like myself, he was engaged in horticultural research, and our private interests are very, very similar. But our grand purposes in life are similar also. Through him many doors have opened, of which I sketch here a few:

1. Yusuf Wali is also a horticulturalist and claims to be a disciple of the living *Qtub* [one who functions — usually secretly — as the spiritual guardian of the world, according to the Sufi traditions — ed. note]. I have heard from others that this honored person now lives and functions in this region. Yusuf has given me reports on *operative Sufism* which are entirely in harmony with what I have been taught or believe or have experienced. I hope to see him further, inshallah, before I leave the country.

2. I have attended many *Zikrs*, chiefly of the Shadhilis and Rufais and have seen some of the other orders. I am hoping soon to go to Tantah, which is a large city inhabited chiefly by Sufis and Dervishes and is the headquarters of the Bedawi Order.

3. I have been blessed with visitations of saints and Rassul-lillah, and this week am to make a complete report to Sheikh Amria. I have also met and love deeply one Sheikh Mohammed Dessougi, and one Dr. Sharabasi of the Rufai Order.

I must record one incident. I entered the Sidi Sharani Shrine one night on the occasion of this saint's birthday celebration. There were thousands of people present. As soon as I took off my shoes and crossed the threshold, two arms seized me. I thought: "Now your presumption has caught up with you; you have dared too many times to enter holy places without permission." Instead, I was immediately conducted to the microphone and found myself the guest speaker of the evening! One does not know how these things occur.

Much more could be written, all of a cheerful and hopeful nature. I have lived under many conditions, and now at a later era in my life Allah has removed many of the burdens and brought either the fruit of effort or the Grace which is needed to follow the pathway of a Khalandar in life.

My love to all.

In Egypt, 1961

CHAPTER THIRTY-ONE

Newspaper Article:

Science is Stirring in the Mid-East

—*from the* San Rafael Independent Journal, *January 21, 1961*

The last time wandering Marinite Sam Lewis of Mill Valley made headlines in the *Independent Journal,* he was just back from a tour of the Orient where he became a member of the mystical dervish orders of Chisti and Nakshibandi.

Today, he is in another distant country—Gamal Abdel Nasser's United Arab Republic.

Based in Cairo, he is carrying on a campaign with two general aims:

1. To assist the country in increasing its food supply.

2. And in so doing, to boost American prestige and reduce communistic subversion.

More specifically, Lewis is dedicated to the bringing of helpful American agricultural and scientific bulletins and magazines to the Egyptians to aid them in enticing more food from their soil.

The project, he says, is the result of his visit to Asian countries in 1956 and a talk which followed with the U.S. Department of Agriculture in Washington, D.C.

The idea explored there was to promote the introduction of suitable trees and crops to help countries deficient in food and timber. . . .

Lewis has paid several visits to the UAR's National Research Center where the leading scientists of the Near East coordinate their research efforts.

"I should say that their methods and effectiveness are in general on the level with the best that I have seen in the U.S. and Japan," he reports. "Whenever and wherever possible, they have the best equipment. And personnel is highly trained. Most of this personnel is Egyptian, but large numbers are graduates of American universities, and half of these come from the University of California." . . .

Lewis says the UAR Information Bureau has furnished him with considerable literature on the progress of that country under Nasser.

"In contrast to what appears in the newspapers or even in the magazines, this information is calm, sedate, factual and actually more optimistic than the emotional propaganda.

"With all the faults here, I find progress has been much more rapid and secure than in many other lands."

Lewis also says that the stress which has been placed on the UAR's position in world politics has tended to obscure its growth and importance in such fields as science, technology and commerce. . . .

Of Nasser's influence in his own continent, Lewis says:

"The new African nations and some others are watching Nasser, and they have been favorably impressed by him. So when the time comes, they will vote with him or for him or both. They probably don't like China and may abhor Russian communism, but they can't understand us."

Lewis has praise for one facet of the U.S. effort to solve this dilemma.

"We are now sending musicians and singers to these countries who can meet people at their own level," he declares. "We are changing the policy of wasting millions of dollars on symphony orchestras and ballet troupes which reach very limited audiences, and are soon forgotten."

He says the most successful touring orchestra he has seen and heard was a group from the Philippines.

"They played almost entirely American and Latin American music, along with a few tunes from their own country," Lewis says. "There was nothing European on the program."

Goodwill ambassador-observer Lewis, at home or abroad, does not confine his activities to the scientific and horticultural fields. One interest is the writing of epic poetry. Egyptian scholar Dr. Kemal Hussein, Lewis reports, has written a favorable review after an advance look at his newest piece of poetry entitled "Saladin" which is dedicated to that great warrior and his country. "I write epic poems to prove that Americans can understand the peoples of distant lands," Lewis says. . . .

In his special field of horticulture, his next project will be research on edible common flowers, he says.

"This looks like a good lot for one man," he admits. "But," he continues, "I take the cold war seriously because all the information I have obtained here is that population is going up and agricultural production down in many lands. I think we can help to correct this situation."

Lewis says his efforts are not so much based upon anti-communism or "anti-anything" as they are pro-American.

CHAPTER THIRTY-TWO

Excerpts from Letters-Diaries:
Egypt, Winter 1961
(Part II)

January 29, 1961

I have been going to Al-Azhar for some special training in Quran and also to Mosques, especially those of the Rufai Dervishes. Tomorrow I am going again to the tombs of the Maeluks to meet the Sufis there. I want to get as much material as possible.

They celebrate saints' days here even more than in India and Pakistan. It is partly an inheritance from Christianity, partly from older religions and no doubt came to fruition in the Fatimid Period when Shia Islam was in control. They have *moulads*, which means festivals, like the Mardi Gras and includes everything. Last night I attended a circus, which is largely in the form of side-shows, but one side-show proved to include the main events, beginning with lion-taming and having a combination of a vaudeville and animal show. I saw the native dancing, perhaps as good or better than at the casinos and much less coarse.

I had to buy the candy, which is supposed to contain the *baraka*. Later I may go to Tanta, inshallah, where the Bedawi dervishes hold forth, whose candy is particularly sacred. Evidently just as monks made wines or liquors, dervishes make candy. It is quite different from most forms at home, although they do have some like peanut brittles and New Orleans types.

At the moment, with my interest in dervishes, I may seem over-enthusiastic. Religions are like trees and when we try to describe them in seed-form, we are projecting and differentiating and not describing. Islam, even more than the Catholic Church, includes all sorts of phases and institutions. To regard them as "wrong" is like regarding the oak as a "wrong" rose-bush or "wrong" pine tree. There is no "right" or "wrong" about the so-called accretions. They are there, they are part of life. We can study and even come to understand them, but to give them moral or personal judgments is totally nonsensical. It prevents communication and lack of real communication prevents understanding and peace.

January 30

Beloved Ones of God: Toward the One, the Perfection of Love, Harmony and Beauty, the Only Being, United with All the Illuminated Souls who form the Embodiment of the Master, the Spirit of Guidance.

One is forced constantly to choose between a personal report and a sermon. I would much rather the personal report, but it is received as a personality report and not so much as an objective one. This makes communication very difficult. One cannot compel the surrender of any ego, but despite all the words in all the scriptures on "surrender" it is not usually a living function.

In Pir-O-Murshid's original teaching, there were two paths distinctly marked out: a) the path of progression in Zikr; b) the path of progression in *fana*, which comes in three stages, *fana-fi-sheikh* [effacement in the teacher], *fana-fi-rassul* [effacement in the Messenger], *fana-fi-lillah* [effacement in the Only Being]. In practice, there has not been too much understanding of these ways of progression and I can only refer to them here as part of one man's biography, regardless.

In Hazrat Inayat Khan's teachings on "Moral Culture," we have reference to the Law of Reciprocity, Law of Beneficence and Law of Renunciation. Reciprocity is the Moral Law for ordinary persons. Call it karma or not, it operates, and in the teachings one should take advantage of all the suggestions. Beneficence comes from the Spiri-

215

tual Path or *Tarikat*, and in Holy Quran we find *Bismillah er-rahman er-rahim* [We begin in the name of God, the Compassionate, the Merciful] which indicates the identity of surrender (fana) with beneficence. But people identify these qualities with God and do not usually try to live *akhlak Allah*, that is, in the manner of God or in the presence of God.

I find myself at a distance from Orthodox Muslims who place all the virtues in a Deity and do not try to develop these in themselves. No doubt, it is a first step to see them in God, but it is not a last step, and it is not a Path or Progression. Whatever way you place religion, it universally teaches: "Guide us on the Right Path," but it is not the prayer, nor the words, it is the adaptation of the life within oneself. This is the "Greater Jihad" Mohammed spoke of.

Paul had to correct the people of his time who paid too much attention to fana-fi-sheikh; he tried to universalize fana-fi-rassul, whether people were ready for it or not. In bringing the Message to the West, people became enamored with fana-fi-sheikh and they do not rise to fana-fi-rassul; the words of the prayer Salat become empty. They remain just words. If a man wishes to change these words into truths, he will likely be misunderstood, but he may also gain understanding and perhaps wisdom.

Here there is a great deal of difference between any invocation of "United with All the Illuminated Souls Who form the Embodiment of the Master" and the direct understanding thereof. It has been insisted by many that there is a living *Qtub* in this area. I cannot argue though I have not met him yet. But I have met many Sheikhs and from them received so much love and baraka that I can never thank Allah enough.

Years ago, I wrote "The Bestowal of Blessing." Most of the copies were lost or destroyed except for one which a friend may have in Santa Barbara. I wish to get ahold of it again, for it would be much easier to explain the whole science and art of *baraka*. In "Marriage and Morals in Morocco" much is said on this subject, and I think there is a *Tractus berachoth* in the Hebrew Talmud on the same subject. Jesus started with the Beatitudes, but there is a dichotomy between bliss and happiness, that we do not see "blessings" as "bliss" or "bliss" as happiness.

Actually, there is a living function here. I have received baraka both from human beings, usually sheikhs and khalifs, but also in the mosques, especially the Rufai mosques. But there is another form of baraka which comes in fana-fi-rassul.

Pir-O-Murshid gave us a long list of Messengers ending with Mohammed. I have experienced the fana-fi-rassul in and with Mohammed, but immediately after that with Jesus; and in the course of time with Buddha and Siva and then under the guidance of Mohammed with all the prophets of God of all religions. In theory, this completed the path of fana-fi-rassul. [This experience is recounted in Samuel Lewis's epic poem "Saladin" published in *The Jerusalem Trilogy*—ed.] But when one regards God as the Only Being, one does not—maybe cannot—of himself distinguish between fana-fi-sheikh, fana-fi-rassoul and fana-fi-lillah; nor does one care for, as Pir-O-Murshid said: "Thy light is in all forms, Thy love in all beings...in an inspiring teacher."

Following the literary method of the Zoroastrian religion, I must paraphrase for my own record the teachings in fana-fi-rassul received today wherein Mohammed seemed to play the part with me that the Angel Gabriel did with Him:

Sage: What is the difference between prayers in no direction, as Kabir and others taught and prayers in a direction, say, as inherited from Judaism?

The Spirit of Wisdom: In effect there may be none. If one accepts the Fatherhood of Allah, there, He is everywhere in everything. But if one also accepts the Brotherhood of Man, there should be *kibla* [the point one directs oneself toward in prayer — ed. note]. The effect of the apparent universality of Kabir, in breaking down certain Islamic institutions, has been the dissolution of the spirit of Brotherhood. The Sikhs carried the "logical" argument to the extreme and analytically were right but instead of Brotherhood, nothing but strife followed. So kibla is advised.

Sage: What is the difference between Jerusalem and Mecca as kibla?

The Spirit of Wisdom: Jesus spoke of Jerusalem as being the city which stoned its prophets. Despite the Hebrew claim that only Jeremiah was persecuted, we have no record of any prophet of God actually being welcomed in Jerusalem. Indeed, the historical career of Jesus ended in failure there.

On the other hand, Mecca has been the kibla of success, both with Abraham, the Friend of God, and Mohammed, the Messenger of God. One does not like to put forth the argument that Jerusalem has been the kibla of failure, and Mecca of success, but you can still see the Christians fighting each other and the Zionists are all divided as to religion.

Sage: The Muslims always mention your name with a special praise.

The Spirit of Wisdom: That is all right, but it is not my way. Quran distinctly says that there are no distinctions between the Messengers of God. And although it is said that prayers are not made to me, there is psychological intercession. The psychological intercession falters if it becomes merely theological, which it usually does; and benefits when men learn to pray *with* the Seal of the Prophets, and not mention his name at all.

This is very difficult, but the errors in religion usually come from too much zeal; zeal alone is not bad, but it becomes a substitute for morality and selflessness. There is too much praise for literature called Holy Quran and Hadith and too little concern with the contents thereof. The same is true with most scriptures.

Sage: What, then, is the right path?

The Spirit of Wisdom: Allah has already shown you that Path, and therefore it is not for me to add. Many will reject you, but that is of no importance; what is important is what you accept and do, not what others say or think about it.

* * *

Now the initial stage in fana-fi-lillah follows the same pattern as took place with Pir-O-Murshid in his 1911 career. Then he was using mostly music and concentration. He often broke into ecstasy and sang loudly in praise of Mohammed. This probably did not go over big. But I have found there are three sorts of praise of Mohammed, and they all look the same, but are different:

A. The initial stage is that one praises Mohammed, and it may even be that he has inherited this phase of religion. He is using it as a crutch, and it may be a crutch; he is using it as a ladder, and it may be a ladder. Actually, it is no better or worse than the praise of Jesus, Buddha, Krishna or anybody, but neither is there any gain by dispensing with it.

B. The second stage is that one praises Mohammed, because that is the experience. He is really talking about himself—and he is not talking about himself. The change from fana-fi-sheikh to fana-fi-rassul in one's life is revolutionary. One is no longer restricted in vision or in faculties, and he finds a tremendous universe before him. Time and place and stage and condition become small things. He cannot prove this nor is he doing this by himself.

In his first sessions on Sufism, Pir-O-Murshid placed Mohammed as the Perfect Man of All Times. I shall explain this a little below. I think the Sufi in Islam generally works from this position.

C. The third stage seems impossible, that while one is being immersed in God, the praises of Mohammed become grander. Dante had it of Jesus, but I don't think Dante reached the highest stages. He held onto selfhood. Even the mystics of Christianity—except a few like John Tauler—never got above the selfhood or to the unitarian realization.

Nor does it seem that God praises God. This seems a contradiction. There are two aspects of Allah, the silent and the creative, although neither of these words is exact. The silent praise is discussed in "The Mysticism of Sound" both in the chapter called "The Silent

Life" and in the final chapter which is partially a dissertation on Zikr. [These writings by Hazrat Inayat Khan are found in Volume II of *The Sufi Message.* — ed.]

The Bible says that God created Adam in His image, but Adam is usually associated with "sin." There had to be a "perfect man" for redemption. Now, there are all kinds of differences between them. But the Buddhist does not live like Buddha, nor the Christian like Christ nor the Hindu like Ram or Krishna. We wish to live in an operative world — to raise families and go into business and study and do all those things which we consider human. It is on this point that Mohammed excels. He does not excel in being nearer to God, the Creator, but he does excel in being nearer to man, the created.

Anybody has a perfect right to differ from me here, but the point is not argument, but demonstration. He does not see people demonstrate what Jesus did, or Buddha did; we do see people demonstrate what Mohammed did.

Therefore comes the idea that God created the world through Light, and this was a living light which also had to become the essence in and of humanity. The idea of Adam, derived from *dam*, earth, is that the Light of Allah had to come through the earthly forms. But how did it come? In "Masnavi" (by Mevlana Jelaluddin Rumi), the cosmic evolution is taught ending in man; and the cosmic evolution continues until the perfect man, or as I see it, the perfect-perfect man.

Buddha was a perfect man who showed the way to Nirvana, and in the Southern Buddhism, this teaching is kept. But it is a limited Nirvana, not the true, if you have to become a monk to reach it. This assumes that the layman cannot reach perfection. But the layman has received perfection, and so the later Buddhists said that creation and Nirvana were identical. Only this means that the common man could attain perfection. But what common man has attained to perfection? One cannot call Rama common, because he was a king; Krishna also had a special place in society, and Jesus and Buddha became monks. There was only one ordinary man who represented both Adam and perfection. So with Mohammed the revelation was sealed, which does not take away from any scripture or teaching. I do not wish here to go into stories about Mohammed which substantiate this point. What I am really telling you is my experience. As Al-Ghazalli said: "Sufism consists in experiences and not premises." Only previously, I told my experiences, and there is a personality reaction. So I have clothed what I am experiencing in philosophy, which is a veil over it and is not *it*.

I have written before that I came here with three missions and have accomplished a dozen. Pir-O-Murshid Hazrat Inayat Khan and Pir-O-Murshid Maulana Abdul Ghafoor have given me the whole world to work in and with the intellectual people. So I transfer my experiences into philosophy. But some day when people want truth and will accept from the simple man, he will give the simplicity. As the simplicity is rejected, he gives the philosophy.

Jesus taught that one must be like a little child to receive the kingdom of heaven. One can always be open to blessings. One can always listen to the "voice which constantly cometh from within." But if we keep on using the mouthpiece, we can't hear what is coming over the receiver.

My destiny sometimes seems to follow the career of the dog in one of Pir-O-Murshid's stories. This dog took 2 days to go from Basra to Baghdad, instead of the usual 12. "I owe it all to the kindness of my fellow dogs," he said. "Whenever I stopped to rest, they came and barked at me." So the more humanity barks, the faster the progression. Every time a rejection or seeming failure appears, Allah comes and brings me blessings and success. This will probably be my career until I am called hence. I, Samuel, have nothing to do with it.

There has been a school of Sufis called "Malamatiyya" which sought out public blame as part of its practice. I do not seek and am not checking on reactions. Every rebuff is followed by meditation and/or prayer, and in turn, something pleasant follows, usually much more pleasant than conjectured. So one comes back to the first lesson: Subhan Allah, Alhamdulillah, Allaho-Akbar.

February 6

On January 30, I was to submit a full report to the Embassy on my experiences including many of the past, and my proposals. I no sooner filed this report when a group of Kadiri Sufis came to my hotel. At that time, I could not see them for without any notice I was asked to go to Alexandria, which I did.

I spent January 31 at Abis, which is the joint undertaking of the Egyptians and Americans (EARIS — Egyptian American Rural Improvement Society). In a sense, I found myself in a new world — brave or unbrave. In another sense, I saw exactly the society forming which had been previously "revealed" to me and recorded, though never taken seriously. It is here, now, and will have to be taken seriously.

My works on social reconstruction and brotherhood were much more prophetic than logical, psychic than physical, but they are here now. The dispossessed are being placed on reclaimed land, given small homes, private barns which can also be used as storage, farms, animals, seed and a small space for a home garden of any kind. At present, people are not settling as fast as necessary; perhaps this is because the Egyptians have in all ages been good builders and not nearly so good in some other aspects of life.

The next day it poured terrifically and I went to the Tourist Bureau in Alexandria. There I met Nadya, one of the most beautiful women I have ever seen; this attracted many men there who were not interested in tourism, but in Nadya, and that meant I met a lot of notable persons and had really a wonderful time.

I did not have much time to get acquainted with Nadya when her supervisor, Fuad Leithi, walked in: "Ah," he said, "there you are. I have been waiting for you. How much do you remember of your previous incarnations?" Shades of Paul Brunton, that was it. I did not get it at the Valley of the Kings, but at the Tourist Information Office, Alexandria.

He told me I was travelling to escape, that there was a woman in my life, and I could not think who it could be. When I got back to

222

the hotel (Leroy), I did remember one such woman with whom I have had a sort of aeonic romance, but she has long gone out of my memory. I had forgotten all about her; but whether it is she or not, I don't know. However, I have had my fortune told five times, all the same and all stressed romances—Sufi Sheikhs, card readers, everybody—so we shall see.

Fuad claimed to be telepathic and clairvoyant, and you can put it in my book: he is. He read many things which I have told nobody, almost secret experiences I have had at holy places and which, in a certain way, affect my international peregrinations. I told him that his eyes and forehead look very much like those of an adept mentioned by Paul Brunton in the final pages of A *Search in Secret Egypt*. He told me that all adepts here are Sufis.

Among Fuad's many visitors (or Nadya's, rather) was the District Attorney of Alexandria. He began by challenging me right and left and ended with cordiality; we had a delightful time. The result was that the conversations reached a higher and higher pitch during the day. I stayed until 7 p.m. when we went to the studio of Alexandria's greatest modern painter, named Wanli. . . .

Yesterday was a theoretical "Sufi" celebration being the anniversary of the death of Pir-O-Murshid Inayat Khan. I had one of the dreams of my life fulfilled—riding an Arab horse. Went from the Pyramids to Sahara city and back. I originally took up horseback riding, because I said that someday I would go to Arabia and I might as well learn. I had forgotten all about the incident. But the reason I went was quite different.

I had gone to Mena village (near the Pyramids) at the invitation of two close friends, and they introduced me to a Sufi Sheikh. He earns his living by renting horses. So on account of this I hired him. On our way back we had a "crazy" time chanting sacred phrases. I don't think any Egyptian ever before had such a client. He then took me to lunch, but while waiting I danced for his children. I also left a good gift for them.

Came home, took a real hot bath, then hot chocolate and off to the

Rufai dervishes where I stayed two and a half hours and then went home, only to meet a delegation of Kadiris from Iraq. They wanted me to visit their country for spiritual reasons. I have neither the time nor money but will visit them and then take it up with the U.S. Embassy. I think one of these days some foundation or somebody should come to my rescue. I am working all alone in a terrific vineyard with an unlimited harvest and nobody else there.

February 7

My dear Abdul Rahman:
I am scheduled to sail from Port Said on the 20th and to arrive in your country at Karachi on March 3rd. It is possible that the ship will sail earlier, so I will be there four days ahead of time.

My visit with the Islamic Congress was long and involved. There has been a complete change of administration, and the former secretaries took off with my papers. I have no time to write them again. It took me hours upon hours and that looks like it's wasted.

I had to go over the program for San Francisco and the the United States. They spend more time crying because the Zionists are strong than in doing anything. The Zionists are strong because Muslims just sit back and cry. They don't send anybody to present their side. Besides, this is political. Then I had to argue against Arabism. I told them I was interested in Islamic teachings, not in the Arab language. If I wished to see more Arabic, I would be studying the language. I told them that one of the great troubles is that everybody says Islam has Five Pillars, and when it comes to practice, one finds everything but those Five Pillars. Instead of Shahud [experience] and Salaat [prayer], I find zeal for Arabism, converting everybody else to go to Mecca without going oneself, more insistence on others performing *wuzu* (ablutions) than prayer and devotion and a whole lot of crying about the Congo. In this, Allah is lost, and I did not see how they could stop others from spreading Islam while they were wasting time in politics and unnecessities.

There is no question but that the Kadianis and the Ahmaddiyas have gone ahead, because they are teaching religion, not Arabism, not politics, not agitation and were trying to bring peace to the world. Actually the Islamic Congress is not against the Ahmaddiyas. Its purpose is to get all the Muslims to work together. The Buddhists have done this. They have a single mission for sending people abroad and do not use funds competing with each other. On the other hand, you have all kinds of missionaries from Pakistan ignoring each other, in competition and so causing confusion.

People are concerned with Algeria one day and the Congo the next and then Laos and Cuba and everything else. There is another way to win, and that is by surrender to God. I have seen the ways of victory through surrender, and evidently I shall have to lecture on this subject in your country. They say "Allaho Akbar" millions of times, but what does it mean?

We came to agreement at the Congress. We placed all our differences down and agreed. They want to see Islamic teachings in the U. S., and they want all Muslims—Shias, Sunnis, Ahmaddiyas of every kind working together.

February 13

I am trying to write some notes in my crowded last moments here. There is no question but that I jumped into a grand salon of vacua which invited international relationships, but into which practically nobody has gone and, in some cases, not dared to go.

What has been called "diplomacy" is nothing but a fancy game for an imaginary thing called "honor," the nature of which is not quite clear. On the other hand, to me at least, hunger is quite clear. Although I primarily started out with the mission of the exchange of international information in horticulture, the contemporary populace/food ration, the failure of crops in certain lands (chiefly behind the Iron Curtain, the Congo mass starvation, plus a lot more things) make my position logically exceedingly strong. . . .

I had written to Senator Engle on an ironical situation: I come here on my own and pay income taxes. There are several organizations in the U.S. collecting funds to bring better international relations and that is what they are good at— collecting funds. There is one in particular that has been collecting funds for fertilizer and spray equipment. You give to them and get a deduction on your income taxes, because they are a privileged non-profit organization. I found they were not even functioning here, except in campaigns for more funds, eaten up by more rents and more secretaries.

Marin Man Watches Rioting of Cairo Mob
(from the San Rafael Independent Journal, *March 2, 1961)*

A Mill Valley philosopher saw Cairo mobs throw fire-darts at the Belgian Embassy and smash windows of the U.S Information Agency because of anger over Congo developments.

But Sam Lewis, "good will ambassador," also reported in a letter to the *Independent-Journal* today that "the bazaars are buzzing— they don't want to lose trade, and friends.

"Even close associates of Nasser admit there is no ground for criticizing the U.S.A. for its stand in the Congo," Lewis asserted.

Lewis wrote his impressions in a letter mailed from Aden, a southern Arabian port, on his way to West Pakistan after a stay in Cairo.

Describing the episode of the fire-darts, Lewis said that some took effect on the Belgian Embassy.

"There were police around, chiefly to see that they did not harm other buildings," he wrote. "There were some smaller boys, but few adults. At the pension I was told that these boys had been given a recess from school for this very purpose and perhaps the ringleader had received a bribe.

"An hour later, they turned on the American Embassy and first smashed all the windows at the USIA library, then the embassy buildings in general. The police came this time, but too late to save the glass.

"Pictures reveal that the mobs consisted almost entirely of lads. Smaller boys gladly join their big brothers without knowing what it is all about. There are comparatively few adults in the pictures I have seen, nor did I see many adults in this or in other 'riotous' crowds. Indeed all the riots were well ordered."

Port Said, wrote Lewis, was mobbed just before his arrival.

"But to substantiate that there is little popular support in anti-American demonstrations," he said, "the main street has a huge sign in English: 'Gamal Nasser, you have gone mad.'"

Lewis paid his respects to "hypothetical, metaphysical pablum that passes for Near East culture in many of our institutions" and said that "in the midst of an Arabian culture, authors prefer to consult European 'authorities' for their (mis)information than interview Arabs."

At least six Arabs should be found to lecture on Near East culture in the United States, according to Lewis. He said he had been told Arabs would accept jobs but there are no offers, though "we must have Zionist and European experts."

America should "stop 'people to people' programs without meeting the people," declared Lewis.

February 17 *Port Said*

I left Cairo yesterday travelling by bus.... I was given a farewell tea by a Sheikh and his friends. Next morning I made a final plea to the American Embassy, for God's sake, to have Arabs teach about their country and don't subsidize English, Germans, Hungarians and Polish Jews to do it. I made my point, but too late for the mob. I had warned the USIA long ago that they would remember my words when they were mobbed, but the man I had warned was away....

I ate well and then went to the movies. The cost here was absurdly low. It cost me one pound for a ticket at the football game, which at the official rate would be $2.80. I think it cost about P.T. 6 for a ticket at the movie, first class, which is around 15 cents. There was one western movie, not bad; the scenery was excellent and the plot, though it could be figured out, was somewhat different. Then an English movie, "The Dangerous Refugee" or something like that—better acting and more "scientific" or artistic lighting, but I preferred the American—give me hamburgers! I think this is all the nonsense in my mind at the moment, the rest being pretty much of a blank. If you can make this out, let Evelyn read it; if you can't, let her read it anyway and then feed it to Cha-cha.

February 20   *S.S. Cilicia*

I am glad to have a chance to sail on a different kind of ship. I feel quite happy to be on board, although just now it is more like river- or steam-boating on a lake. At least, I shall be "house-broken" by the time we reach the Indian Ocean. . . .

We are now on the Arabian Sea south of Hadramaut. We landed at Aden, and although I did not want to spend money, my friend Abdul Rahman wanted a camera. We were taken to a shop (*taken* is the word), and none of us bought. In the next shop, I noticed a man with prayer beads, and the next thing I mentioned was that I was a dervish, and then I found the store owner was the Rufai Sheikh there. We almost fell over each other, and the next thing I knew he was dropping prices like crazy. So I spent more than I had expected and can only hope Abdul Rahman will be satisfied. I know I got a bargain, but I can't tell what the Pakistanis will charge for customs duty. . . .

I have been playing around as "Puck of Pukhtunistan." I have been writing at length about this real-imaginary country. Yet the fact is that on this ship, the Pathans have sought me out and taken to me like a duck to water, acting as friends and protectors. It is seemingly fantastic, but might be explained by reincarnation or otherwise.

CHAPTER THIRTY-THREE

Excerpts from Letters-Diaries:

Pakistan, Spring 1961

March 4   *Karachi*

I have now been in Pakistan four days and have had a very rapid start. . . . I went to the US Embassy, where I had three long and successful interviews. In the U.A.R., I had to take certain rebuffs from Americans on intercultural exchange, and though I lost the discussions, regretfully my prediction of the mobbing of the USIA library came true. At the Embassy, there was also a letter from my close friend Robert Clifton; between us, in a sense, we cover the whole Asian continent, and have been uniformly successful with Asians, and unusually unsuccessful with the press. . . .

March 12   *Multan*

Multan is known as the city of flies. When I was here before, the Chief Engineer begged me to do something to help eradicate the fly-nuisance here. I spent some time with Dupont people, who told me they had agents in Pakistan. I asked them if we had to wait until the Russians had a fly-swatter or spray before we would rid this region of flies. In an earlier age, we did wonderful work in Panama, the Philippines and Cuba in eradicating an insect problem— no politics were involved.

I have learned that today some work is being done with spraying and the army engineers are active in the region. I also learned that there is a large fertilizer factory some eight or nine miles from Multan, which I would like to visit. There are several problems here, chief of which is the high salinity combined with a high water-table. There is not even the rainfall of the Alexandria region. The soil is either very, very friable (brittle) or clayey. This city is noted for shrines, and today I found that the hilltops where these shrines are located have been landscaped. The hilltops, of course, are above the water table and there is no saline problem there.

Dr. Farook is the assistant to the Agricultural Attache at the US Embassy in Karachi. I laid out my plans for him, and they were well received. The next day Dr. Farook took me to a Junior College which trains young men to become agricultural inspectors. This is a worthy step. Before, we had high grade specialists trying to communicate with peasant farmers. Now we are training sergeants, so to speak, who will act as intermediaries.

M.A. Cheema was my contact on the former visit to Pakistan. He is now Secretary-General of the Ministry of Food and Agriculture. He is also a close friend and associate of Dr. Farook. My visit with Mr. Cheema was short and to the point. I gave him the packet of tomato seeds with the exception of a few to Farook. He told me that my best contacts would be at Lahore and Lyallpur.

March 16

My dear Harry:

I cannot escape it. It is inevitable. I follow the old E. Phillips Oppenheim dictum: "Fools for Luck." I could not get accommodations when I arrived at Lahore and I was shunted to the Imperial Hotel, which is an old group of buildings made into a new hotel. They may be charging me a lot or a little, but for the moment, it does not matter. For I wander around alleys — they are not dark in this section of the city — and the first thing I see is a building: "Agricultural Department." So I nosed in and sent my card; in about two minutes I meet Mahmood Ali Bokhari.

I tell him about deserts and desert reclamation, and that is what he is interested in. I tell him about salt-water from the ocean, and that is what he is interested in. I even tell him my private ventures, and that is what he is interested in. Why go on? The net result is that I may come to this hotel again and show him my "etchings"—or rather, all the agricultural bulletins I have which you so kindly helped me collect and for which everyone gives me the benefit.

At the moment, Lahore is very beautiful, and I am not far from the Zoological Gardens. The whole city is in flower: dahlias in full bloom and hollyhocks seeking salvation in heaven and cosmos all over the place. This is springtime, *n'est-ce pas?*

Tomorrow and the next day are the biggest feast days of the year. Trust me to get in on them. I used to know a song with a refrain: "If our legs hold out, we'll stay," but with me it is mostly, "If my stomach holds out, I'll stay." I have arranged sundry lectures on everything from Islamic Philosophy to research in Genetics to how to get around in modern Cairo.

So far I have met only one lady. I hope she is still married. She is head of the Fine Arts Department, wealthy and mature, of Jewish birth and now a Muslim. I don't know if this means anything, but I am a confirmed bachelor, to which applies the saying: "A man is old when he stops looking" and I have not stopped. Besides, my friend the fortune teller was here, waiting for me, and he told me I am going to live a long, long time yet, so might as well be resigned to it. Which I am. For if life began at 40 for me, it got bigger at 60 and is still growing.

March 23

My immediate host is Abdul Rahman who has long been an American citizen and lived in San Francisco. Tomorrow is Pakistani Day, and I am on the program. The morning and afternoon will be devoted to parades and sports; the evening to intellectual matters. I shall read from "Saladin" and also perhaps one short Islamic poem. Some of "Saladin" may be translated into Urdu, and it is possible that all of it will before I leave the country, inshallah.

I have signed many papers which grant me the right of residence for one year, but I expect to leave this region in September, inshallah.

March 27

The other day a Mr. Qureyshi came to my rooms. He is descended from an Arab family which became custodian of the Moghul Court Jewels. They are supposed to have disappeared. I have seen them. He has been negotiating with a Los Angeles firm to sell them. I saw by far the largest and purest rubies in my life and some very ancient specimens, too, from this region. The immediate transactions will run up to six figures, and he calculates the heirlooms easily run into seven figures. If God wills, I may even get a small commission if my contact with Conlon Associates in S.F. works out. If that happens, it may change my financial status; my former trip was helped by a similar deal through the sale of Thai zircons.

Qureyshi Sahib also has a lot of uncut stones. This is his own profession, as against the heirlooms. He told me there are many gems in this region and I hope to see some of the mines.

Qureyshi has also kept his genealogy and historical records. This involves both his Arabic background and some Moghul history. I have sent a carbon to Prof. Park at Ann Arbor and may shortly be writing to the South Asian Studies in Berkeley.

Through Qureyshi I met Chisti Sahib. This man is a real Sufi. He was being mobbed recently, because he denied the efficacy of political prayers. I was told he is very poor. I called on him with Qureyshi and one look in his eye was enough—full of love. He speaks only Urdu and Persian, but Qureyshi knows both and English, so we had a very fine session.

Most of the time he explained Moineddin Chisti and Jelaluddin Rumi, both of whom used music in their spiritual training. He went on at some length, and I gave him the flute chant to show him I understood Rumi. Afterward, he said, "Yes, the real flute is in ourselves." From the occult point of view, the Chisti stories were the most interesting. Khwaja Sahib had many powers, and he was able to control the water supply at Ajmir. I told him I had been at the very place, and it is mysterious to find a lake high up in the mountains above a desert. I often wondered about it.

The essence of Sufism comes in the *auliya*—saint or hierarchal development, and a master learns to have control over the elements. This is not nonsense. I am pretty sure that Chisti Sahib has both power and wisdom. He also told part of my future, which corroborated in every detail what my fortune teller friend the Munshi said, but added more. He gave me his blessing, and I hope to see him often. Both he and another man here are really "disguised saints" operating as very poor men.

March 28

Insidious Propaganda. Puck visited the Ismailis in Karachi. He did not know much about the Ismailis:

"There is no God but Allah, Mohammed is His Messenger and Aga Khan is not a Pope. Women are equal to men."

That is all, but. . . . He was given to understand that Aga Khan is not a Pope and he should keep on repeating this—all good Ismailis do. Puck soliloquized out loud: The Americans may not accept Allah, but they might under duress accept Mohammed. As for Aga Khan, they already have accepted him. There is no question about that. Why don't you start a mosque in Hollywood. Dim visions of a grand conversion of movie actors to Islam and dim visions of a grand conversion of $$$ to Puck. It was accepted at once. Besides, in Ismaili mosques, women pray and they are regarded as equals to men. In Al-Azhar, they are not regarded at all. The Azharites believe in the equality of all men, all races, all colors and all money. Period. Women, dogs, donkeys and camels don't count. Why Allah created them is a mystery. But the Ismailis don't accept such mysteries, they just accept. And Puck is thinking of accepting. Sheikh Puck, Imam for Aga Khan, Men, Women and Horses!

March 29   *Abbottabad*

Health has been generally good. Resuming playing ping-pong and hiking. Boys here play cricket, which is more fun to watch than play. There are plenty of fields for hockey, football and basketball, but so far empty when I visited them. I am reading every Perry Mason book I can get hold of, and there are lots of them here.

March 30

I have been the guest of my friend Judge Mohammed Rabbani Khan, whom I visited before and who has been in San Francisco. In our first conference this time we talked about 1.) Agriculture and reforestation in this region. 2.) Establishment of the World Congress of Faiths in California. 3.) A serious program of actual cultural exchange between this region and the U.S. without any more intervention of European and sometimes Hindu obscurantists. 4.) Semitic Archeology: there is evidence that the Lost Tribes of Israel came to this region. I have the green light from Harvard (Professor Cross of the Dead Sea Scrolls research) to ask for a permit for the Department of Semitic Archeology to work here.

I am at the moment writing to both the *Pakistan Times* and the *Civil and Military Gazette* of Lahore. I am now ready to disgorge my scientific and horticultural notes and papers, which will lighten my burdens. I shall just keep the bibliography which Harry Nelson got for me and will work on that later on.

The other night I was the guest of a doctor. He told me that most of his patients suffer from malnutrition. The chief crops here are grains: wheat, rice and oats. But the "lawns" are filled with dandelions and the fields with wild mustards—and the people suffer from lack of vitamins. I think I'll tell them how to use the outside cabbage leaves, if they can't afford more. There are oodles of cabbages on the market, as well as turnips, spinach, oranges, carrots and things that look like cresses. They are not too popular here.

April 4

The next thing is a "Puck experience." I found myself with three men: one trying to teach me Pushtu, the second Urdu and the third Punjabi—at the same time. My friend Prof. Park returned from India and said it was of no value to study Hindi if you went as a technical expert, because the language changed every 50 miles. And Park, unlike Burdick and Lederer (of *The Ugly American*), visited villages.

My friend Rabbani Khan, the Pooh-Bah of the district to the north, took me to the law court. I had already written: "Anybody who finishes a sentence in the same language he began it, will finish a sentence in jail." Actually, an attorney here has to be acquainted with Islamic, Indian, British and Pakistani law; the end result is that each case is tried on its own merits. But the conversations. . .linguistically they would have made (if I may give it a name) a *Desperanto*: you would despair if you had to translate a conversation into any one tongue.

April 4

Dear Jack:

I called on the Maulana today, and we discussed religion. I said that the Muslim kids had little diversion. He felt that cricket was a great game, for it gives every man an equal chance to bat. I agreed. He also said the Prophet was a great one for sports and his favorite sport was that of kings, sultans, conquerors and wise men—to keep you in suspense—horseracing. Of course, this is against "Islam": everything is against the so-called "Islam" which puts women in prison and makes second class citizens of everybody except the privileged. This was a new one on me, that the Prophet liked horseracing. One Aga Khan, who is his chief descendant, goes to the track, and so on. He has the family records—the genealogy of the horses as well as of himself.

Later in the day, Chisti Sahib came in. He made his living by picking out winners on the track, and it was a good living. Then he got converted to being a Chisti Sufi and the money came rolling in. It does not always happen that way. After he got religion, he began buying and selling horses, too, and running his own. Being a Sufi, he had a sort of prevision and, of course, was always in the chips. When India got its freedom, the Hindus who made their livelihood squeezing Muslims were also losing it all at the track. So they said they were sorry for considering Chisti Sahib a pig-of-a-dog or a dog-of-a-pig to whom they had to be kind, that he was a mere outcast, so they outcasted him and grabbed his home, money and everything. So he and his family fled to Pakistan.

This enlightening series of events made me humble indeed, and I must, according to the dictates of real religion, absolve you from having to bet on horses with Arabic names. You are under no compulsion to lay it on the line for Nur-ed-din, Shah Jehan or Sonovabitch (I think the last one is of Russian extraction, anyhow). I have not yet cracked the code by which Chisti Sahib was successful, but if I find out more will advise you.

April 5 *Abbottabad*

Abbottabad is like a misplaced Marin County, California. I have visited Begum Selim Khan here, widow of the first Consul General from Pakistan to San Francisco. Her garden is so much like those around Ross, and she has made it deliberately so: a multitude of irises and daffodils.

Basic Democracy. There is a movement here toward a real Asian type of democracy. The village is being organized on the same basis as that of ancient Aryans, plus some features that look like New England town meetings. Begum Khan has taken the leadership with the women to instill a political consciousness in them.

I visited a place called Khwaja Gan as a guest to one of these meetings. It is also the junction of territories where Pathan is spoken in one direction, Swati in another, Punjabi in a third and Urdu in the fourth. They are learning a common national patriotism and are delighted with it.

Pukhtunistan. There has been a great deal of propaganda on the subject of a separatist movement here, and the Afghans and Indians have been accused of fomenting it. I have met many, many Pathans, and they are all strong for Pakistan. The reforms of Ayub interest and excite them. Besides that, there is a rush toward education that is tremendous. There are many Pathans in college here, and of course, those at Peshawar are filled with them.

Pukhtunistan and Russia. There is always another Laos or Czechoslovakia or Viet Minh in the making. American reports have been turned aside by the press who then criticize the State Department. My reports have been accepted by the Foreign Service here. The Pukhtu leaders have been subsidized by Afghanistan. They have not been very successful and one, the leader, has gone to Soviet Russia. The Russians are encouraging a very reactionary regime in Afghanistan, but you can be pretty sure when it is overthrown, it will be by a "Castro-Junta" to our dismay. The people here have in many instances asked me whether it would not be better to "trust" Russia, whom they can honestly mistrust, than the United States which never seems to be with them in crises. One can almost say that someday, the corrupt government in Afghanistan will be overthrown and we shall have another Viet Minh. I hope you will take this seriously.

April 9   *Rawalpindi*

In re: The EPOOP, or European Professors of Oriental Philosophy.

In the past 24 hours I have met about 100 persons. I am at the moment the guest of Radio Pakistan. Last week I visited a meeting of the Basic Democracy movement. It was presided over by a Sufi. The Epoops in California unanimously deny there are any important Sufis today, or if so, they are not in politics. You cannot dispute with them or you will be in serious trouble.

The manager of Radio Pakistan is a Sufi. My former host in East Pakistan, a retired general, lives in Rawalpindi, he is also a Sufi. He told me there are many Sufis in high places here. The late Ahmed Bokhari spoke to a large crowd in S.F. in 1957, but the Epoops ignored him—they had to. If Pakistan is classified as an Islamic nation, the "authorities" are Epoops or Zionists. If it is classified as a South Asian nation, the Zionists are displaced by Hindus. No wonder Russian grapevine propaganda is successful. Lies are spread, but the absence in the United States of genuine cultural interchange is something we cannot overcome by conferences or lofty editorials. These things never reach the masses; subtle whispering does.

I told my friend Ansar Nasri, Director of Radio Pakistan, that I found at least six cultures here, exclusive of Indian influences: Indus Valley, Hebrew, Greek, Gandharva, Afghan and Moghul, although I do not consider the list complete. Pakistan is large enough and populated enough to be given equal treatment with Italy and superior, let us say, to Sweden or Spain. Urdu is a cultural language with immense literature, hardly touched in the West. Back of Iqbal, there is a whole procession of geniuses.

April 16

It is morning, and I hope to meet a Pir-O-Murshid and other Sufis today. In some books, Sufism has been identified with Bhakti. In the Bhakti I have witnessed, outside of Swami Ramdas, there is an ecstatial relation with what one calls "God" in some form, which is nothing but transcendental infatuation. It brings ecstasy but not breadth of outlook or being. Real love is a universal communication which runs in all directions. In the spider-web, each ring is connected not only with the center but with each other. Thus the love and brotherhood go together.

The other teaching comes from effacement before the teacher. The teacher is real and living. I have read a lot of books about spiritual teachers and the books, as such, are generally true, but the writers often have no capacity for surrender. This is not abolition of self. In the prayers, one puts one's head to the ground and raises it up. In discipleship, there is something of the same thing. In the mystical side of breath there is the same thing, but none of the professors who ever taught at the Academy knew this. Some of the swamis know it, and therefore I am still compelled to place Ramakrishna and even the Vedanta Society way beyond the empty intellectualism of most professors.

Last night, after finishing what I had written to you, two young men came in. The father of one of them works for Radio Pakistan and is also a Sufi. The young men have been troubled at the seeming dichotomy between traditional religious instruction and modern scientific instruction. I had no trouble in answering their dilemmas. Actually, there is not much difference between the scientific outlook and the spiritual outlook, only as the world stands, the metaphysician has gotten in between the scientist and mystic in the West and sent up clouds of effluvia and fog. In Egypt it was not so, and here even less. The egocentric metaphysical outlook is not strong, excepting where the German and Greek cultures came in. These cultures were better than the Jewish culture in being broad, but they lacked devotion entirely, and their "god" is a mental abstraction, not the center of worship. On the other hand, the Jews, while worshipping, have turned this into an egocentricity. Being egocentric, they symbolically "crucify" Jesus who is the opposite spirit, that of surrender and universality. But the teaching of Moses was one of surrender and universality which he tried in vain to impose upon the Israelites.

April 22

International Art as a Conveyor of World Peace: You know, I was mixed up in the Roerich complexities, and wrote a minority report saying that Art would never become a means to world peace and understanding unless the artists themselves were the leaders. Roerich accepted the goodwill of every politician and international gangster, and in the end lost everything. His personal losses may or may not have been important, but he started something which has continued: *personnel* as the nexus of world peace through the Arts, so it becomes individual persons, rather than movements, which become the center of the stage. . . .

Ansar Nasri introduced me to Q.U. Shahab who is not only a top intellectual, but Secretary to President Ayub. Shahab accepted every single one of my projects and then, with General Ayub's approval, added one more. The most personal of these was my poetry, and that was demanded on the spot, in his home. I had to copy one section immediately for translation into Urdu.

April 26

At the moment, world affairs are very much my affairs. I am enclosing a copy of a letter to the Second Secretary of the Embassy at Karachi. When I visited Lahore in 1956, the Consul General confided in me and begged me to go on several errands without mentioning his name or the source of my projects and information. Every one of his proposals was turned down flat. You can understand then, why I took so much umbrage at *The Ugly American*. The guilty classes were blaming the innocent for the "crimes."

The new psychological policies of this administration have been wonderful. All that is necessary is to treat Americans as if voting, responsible citizens. And it is that simple idea I am working for—not sending college graduates into fields, especially where their fellow Americans have preceded them. Some European governments require all returning citizens to tell them of the lands they visited. On the whole, the U.S. has discouraged this.

My play-game about "Pukhtunistan" has brought me nothing but refreshing and delightful experiences and reactions. People like to be considered as if you were one of them and they one of you. It does not need much insight to see that.

240

April 26

It may be hard for one at a distance to understand what is happening in my life, because I, who am in the midst of continual adventures, do not always understand things myself. Part of it is no doubt due to what the Hindus call "karma," which is now "good." But from the Buddhist and Sufi point of view, it is the harvesting of life and some of this harvesting has been favorable.

The Buddhist explanation is better, because while it also teaches that we reap according as we sow, it is not always through the same persons. I started out early to be a sort of foster-uncle. When my first boy, who was the nephew of a young companion, reached the age of 16, his father suddenly appeared in S.F. and took him away. This has been my history, that the boys and girls whom I have looked after were often suddenly "discovered" by their parents. But those to whom I was especially attached sometimes died, and in a few cases jealous relatives poisoned them against me. Now here I am called "Mama," which means "maternal uncle," and my pal, Abdul Rahman is called "Chacha," which means "paternal uncle." You see, you are not the only one who has a "cha-cha." It's funny how the earnest things and the jest things always get mixed up. . . .

My belonging to the Chisti Order of Sufis has been of great social and material assistance to me, although that was not in mind. The strange and immediate acceptance of my poetry plus the O.K. given on all my projects at the highest level has undoubtedly somewhat unnerved me. If you struggle and struggle and get a sudden release, it is not always easy to adjust.

April 27   *Abbottabad*

Young Arif Khan came in after lunch and asked me if I wanted to go mountain climbing. My hiking shoes were in the middle of the room, and before I could answer the shoes were on. We climbed a mountain on the west side, and the country looked like the hills between Fairfax and Woodacre (in Marin County, California). There was a lovely gorge which had fresh spring water. Below that was a lovely presidio where the soldiers live, a park-like section with pines, cypress and eucalyptus.

I have been most fortunate with my dervish connections. The hostel here is run by one, and also the hotel in Rawalpindi. Now I had a wire from my friend Major Sadiq. We swore "eternal friendship" in 1956, but then lost sight of each other. In fact, my old address book was stolen. As soon as I located him, he wired me that he is living in Lahore, which has been the most expensive place for me. At the moment, this cooperation of friends makes it appear I will be well in the black....

It seems fairly certain that the Lost Tribes of Israel came this way, and also the Greek armies. There is plenty of evidence for both, but they have never been properly studied. Most of the students here are Pathan speaking. While my friend Mr. Qureyshi was describing the Swatis to me, and showing me on the map where the "purest" Greeks are, I began showing them sections of Greek dances. All the college boys around applauded and said that these were very much like the dances in their country.

The last time I spoke to Ansar Nasri, a whole hour was taken talking over folk music and folk dancing. The current campaign seems to be to instill people with patriotism. I am running a companion campaign trying to instill people with pride in their cultures, past and present. This is much more attractive, because it implements the raw words "patriotism," "loyalty," and so forth with content. In fact, it reached such a peak that I shall likely have full cooperation in regard to securing folk records and introductions. I already have to go into many of the areas where the traditions are strong and there is a likelihood of picking up dance steps.

The Hebrew and Greek traditions here excite me; the Indian elements leave me cold. The popular Indian dance elements have no depth to them. By depth, I mean, something physiological and physical—what causes the whole body to resound or thrill; then a psychic element is added which I cannot verbalize but which everybody knows—it gives the impetus to dance.

I am not concerned with morals here. There is little hip swaying or buttocks movement. I think this is due to an ancient "snake" tradition. I mean, just try a "rooster-chicken" dance, an elephant dance, a horse dance or a bird courtship dance and the body becomes different. With the snake, the outside of the body seems to move, there is gliding; the Indian dancers not only seem to move their bodies externally, but they move their "space" that way, and it extends into choreography. Compare the Greek dances or even the slower Kolos where the whole body is involved. I think when the whole body is involved, there is something deeper not only physically, physiologically and psychically, but even spiritually.

May 4   *Lahore*

It is now over 100 degrees in Lahore, and I have braved the weather to come here; it is not easy for me to write.

Tomorrow I understand I shall be speaking in a large mosque. Thursday night I was taken to the tomb of Dada Hujwiri, a great Sufi saint whose works I studied first long ago. I was met by a guard of honor and escorted through the place as if I were a very important dignitary. I was first a guest of a Sheikh and then of a Nakshibandi Murshid who has 500,000 followers. Garlands upon garlands were thrown over my head and a special turban given me for the evening. I spoke briefly before the Sheikh, and the Murshid has asked that I come again Sunday night. From the American point of view, this was fantastic and impossible. From the Asian point of view, we—the Americans—live in a land of dreams and fantasies. Someday, inshallah, we shall look at Asia as it really is.

May 7

I am at the moment living in the house of Major Mohammed

Sadiq, a brother Sufi with the same spiritual teacher. We are in the strange position of seeing in each other a person who has advanced much in the last five years.

Major Sadiq has been blessed with a healing gift, which is both spiritual and occult. He prefers to hold to the former, but will apply the latter when necessary. He has the gift of healing by touch and of magnetizing water and food with super-physical vibrations, which seem to have remarkable effects on the health. He has even "cured" people who have been to Lourdes. His "legend" has spread far and wide and every day we have a strange sight here — long lines of people, usually peasants, to meet him, and scholars to meet me.

The general basis of his faculty, which we both hold is a grace and not a possession, coincides with the "theories" of Pir-O-Murshid Inayat Khan and some of the details of the applications are the same. If we begin with the theory of Jesus Christ that the body is the temple of the holy spirit and continue on to include some of the teachings of a Pir who recently died here, we can apply a complete method of "cure" and sanctification which is entirely in line with the original idea of "savior," which has little to do with divinity or theology, but meant, in a sense, a metaphysical or superphysical healer.

May 7   *Lahore*

There is no question that there is a "clair-tactic" power, and it seems to both the Major and me that the higher psychism, as against mediumship, is clearly related to the opening of centers, particularly those which we identify more or less with the pineal and pituitary glands. We are going today to zikr meetings of the Naqshibandi school of Sufis, which sets great store on the opening and development of these and other centers.

By entering into meditation, Major can function clairvoyantly, locating the focus of infection and also, through chromatic clairvoyance, occultly determine the nature of disease. He has, in a few cases, corrected a wrong diagnosis which had prevented physicians from effecting cures. After this correction, the physicians succeeded.

Here he does not take money for healing, though people have spent considerable sums to visit him. In the U.S., this might be on a different basis. But if we do come to the U.S., the funds will probably come from this end.

Also, all my agricultural contacts have been a series of successes. Yesterday I turned over my materials to the institution handling the problem of saline soils and learned there is developing a steady stream of cooperation between the University of California and Pakistani officials.

Lecturing in Pakistan, 1961 (photo from Daily Kohistan, Lahore).

245

CHAPTER THIRTY-FOUR

Newspaper Article:

Misplaced Marin County Found in West Pakistan

—from the San Rafael Independent Journal, *April 13, 1961*

A misplaced Marin County has been found in West Pakistan by a philosophical dervish from Mill Valley.

Samuel L. Lewis, member of a mystical Moslem fraternity and self-styled ambassador to various foreign parts, thus identifies the region of Abbottabad, Hazara, in a letter dated April 5:

"Abbottabad is like a misplaced Marin. I have visited Begum Selim Khan here, widow of the first consul-general from Pakistan to San Francisco. Her garden is much like those around Ross, and she has made it deliberately so."

Being a dervish paid off for Lewis, he reports: "This country is full of dervishes. They are coming to my aid."

"They are leaders in politics, education and community development despite all the misinformation we swallow."

Of pictures showing Lewis with the *wali*, or guardian saint, of the tomb of the mystic Shamsi-Tabriz, Lewis writes: "I was welcomed and am the first foreigner to have given them a talk on their own philosophy and teachings. Penalty: they all embraced me."

Lewis says U.S. Army engineers are doing a good job of sanitation and pest control in a place where "the fly, not starvation, space-conquest or communism, has been the bane." He believes "there is a movement toward a real Asian type of democracy."

CHAPTER THIRTY-FIVE

Book Excerpt:

Shrines and Saints
(from *The Lotus and the Universe*)

ON MY RETURN VISIT TO PAKISTAN, I WAS UNABLE TO FIND ANY of the Naqshibandi Sufis whom I met on my previous visit. Death, illness and change of address took them from my life. But as Allah has willed, many of my movements have been associated with Haji Sarfraz, whose Khankah is on the Mall in Lahore, across the street from the offices of the Asia Foundation.

In the Naqshibandi School, there is more stress on sobriety and in the Chisti meetings, one finds more people going into "spiritual intoxication." This state called *sukr* (corresponding perhaps to the Hebraic *shikkor*) is fine for the young for it helps them to dominate "lower" forces. But when it becomes an end in itself, it may lead away from the Goal, not towards it. At times it would appear to have the same psychological significance as drug-taking, but at other times it can be most elevating.

The Naqshibandi methods certainly keep one away from every sort of drug and artificial stimulant. In Sufism, *hal* indicates a state of consciousness and is often used interchangeably with *sukr* or *wujud,* but it does not imply the intoxication that the latter two terms do. An extreme, but perhaps unfair parallel comes in the story of the Hare (the Chistis) and the Tortoise (the Naqshibandis), but the Bedawis and others seem to be more "hare-ish" still.

When I was living with Major Sadiq in the Cantonment in Lahore, I was approached one Sunday by two delegations. One was of Kadiris, whose Murshid has been most kind to me on many occasions; the other was of Naqshibandis. I do not know how they found out where I was, but it was the continuum of the same group who had hosted me in 1956. The Murshid and Khalif had both departed, and they had moved to a suburb called "Sufiabad."

The great center for all the Sufi orders in Pakistan is the tomb of Ali b. Uthman Al-Jullabi Al-Hujwiri, known as Data Gang Baksh, where thousands gather constantly. It is even more disconcerting that the shrine is almost within walking distance of our Consulate in Lahore, and still less distant from the various universities where Americans teach. Yet I have met no American who visited the place, and many go right on acting as if there are no dervishes and no Sufi orders.

On every occasion when visiting the shrine, the Saint appeared. The first time there were rival ceremonies of the different orders, dominated by two Chisti groups who were singing loudly and simultaneously. Yet such is the nature of a holy place that communion can be much more powerful. There, and at all subsequent visits to other shrines, there manifested something like an oracular power, or evidence of *shahud* (seeing-experiencing).

Muslims all say and repeat throughout their lives: *As-shadu an la illaha el il Allah, As-shadu anna Mohammedar-rassullillah.* (I see-experience that there is no reality but God, I see-experience that Mohammed is the Messenger of God.) Yet do they see, do they experience? It is still mostly an act of faith, not yet of knowledge.

After this sort of initiation, the tomb of another Sufi, Mian Mir, was visited many times. There is a close personal attunement with this saint who taught the children of Shah Jehan. They learned to "love" Allah, but not one another. The great lesson learned from Saint Mian Mir is that *"Allaho Akbar"* (ordinarily translated "God is Great") may be interpreted as "Peace is Power," in such a way to explain the whole of physics and metaphysics alike.

On another occasion I visited Kasur to go to the tomb of Bhulla Shah. The methods of this saint have made such an impression that I hope some day, God willing, to give instruction on those very simple principles which at the same time become most profound. Bhulla

Shah became an adept, because he found all the mysteries of the universe in the Arabic letter Alif—the straight line—and the Divine Unity.

The world is very much divided on the value of visiting holy places. In the West there has been a reluctance to accept the "miracles" of Asia on an equal basis with those of Europe. And even a greater reluctance to accepting reports from Western persons on the unusual in the Orient.

Gates to the tomb of Hazrat Data Ganj Baksh in Lahore (news photo clipping from Samuel Lewis' scrapbook).

249

CHAPTER THIRTY-SIX

Excerpts from Letters-Diaries:

Pakistan, Spring 1961
(Part II)

May 8

I have been given a grand ovation in one mosque and spoken now to many assemblies of Sufis here. I am next invited to Malaya to come as an American Sufi. The whole background and conditions are so against our newspaper traditions and psychologies that they cannot and would not believe this invitation comes through the chief Buddhist!

In Cairo I attended the reception of Ambassador M. Hussain, whom some of you may have met in San Francisco years back. I was introduced as an "American dervish." The whole Indonesian delegation immediately surrounded me, and I did the unpardonable thing—won their friendship right in front of the Czechs and Russians. This was "unpardonable" and entirely against protocol, because I was the only non-diplomat at the affair. The Americans! They were too busy with cocktails and chit-chat with NATO allies to bother with Asians.

I do not know what these affairs are for, nor our tactics of entertaining our citizens abroad and thinking we are accomplishing something. Our farm exchange program is exactly of the opposite nature, and I am beseeched with requests to increase it. Most of the people from here west are Muslims and agriculturalists.

People have, of course, every right to reject Sufism, but in a world of international relations, we should at least know something of its operations and personnel. I have failed, and perhaps it is my own fault, to reach the Near East Department (which relies on European humbugs, too). I have a list of untouched subjects for research ranging from Aramaic archaeology to the music of the dervishes, and from the natural resources of Pakistan to the continuance of the caste system in South Asia.

May 9

My dear Wesley:

I have just heard from Leonora that you are in the hospital as a cancer patient, and I am writing to you because this is strangely in line with some "coincidences" going on here.

All my affairs at the moment seem prospering, especially on the higher levels in ways which may be appreciated but not understood in the United States. There seems little hope for the world, for it has divided—not into "haves" and "have-nots"—but into potters and clays. Certain nations insist they are potters, and at the moment are having "cold wars." They cannot see that humanity is *not* divided into potters and clays.

The first thing we have to do if we are going to have peace is to stop this nonsense. Clemenceau was a very wise man who said that war and peace were too serious to entrust to generals and diplomats. We do not need a "peace movement" so much as a Clemenceau movement to entrust peace to others than diplomats and generals. But the international protocol protective association of generals and diplomats want to be left alone to carry on their cold war and consume the wealth of the earth in so doing. It is not Russia that is to blame, it is not America that is to blame, it is protocol. Both Russians and Americans worship that common god.

For instance, the Russians send out a ballet troupe to "Kohistan" and 2,000 people watch it. The Russians seem to think they have won a diplomatic point. The fact that the 2,000 people were mostly nationals of the NATO nations who happen to be in Kohistan is unheeded. The NATO people spend millions to arm themselves against the Russians and large sums also to be entertained by the Russians and to entertain the Russians.

There can be no peace without friendship. Otherwise, it is just status quo or armistice. Getting rid of arms without getting rid of hatreds is wasteful and useless. We talk about "education," but half the time we mean propaganda. We do not know what is going on in the hearts and minds of exotic peoples.

I am in Pakistan, in the Punjab, which has been the site of innumerable cultures and wars. We do not know much about these cultures or wars, and we know even less about the hearts of peoples. Wesley, there are sciences of the heart as well as of the mind and body. We live in a body which we do not study. Every time the heart beats it sends a flood of fluid through the organization. This flood of fluid feeds the cells and takes away the wastes. If we do not feed the blood rightly, it cannot feed the cells, and if we do not feed the nervous system rightly, it cannot help take away the wastes.

I am living in the home of Major Mohammed Sadiq, who has the gift of healing. We have studied sciences of which the West is not aware. We have both had the same teacher, a marvellous man whose name is Maulana Abdul Ghafoor. From him I have learned to treat the world as a whole single body and to learn to appreciate the hearts and minds of other people; so I do not travel as a stranger.

I was thrown immediately into a cancer problem with the Major. The major works with medical doctors, and there was a case where he and the doctor had "lost face." The patient was a brother of the doctor, who was also the head of a large hospital, so the loss of face was serious. Besides, the Major seldom loses cases. He took me to the patient. I said the man was holding a secret, either a loss or worry or there was somebody or something he hated or feared, or there was an event in his earlier life wherein he felt he had committed a "sin"—a sin and not a wrong. For a "sin" is a mark on one's conscience for having done something against a code and is a mental more than an ethical tort. But whether mental or ethical, it established a focus of infection, and that focus could not be destroyed unless the patient stopped blaming himself. As the semanticists say, "God may forgive your sins, but your subconscious mind will not." The patient denied this entirely and said he had a clear conscience.

His case did not improve. The Major went again, the patient was adamant, but his pain was terrible. Then the Major demanded a show-down and the patient broke down. As soon as he broke down, the Major's methods were effective, and in the last days there has been a great improvement.

This is effected in part through magnetized water, and when I referred your case to him, he said he will send you his own magnetized water.

May 18   *Abbottabad*

My dear Harry:

You may remember that I hinted to you that I had had a past, and it was not a particularly glorious past. Today I see the flowering and harvesting of every project I ever undertook in my whole life and going on at the same time with a fury that is both delightful and complicated.

Take the case of my poetry. When I was a little boy—and at 13 I was still mighty tiny—Archie Cloud gave me his blessing. It was only in the few months before I left S.F. that the poetry teachers of the University of California discovered that I had something. It was a stranger, Admiral Evenson of the American Friends of the Middle East that proclaimed me. The Beatniks feared me for I beat them at their own game, and the nice people do not like serious poetry. Well, I was hardly here when I had met Secretary Shahab, the top civilian of this country, the chief expert on poetry and literature and the bosom friend of General Ayub. One page reading and three men demanded Urdu rights.

When I left working for the Army in 1945, they refused my resignation until I signed the heroes' war book. "I am no hero," I said. "We know more about you, Mr. Lewis, than you know about yourself. No false modesty." I had been turned down more times by the Intelligence and the F.B.I. than one has fingers on their hands, but I realize today that the rooms were bugged, and perhaps I, too.

I have recently written a cousin a letter entitled "Four, Just Men." I have a personal underground which grapevines the whole of Asia. After Pearl Harbor, of which I had been forewarned, I resolved it would never happen again. But it did no good. I may still have my letters concerning Viet Nam and Laos, but I recently received an invitation from one of these men (Robert Clifton) to come as the guest of the Prime Minister of Malaya, which will probably be accepted.

Another of these men invited me first to go to Asia because it "needed me." The fourth is Bryn Beorse, who is one of the grandest men on earth, a cloak-and-dagger hero, friend of Dag Hammerskjold, cousin of at least one Prime Minister of Norway, the clearest thinking man I ever met in economics and long engaged in research to produce fresh water from the ocean at low cost. He has also been in the recesses of the Himalayas, met real yogis in caves and had a long string of experiences. . . .

This is written in a mixture of laughter and tears. Some day some thick-headed editor in the U.S. will recognize that the people of the world are not concerned with "foreign aid," "dialectics," "cold war" or "space conquest." Here there are two problems which dominate everything, and to me it shows that the people are far more sensible than most. Their primary concerns are God and saline-soil problems; anybody coming here not acquainted with these is going to have a hard time. True, the problems of the desert and eroded lands are also immense, but it is impossible to take up all these things at once. I am not an expert on saline soils, but I am an expert in finding out what bothers others and then trying to do something about it.

The imbalance of this report is the imbalance of the facts of life. You may remember how the Japanese were so amateurish in rose growing, although the terrain and weather were suitable for it. And the Thais and Egyptians were very successful, because they made a study. I had long concluded that the lands around Lahore and Rawalpindi were self-sufficient in K (Potassium) and deficient in N (Nitrogen) and P (Phosphorus) just by looking at the flowers.

In touring the Agricultural Experimental Station at Rawalpindi, I ran into the difficulty that Horticultural and Botanical training there are different. The botanists included the "experts," which means they did not dirty their hands; they had fine minds but not green thumbs. The horticulturist had to know how to plant, prune, graft and bud, but without knowing the nomenclature.

Then came one of the great shocks of my life, and I still do not know whether to laugh or cry. Between the ornamental flower and the vegetable-seed section were huge hedges with great bluish flowers, excellent—ARTICHOKES! They did not know they were vegetables and used them in flower arrangements.

Harry, we send out Point Four people and experts from all kinds of branches of the U.N. They are making a survey for the great problem of Pakistan: *malnutrition.* I had to point out wild mustard and dandelions to a doctor at one school; at another school, I found a doctor using parts of even common flowers and weeds for medicinal purposes and to stop malnutrition. As in India, the communications are blocked. This seems to me as terrible as malnutrition itself.

I never saw better artichoke bushes. They are naturals here, and they are one of the plants I have long predicted as naturals. They have a certain amount of Na-CL (sodium-chloride) tolerance and there they were. Wonderful hedges and wind-breaks, full of buds and flowers. I had them pick the artichokes before full bloom for food; when I go again I shall re-check.

At this point, I also feel a sense of deep dissatisfaction with myself. I can almost long to return to study and perhaps I will, but the pressures in other directions are terrific. I am longing to have some good sessions with you as soon as possible upon my return. This "cold war" has made us mad, and we do not look upon the earth and its problems anymore.

May 18

While I was with Major Sadiq in Lahore, there was a feast every night. This was hard because it was very warm in the day time, sometimes getting up to 105 degrees. I could not walk in the heat; besides, everyone treated me like a great person. It was like living in a dream. You see, this is my home and these are my people. In this life, I had to be born in a Western body, so I could bring Oriental teachings to America. I feel at home with both the Punjabis and the Pathans.

I am hoping we can arrange to bring Major Sadiq to America to present his spiritual healing. I also want this on account of my first dancing partner, Mrs. Hazel Reeve of Mill Valley. She has long been paralyzed, and I am much concerned with her. I never had a chance to really fall in love, and by the time I was on my feet financially, she was a victim. I do not know whether God wants me to marry or not. I still feel pretty chipper. In San Francisco, they don't believe I know much about Oriental philosophy, but they admit my age; here they say I know the philosophy, but they won't accept my age. . . .

May 30   *Abbottabad*

The work laid out for me by Pir-O-Murshid Inayat Khan was of world significance; the very magnitude prevented anything I tried from being accepted. Pir-O-Murshid Maulana Abdul Ghafoor added to the above and, in addition, pointed out to me the path of the Khalandar. I guess Americans know this word from the Sheherazade Suite or the Arabian Nights. Khalandars have to go through unusual disciplines and often submit to bizarre or seemingly heterodox methods. Many exercises of yogis and dervishes seem to be nothing but extensions of "control experiments," but in other directions. The Khalandars challenge this.

The other night I met Alfaqir Zulafiqar Ali Shah Mastan. He is a Khalandar and was drawn to me immediately. He explained many things. For example, when I went to speak on Islamic Art at the Punjabi University, I had slides which I had never gone over — it was to be a rehearsal. Instead, all the seats and standing room were occupied. The lights were put out and the words came into my mouth letter perfect from beginning to end. It was like attending my own lecture. He explained that he saw behind me the spirit of Bu Ali Shah Khalandar, and that it must have been his doing.

Pakistan 1961, with guardian of one of the supposed tombs of the legendary Sufi mystic Shems-i-Tabriz.

257

CHAPTER THIRTY-SEVEN

Book Excerpt:

Abbottabad
(from *The Lotus and the Universe*)

MY ORIGINAL "HOME" IN PAKISTAN WAS ABBOTTABAD, IN HAZARA District in the Northwest. It is very much like California there in so many respects. One of my neighbors was Pir Aslam Shah, one of the most childlike persons ever encountered. He used to tell us constantly of his wonderful Pir-O-Murshid. Indeed, he could not talk of much else.

One day he received a cable asking that I remain in that section until the Pir, Haji Baba Abdul Aziz, returned. The Pir lives at Havelian, the train terminus, which is down the gorge from Abbottabad. It was from him that I was to receive the Zemzem water, blessed and from the spring of Abraham at Mecca.

The exchange evoked the divine love that permeates the universe. We live and move and have our being in and with this love, though we may not recognize it and often are unable to maintain it. This is the least that one can say of Pir-O-Murshid Haji Baba Abdul Aziz. He was not to become my spiritual mentor, and I cannot say that my own Pirs were "greater," because in the infinitude this word has no meaning.

Pir Aslam Shah also took me to many holy men and Pirs in that region. One man decried the fact that I did not have a beard (neither did Pir Aslam Shah), and this has made some of the more conservative brethren hold back. But when I asked Allah, the Compassionate, the Merciful, about it, he told me that his munificence also extended to Chinese and Burmese and Amerindians.

Aslam Shah also brought me to strange holy men who were beyond classification. They might regard Mohammed in highest repute and dress and behave otherwise like Hindus. They might be Munis — in at least semi-permanent silence; they were always in "states" of *remembrance.*

Pir Aslam Shah lived across the road from me in Abbottabad. Just beyond him, one could find Pir Ali Mastana, the Khalandar....

CHAPTER THIRTY-EIGHT

Excerpts from Letters-Diaries:

Pakistan, Summer 1961

June 1

U Can, Twin,
Mandalay, Burma

U Can, Twin, there are only two ways of purchasing here. "The Price is Right," which means, for butter, oil and superfluities, you are going to Tiffanys; for fruits and vegetables which you can buy cheap, they all but give you the store. For instance, melons which cost one rupee (21 cents) in America cost less than a quarter of that here and mangos which cost 2 rupees in America cost almost as much in Abottabad. Why they put them on the market I do not know, because the public can't afford them. So they remain unsold and would be given to pigs if pigs were allowed. So they all spoil, because protocol does not permit lowering prices for any purpose.

In America, okra costs about 30 cents a pound and one does not know why. Therefore, because I love it, I wanted one rupee's worth. This is fine, but Puck is Puck, except that sometimes he is "Ah Yaint, a saint." He had with him a big bag for sundries. First they weighed the okra out very carefully down to a single item, but by that time the scales would not hold any more. There was already enough for a week. That was only the beginning. They insisted on giving him the honest weight, then they gave him over-weight, then over-time, then they just gave him. . . .

June 5

Now look at crazy me. The entertainments here have been football, volleyball and Iqbal. I have added to it—softball. I got a softball and a make-shift bat and tried to teach the boys a game we have called "pinkey-on-the-bounce" or "piggy-on-the-bounce." You dare not use the latter term here. Then, out of nowhere a saint appeared—you see, us saints have to stick together. He stood around first base. The batter hit a ball to center field. There was a boy there, but that did not stop the saint—off he ran to center field. The next ball to shortstop— off the saint ran. He backed up everybody but the catcher. He was certainly coordinated to the hitting, and maybe he had inner sight, anyhow.

This intrigued the hard-working (?) college youths who have another strange game called "arsenal." You have nothing like it in the U.S. You sit on a chair and rub the seat of your pants against the wood, and it is a bet whether the pants or the chair wears out first. So it may be called arse-nal. The saint broke up the arsenal league in three-quarters time. It is only the hot weather that prevents progress. And me nearing 65 and throwing balls and having them batted all over the lot and becoming popular with the kids—crazy like the Englishman who goes out in noon-day sun. . . .

This morning, my friend Qureshi goes to Karachi. He introduced me to four things: Moghul jewelry, mines, psychics, Sufis. Someday somebody will recognize that these things are more important than Johnson's hogwash. Well, little Ben Franklin-Sam Lewis, his hand on typewriter, went to it about the Moghul jewels. For nothing, abso' nothing. Nobody believed. But Qureshi has a deal on, the jewels are on the market and there will be red faces.

Qureshi's efforts to get me in touch with the psychics have not been successful, and if there is wisdom in the universe, you can see it from what is written below. He introduced me to a Sufi. This man was a poor decrepit person like all Sufis are supposed to be in the storybooks and legends. Yet what he told me is exactly the same as what others have told me and are telling me.

Roughly, the Sufis I have met are of two different types— intellectuals and seers. Yet the intellectuals can't be Sufis, because the Encyclopedia of Islam and Prof. Von Plotz and others say so. They are, in fact, all over the place, including most Pathans, which also means most generals which also means the tops in the govenment....

We are, of course, going to send more top-level entertainers here and spend millions of dollars mainly to entertain Americans and NATO nationals abroad. The people will go right ahead not knowing about it or caring very little. We can't send tops, jump ropes, hula hoops, coasters, dolls or baby swings — it jest ain't done. Maybe the Russians will.

I feel wonderful, damn it, in the 100 degree weather. This is awful. I must be losing my nationality or something.

June 14   *Abbottabad*

My Blessed Pir-O-Murshid (Maulana Abdul Ghafoor):

There are times when one has unusual experiences and these are tests, no doubt, of one's spiritual and personal ability. Jesus said, "Let us not into temptation," and I do not know whether what I am facing is temptation or not. I have met a Khalandar whom I see almost every day. He claims to have many followers, including the Chief Justice of the Supreme Court. He is planning to go to America. He wishes, or is guided, to bring the message of spiritualism to my country and to other countries.

He has given me many evidences of his powers and what he calls "*kashf* [insight, intuition]" but it is not the same as what I call *kashf*. That does not mean that I am right and he is wrong. Only his *kashf* seems to be concerned with seership and the ability to escape from the body, to function in the "heavens," to meet saints and to have grand faculties.

All this is excellent, but to me it is not *Tauhid* [Divine Unity]. On the last day I was in Japan, I had tea with the Ambassador of Pakistan. He told me the story of Farid. Farid practiced austerities and one day even made a flock of birds die and become reborn to fly away. Later, he came to the house of a lady and demanded food. She was very slow. Finally, he grew impatient and seemed to threaten her. She said to him, "Do not treat me as a flock of birds that you can cause to die and be reborn." This amazed him and he asked her for the details of the story, which she gave him.

Now I am receiving instruction from the Khalandar, who believes he is one of the most powerful men in the world. Maybe he is. He says he has 38,000 followers who will help him to travel. I have no follower. I am going over the globe a second time, I have crossed the United States many times, sometimes without having 50 rupees at any time, yet lived in both fine homes and poor places. I had nobody but Allah and He showed me. This was a different kind of *kashf*.

The Khalandar asked me to ask Mohammed where he belonged in the assemblage of saints. I am only in the rear rank of the assemblage. But I told him I could not ask Mohammed, because I had already asked Allah. He did not seem to realize that if I could ask Allah, this might be greater than asking Mohammed.

I told him he was greater than I in all but one thing—I could be a greater pupil than he. I could learn from him, I could listen to him, but he could not listen and learn from me. Although in breathmastery and insight and teaching he was far above me, I was a greater student. This rather surprised him.

I cannot believe that the higher stages — Haqiqat and Marifat — can be fathomed by the human mind. I have not often been in assemblages under Mohammed. I have been in one assemblage under Mohammed as Abdullah — Servant of God. Mohammed said in his lifetime that he was over everybody as Messenger (Rasullilah) and also slave of everybody (Abdullah). I have seen him many times clearing and cleaning a great Mosque. He does not use any magic nor any power. He uses love and humility — and such love and humility that I cannot compare it with anyone else's. It is as if everybody were a baby and he had to look after everybody with love and sweetness.

He is not exactly assisted by Jesus. Jesus washes the feet and looks after the shoes of the devotees that come to this Mosque and does other very simple things. I have seen this many times. Mohammed says this is his work as Abdullah, not as Rassul-lillah.

I have seen him in two other assemblages. In one were all prophets mentioned in Quran. In the other were also those not mentioned in Quran [e.g., Ram-Sita, Krishna, Buddha]. These are described in my poem "Saladin." In it, I was shown a Miraj (journey through the heavens), not exactly as it appears in the record, but he told me he wished to reconcile Quran with Bible and I had to write it that way. Also, in the highest assemblages, he made me write what I have not believed and I do not think many Muslims believe.

Now I am receiving another poem called "Rassul Gita." It is to be, inshallah, the Islamic answer to "Bhagavat Gita." It is very deep and requires me to be in states and stages of receptivity. I have to listen, not see, and to feel and feel more in the heart. There are many things given to me which I have either not believed or not known.

The poem is divided into two parts:

I. *La Ellaha* (There is No Reality)—which deals with *fana* (efface-ment), the Kingdom of the Cipher and the Conquest of India— meaning every sort of "other" worship.

II. *El Il Allah* (Except for God)—which deals with *baka* (expression of the real), the Kingdom of the One (Tauhid), the Conquest of Pakistan and the Resurrection of Pakistan.

It is based on Nimaz [the Islamic prayers] and then further. Any-body who has studied the sciences, inner and outer, knows that cer-tain *principles* are found there—not certain personalities. The whole poem is based on principles. It is also based on fana-fi-Rassul (efface-ment in the Messenger).

People are unhappy, uncertain and do not have enough food. I have been sent here as a servant of Mohammed, Abdullah, and he wants me to follow him as servant. People call him "Messenger" or "Prophet" and go contrary to his words in Hadith [the Traditions] where he says he does not want a lot of titles like the Christians gave Jesus. If one says that Mohammed has all power, is the greatest of the great and then is concerned with Pakistan acquiring Kashmir, he is a liar. People here are concerned with Kashmir and Mohammed is concerned with Islam. People use the word "Islam" and they know nothing about its meaning—submission; they only know insistence and insistence is the enemy of submission.

"Rassul Gita" is being written in the hopes that it will help spread the Messages of Mohammed through the world. The divines can take care of "rassul-lillah" and they will succeed or not insofar as they follow the will of Allah and not their own.

There is an Australian here. He gave up lucrative work and does nothing but keep the chief Mosque clean. This is acceptance of Abdullah. No talk accepts Abdullah—you do not teach, you do not command anybody and you have to learn love and reverence. This is not easy.

When I left the Khalandar yesterday, convinced of his great power, a flock of little boys followed me. I danced for them and finally bought each one a sweet. . . .

I have met three Chisti Murshids. One does not seem to have any power at all. But all of them had love, plenty of love. You should see the way they cherish their mureeds. They belong to each other. It was the Pir-O-Murshid of Ansar Nasri who gave me the "push" to begin "Rassul Gita" and you who have given me the push to continue it.

The great questions here outside my ego are those of starvation and unhappiness and the need of having the real teachings of Mohammed broadcast. . . .There are those places in this universe above assemblages, even above faculties, which are the well-springs of all blessings. I may just be sipping through one little straw, but if I sip truly then I may be fulfilling the purpose of my life.

Those who proclaim Mohammedar-rassullillah (Mohammed as Messenger), let them prove it by radiating love, peace, justice, tranquility and every sort of healing.

I knew the private secretary of Prime Minister Mosadegh. He is now home in his native village, drawing water and taking it to the people in the hills. This is *ryazat* [spiritual practice], this is Abdullah. This does solve some problems.

Faithfully,
Ahmed Murad Chisti

June 16

This is my badly-neglected diary entry. P.P. not only stands for Puddinhead, Prelate, Potentate, Plenty-potentiary Puck, it also stands for Pied Piper. Well, I asked for it. I have had the crazy, stupid idea that if you ate, slept and danced with people, you would gain friends. Oy! Now I can't walk through the streets without: "Natchna!" "Natchna! [Dance!]" It came to me that "natch" —from which we get the word "nautch," means "dance." And then some. In the last week I have gained the friendship of scores and scores of kids. I have now given the boys at the Catholic School three softballs and intend to play more with them. And for the others, both boys and girls, I dance.

June 21

So I natchna and natchna. Only the paths are stony and it is fortunate where and when I can find a grassy spot or courtyard. I dance with a brick on my head or I dance with castanets or I just dance. But it is the unanimous opinion of the sires that I must take tea with them and of the children that I must dance for them. The Pathans are called "submitters," but if any people on earth do more insisting than the Pathans, I have yet to meet them. If they were not Pathans I might object, but again Puck axed for it and the axe has descended.

And what an argument I had in the bazaar! I mentioned "Pukhtunistan" and people paled white. It is a forbidden word. *Nobody* believes in it. I said, "You are wrong. Pukhtunistan is not part of Pakistan, Pakistan is part of Pukhtunistan. Who is your President? Ayub Khan, and what do you think he is? Who is his chief assistant? Lt. General? Sheikh? Where are they from. Who are the top bananas here? Murshids, professors, engineers, scientists? Pathans—the

266

whole bunch. They run East Pakistan and West Pakistan. Can you name one honest man in office who is not a Pathan?" Boy, what a session! And my friend, Abdul Rahman from S.F. just sits and laughs and laughs. He came from the Pathan district himself!

June 24

My dear Harry,

Outside my work in the fields common to us (horticulture), my largest project is in the philosophy of Integration. My leader in the U.S. is Prof. Oliver Reiser at Pittburgh U. The Integral approach is compulsory in the engineering field: you cannot omit anything and many formulas are based on integrals. But the medical field is exactly the opposite. We have diagnoses and diagnoses, but putting jig-saws back together is not always accomplished. The Gestalt Psychology offers another approach in integration or near-integration. . . .

June 24

Jack, I must advise you when travelling abroad that the most important thing is to become acquainted with the top police. This is one of the first themes for my unwritten book, "Not So Innocent Abroad." I have been threatened with arrest but with three police stations on my side, from tops to bottoms, and having eaten with the common cops, my erstwhile "enemy" has probably had a hard time finding someone who would deliver a warrant. . . .

Interlude for breakfast. Now I am not only in a jam, a jam is in me. That's a joke, son. Dog did not show up. I fed him already. To show you how poor Muslims they are here, dogs are treated well and cats nix. In Egypt, where the "pure religion" is taught, the cats are kings and the dogs scavengers. This has been since 60,000 B.C. and in China, too, but here dogs are not curs, simply mongrels. I have to play with him every day, too. Also push kids on swings and dance.

June 30   *Abbottabad*

Agha Faqir Shah is an engineer who has a home nearby. His hobby is color experimentation in plants. . . .The soil in this region is predominantly alkaline, high Potassium, but there have been few analyses. I may have to bring a soil-testing kit next time I come. My first reaction to failures in Rice is that it is planted in soils of high pH. There is no good fertilization program; the farmers are in revolt against the synthetic Ammo-sulph approach. The Chinese farmers were successful in both Hong Kong and Thailand; now only complete fertilizers are used in the former and only organics in the latter. In the next place, Ammo-sulph is detrimental to soil organisms and there are not many organisms as it is in lands which divert manures.

My friend the Superintendent of Police has three compost heaps— night-soil, buffalo dung and vegetable wastes. I have suggested a partial combination of the last two and another pit for pine-needles. It snows here in the winter and they do not know about mulches. He has already introduced the persimmon, and I have suggested mulches for both this and the roses.

July 1   *Abbottabad*

My dear Mrs. [Leonora] Ponti:

I am very, very relieved. As a student of religions I have been most struck with the problem which Buddha faced of human suffering. I am even now writing another epic in which a love-theme arises, that there are certain forms of expressed love that are devoid of sympathy. On the one hand, we have the love of passions and on the other a divine love, the former seems to me uselessly hot and the latter uselessly cold. Still, to be "sympatico" is not easily expressed.

It may be odd for me to say that the greatest favor you ever conferred on me was the experience of being able to share your pains and burdens. It was only that I was tied down, perhaps with a dream. This dream was and is now so much like the theme of "Lost

Horizons" that I am becoming bolder and bolder in relating my "Lost Horizons" experiences in letters. Sometimes an endless urge drives one on, which one cannot explain.

I was engaged to marry, and a former lover crossed the lady's path. The temptation was too great. The results have been ironical as have the results of all my broken romances; they always end in irony. But even without the lady, and perhaps because there was no lady, I met the very top people in Pakistan that it seemed to be in the cards to meet through her. In turn, she has through her marriage accepted a much lower strata in society.

On my previous visit, the seers insisted I would be married. Now they are insisting even more—men in different places who do not know each other. They all see the same picture; one man went so far as to give her first initial—and I don't know any woman with that first initial. However, they agree that she will be a rich widow. I am not putting any stock in it, and I am not ignoring it, for the man who wrote "I Led Three Lives" was a simple person compared to us — Sam Lewis; P. Puck; Ahmed Murad; Ameer Ican; Ah Yaint, A Saint, etc.

I have lost 30 cents. I have just written Wesley a long air mail letter. We were much closer than many knew, and there were many secrets that we felt even more than knew. I am told on one hand that I shall live a long, long time and on the other I see all my best associates in the West go. If so, it means one of two things — recognition or residence in Asia. Either is possible. . . .

There is one thing you have to learn—all religions to the contrary—and that is that God and the Devil are often on the same side. At least, they have both joined me in a conspiracy several times.

July 3

Across the street has moved Professor Durani. This is impossible. He comes from a celebrated family which has provided hosts of Robin Hoods, caravan traffic cops and "kick out the other rascals" campaigners. He is a top physicist, engineer and Sufi teacher. We are as thick as the thieves from whom he has descended. Durani has invited Puck to a personal tour of Pukhtunistan late in August.

Meanwhile, Puck is not always seeing Durani. "Obdurate" Rahman has gotten in the act, too. Puck twice gave him the Leprechaun sign—never again. Puck is beginning to suspect he is just as much a bas—illegitimate as Puck is. He acts, looks and thinks like a Leprechaun; even his accent is suspect. Anyhow, he sent Puck off to Murree via Nathiagali. Nathiagali is at least 9,000 feet high. As soon as Puck arrived, up walked one Malik Khyber.

"What are you doing here?" he asked. "Why aren't you visiting me at my home?"

"But you are not at home," I replied.

"That is right."

"What are you doing here?"

"This is my 14th honeymoon," said Malik Khyber. "I am almost 80. But what a time I have supporting my relatives and the Pukhtunistan Mortuary Combine. Fortunately, I am wealthy enough. Now, please visit my home and family, but don't tell them where I am. I have left ample funds for them, and I want to enjoy my honeymoon a little." So sooner or later, off to Khyber. . . .

My last dancing partner Leonora had a most dramatic month. She lost her two best men friends through death, and in the middle of it received three proposals of marriage from a business associate and finally accepted. I am relieved, because in the last few years, she has had a hard life. Deafness incapacitated her for most employment, despite her efficiency and made her become a laundress manager. She has had nothing but troubles and worries. But me with my far-away determination could not be mixed in these things any more, and if I do marry—which is always possible—it should be to a woman who has a far-away attitude.

I now have two extremely contrary yearnings—to settle down in one place either to study or work with plants, or to travel to certain parts of Europe: Sweden, U.K. and Spain, and to the West Indies. Maybe I may live long enough, but again I do not care; it is always possible I shall have some sort of recognition. I am getting it here, and it looks as if I shall in India, Malaya and East Pakistan. Now it looks like the cards are all loaded for me—and then some.

July 13   *Abbottabad*

When E.G. Browne visited the tomb of Shah Nimatullah, Persia's most important mystic, he learned that "among the Gnostics there is no difference in sects." So also Professor Durrani is not only a Sufi, he is one of the most complete Yogis I have ever met. I offered one morning that there is a teaching derived from Abdul Kadiri-Gilani that even his followers, the Kadiri Sufis, do not know. "That is absolutely correct," he responded.

This teaching is that Rama, Krishna, Siva, Buddha, Jesus and Mohammed all lead to the same Universal Oneself. The Khalandar came by at that moment and never said a word. He had met the professor before and had acknowledged his superiority, and was a little taken aback to be seeing the professor listen to me.

Then I met another Khalandar—a sober type who gave me his blessing. This was not verbal, but a communication in heart-energizing and magnetization. I may meet this man again, but do not know.

Then last night, the Paymaster (Aslam Shah) took me to a Sadhu Baba who is both a Sadhu and Sufi. He lives a few miles out of the next town from here. He had heard about me and so I went. It was not hard to find him. We sat in attunement and it "took." I was able to renounce the ego and get into both his breath- and heart-vibrations. I had previously gotten into Paul Brunton's breath-vibrations, but not heart; and into the second Khalandar's heart-vibrations, but not breath.

Sadhu Baba is quite an old man and very much respected. One of his disciples gave me a thorough massaging, and I see this is done in some places. I am hoping to go to Azad Kashmir soon and may look into such matters.

July 19

I have protested and will protest against this "Peace Corps." We have our field workers here, all kinds of people from Asia Foundation and Protestant missionaries to farm-exchange boys. We ignore them. The USIS press releases from Lahore report a speech given in San Francisco by one Mohammed Jamil, former president of the West Pakistan Chamber of Commerce.

He said, "The way to help us is not to send over experts to lecture us. I am convinced that the greatest benefit would come from sending over a working farm family, such as I visited in Kansas and Minnesota, and have them set up a model farming operation, the way you do it here, and show us how to make money from it. . . . If we were shown how to organize, I'm sure American farming techniques could easily be adapted in Pakistan."

August 10

Jacob's ladder was no doubt a symbol, but there is an intercession available in tombs and shrines — and even holy men. There are definite "telephone lines," so to speak, between this world and the vast vistas unseen. There is a complete guidance of love, beneficence, wisdom, compassion and even mercy. There are no problems excepting those which are man-made. There is a wisdom in having these man-made problems so that we, as individuals and societies, can grope and grow. 'Therefore fight, O Arjuna" [Bhagavat Gita] must mean something more than poetry, and in a sense, each of us is Arjuna.

August 15

Professor Alfred Cantwell Smith,
Institute of Islamic Studies
McGill University
Montreal, Canada

My dear Professor:

When I was in the U.A.R., I was approached by a group of scientists, who said:

"We are Sufis and we wish the American Government would take more cognizance of us. The Russians are 100% materialist, we are 0% materialist and you Americans stand just between us. The Russians are 100% dialectic, we are 0% dialectic and you stand halfway between. The Russians do not believe in a god, we firmly believe in God and you stand between us. So we are far more anti-communistic than you are or can be, but you will have nothing to do with us. Why?"

The scientists then went on to describe to me their method of counter-espionage and counter-intelligence which is almost impossible for a non-Sufi to understand. I have met other scientists who are Sufis also engaged in counter-intelligence, and I mention this in part because you have placed in your book *Islam in Modern History* a number of "cosmic philosophies" in juxtaposition or opposition to each other.

I opposed Hitlerism in full. I did not believe a man or group could evaluate whole cultures and civilizations by any moral or immoral standard. Neither do I believe nor can I believe in "scapegoatism," and I am afraid that your book has made the "Sufi"—who is not a Sufi at all but a figment of imagination— into the scapegoat. Indeed, I have not found anybody who has refuted Professor Titus Burkhardt's claim that European writers do not understand the Sufis, because they have not faced Sufi disciplines nor learned from Sufi teachers.

August 22   *Abbottabad*

I am assuming I shall be leaving Abbottabad tomorrow. The immediate destination is a place called Bannu, which is the gateway to the tribal area known as Waziristan. The rulers or landlords there, called Maliks, wish to see me, and I understand I am the first Ameri-

273

can who has ever received such an invitation. Other Americans have gone for scientific, travel or political reasons, but not just as a friend. . . .

Sufi Barkat Ali in 1979 (photo: N. Bluestein)

CHAPTER THIRTY-NINE

Book Excerpt:

Sufi Barkat Ali
(from *The Lotus and the Universe*)

IF THE MEETINGS WITH SAGES IN THE NEAR EAST WERE LIKE comic operas, those in Pakistan became like grand dramas. Leaving Abbottabad, my friend Pir Aslam Shah said to me: "Murad, I do not think any foreigner coming to this land has met so many holy men as you have." Yet, in the sense of one of our noted cartoonists, "then the fun began."

My friend, Ansar Nasri of Radio Pakistan, introduced me to his Pir-O-Murshid and by the process of *tawajjeh* [attunement through the breath and eyes] there was an inner awakening which has resulted in much poetic creativity. *Tawajjeh*, in theory, corresponds to the *darshan* practiced in India and is mentioned in *In Quest of the Oversoul* by Paul Brunton. Jesus pointed toward it when he said, "The light of the body is the eye." Few have experienced it to the depth. A similar experience came when I met the Pir-O-Murshid of my friend Huq who operates the Dawn Hotel in Rawalpindi.

But the greatest drama came when life centered around my friend and spiritual brother Major Mohammed Sadiq. In epic fashion, in the year 1961, we were led or pushed from one holy person to another, from one place to another until we met Sufi Barkat Ali, who lives in Salarwalla, Lyallpur District.

All the occult and mystical experiences in books or told through folklore seem to have paled in the separate or common experiences of the Major (mostly) and myself. In many respects a very childlike man, the Major had been told he had healing powers, and during the years multitudes have come to him for help.

The Pir, formerly an aide to Field Marshal Auchlinchek, retired from military and political affairs at the end of World War II to devote himself to the spiritual life. His state seems very high, his stations the most advanced, from the Sufi point of view, yet encountered. He has a vast amount of inner and outer knowledge but devotes himself entirely to recognition of the All-Pervading Omnipresent Deity, and to help humanity to rise from unhappiness, disease and frustration.

He has a simple abode in the jungle, the compound terminating in a Mosque and courtyard used for study, prayer and ceremonies. But sometimes the crowd is so large that meetings are held in an adjacent field. The women meet separately, and one can easily distinguish the Pir's wife with her remarkably brilliant, loving, living eyes—magnetic and electrifying and more. Children are also encouraged in devotions and present indications are that there will be a large Sufi center in that region as time goes on.

Pir Barkat Ali combines the tassawuf of the Chisti, Kadri and Sabri Schools. The Chistis use music mainly, and there have been some excellent qawwals (songs of devotion) presented there. The Kadri teaching takes into consideration the use of repetition of spiritual phrases, mostly from Holy Quran and all in Arabic. The Sabri school has a moral training, not too different from that offered in the Indian *Bhagavat Gita*; that is, so that one can practice a sort of "indifference" under all circumstances, feeling the presence of Allah, whomsoever, howsoever, wheresoever. Thus to Sufis, God is both *being* and *The Being*.

CHAPTER FORTY

Excerpts from Letters-Diaries:

Pakistan, Fall–Winter 1961

September 8

There is one thing definitely wrong with our foreign service. A number of years ago, I heard a lecture in Mill Valley by a Hindu who came out boldly for neutralism; his ground was very simple: "The Russians eat with us and you don't." I do not think many of the audience got the full impact of it. Certainly the foreign service has not.

I again gave a lecture before another college, with excellent results and three newspaper interviews here. If a Billy Graham or newspaperman or a Russian had a quarter of the audiences I get, it would be news and even world news. But a single American is ignored—at home.

The main complaint all over is the lack of mingling. We even mingle with the Russians. Unless the Peace Corps does some mingling—and I think this is very difficult for high I.Q.s—we are going to lose more money on useless projects.

The Pushtu Academy here is being highly commended by its counter-espionage plans—rejected by our CIA, of course. If Afghanistan goes the way of Laos, what a field day I shall have. It is time to listen to Mr. Little who has been there and not to Mr. Big who has not. I am speaking for a lot of Americans—tourists, adventurers, Protestant missionaries and more.

September 16   *Rawalpindi*

I am about to make my final report to Secretary Shahab and also a long report to Secretary Ulema, Joint Minister of Food and Agriculture. The latter emphasizes two things:

A. *Soil salinity.* This is the big problem here and the further I go the more important it seems. We are still sending "experts" here. But I have found nobody who knows about the U.S. Department of Agriculture Research Lab at Riverside, CA, which works in this area. I have presented and will continue to argue for Pakistanis to send both undergraduates and graduates to that region for training and then for primary work in their own country.

B. *Food processing.* I have proposed that at least 12 Pakistanis be given apprentice training by our large corporations or farm organizations in canning, drying, packaging, grading and sizing for market, conditioning and preserving. So far I have had nothing but favorable reactions.

September 18

It is very definite that this pupa is coming out of its skin. Whether he is a moth or butterfly, pest or beneficial insect is to come. The story of "Mr. Isaacs" by Marion Crawford is that of a Sufi, originally of Jewish ancestry, who was protected by the Indian and Buddhist mahatmas and rishis, who fell in love with an English girl, an Episcopalian, but whose lot was to work with the spiritual forces and not marry her. I have always said this would be the story of my life; it is certainly the story of this trip. . . .

The Khalandar invited me to Bannu, Waziristan, and because we got off a lot of letters the Waziris began planning rival potlatch dinners. Pir Aslam Shah insisted I would not get to Bannu. I did not. Instead I had a dream in which I was suddenly sent for by Secretary Shahab, an emergency. But when I got to Ayub, he paid no attention to me. Instead, his murshid (teacher) came to me, gave me his blessing and embraced me, which so startled me I woke up.

When we arrived in 'pindi, the Khalandar told us his own Pir-o-Murshid had appeared and forbidden us to proceed. We then went to the Dargah (tomb) of Golra Shereef, about 10 miles west of Rawal-pindi. When we arrived at the shrine, there was a tremendous cele-bration going on. Then everyone crowded around the Pir and he was having a hard time dismissing them. Then an attendant came and told him a foreigner wanted to see him. He got up abruptly—his back was turned to me—came up immediately and said in Urdu, "Come to lunch." I don't know much Urdu, but you can bet I know the words about eats. Instead of lunch, he took me to a room and gave me the exact blessing I had seen in the dream, in the same way. He added more about my work in America—each holy man adds more. The Pir, Dewal Shereef, it turns out, was one of the teachers of President Ayub. . . .

Now I am getting frightened. The Khalandar has built up a for-tune and in the last two weeks an uncle got it all away from him while he was busy at law-court fighting for a sister. The Khalandar was in tears, but I went and prayed for him. I do this without think-ing. That night, he rushed over to my rooms. It seems that a very wealthy woman who is one of his disciples is unloading her proper-ties and offering him 50% —not commission—but of the principle. There he is, back in the plunks—six figures.

Then I decided not to call on the Khalandar's disciple, Abdus Ravi, but to go to Dawn Hotel to say good-bye to my Sufi brother, Mr. Huq, who operates it. This proved to be right as Ravi was in Lahore and I am to meet him later. Huq, however, was in danger of losing his ho-tel. A hospital wanted it and was greasing the judge-advocate. Nize peepul. So at least I prayed.

The next day there was an auto accident, the judge was hospital-ized and the case transferred. These are wonderful coincidences!

19 September 1961
To the Indian High Commission
3 Bonus Road, Karachi
Sir:
You will find enclosed: 2 Copies form of Application for Visa, 2

Copies Incidental Explanations requested, 10 Rs. Pakistani, USA Passport #1919228, Passport photos of myself.

I think you will find my references quite in order, and I have answered questions with candor. One of my first hosts will probably be Dr. Radhakrishnan, whom I hope to see at an early date; also some of your colleagues in the Ministry of External Affairs.

Faithfully,
Samuel L. Lewis

September 22

My dear Harry:

Takht Bhai is Persian for Mountain Spring. It has ruins of old Buddhist monasteries and cities. Most of the land nearby is owned and operated by Sattar and Jamshyd Khan. Months ago I informed you that I had hoped to visit the best farm run on modern methods, and this is it.

Sugar is their main crop. They plant only on rows and hills and never broadcast. Both rain and irrigation water is used. But we ran into a difficulty—their harvest was much greater than expected per acre and there are not enough mills to handle the cane....I had come from the U.A.R. hoping to find some solutions for some problems. Here there was no problem, except on the economic side. There may still be some trial-and-error in obtaining the maximum of sucrose, but the whole thing at Takht Bhai was combined with the proper handling of labor and utilization of soil....

I also found myself in one of the most beautiful orchard gardens I ever visited. If it had been more Persian it would have been a "paradise," but there were no fountains and few ditches....

The tendency here is to use small modern machines. The operators are happy and proud of their work, but the tradition in this "casteless" society—boy! It is bad enough to have dirty finger nails, but even the kind of dirt is classified!

September 26

Dear Florie,

I come to your statement that "average people are not really concerned with matters that are not tangible." You should come to Pakistan. Hosts of people are only concerned with matters that are not tangible. That is why there is "foreign aid." They don't like to face things. You can go around to any tea-shop or cafe and have a huge audience discussing religion or metaphysics or the coming of the *Mahdi*, but not on the question of soil salinity or desert agriculture. So I live two lives here, as in the US, but they are reversed: here I live the scientific life and preach or write about the spiritual; in the U.S. I live the spiritual life and discuss the scientific.

September 28

I have been urgently urged to write an answer to Koestler's *The Lotus and the Robot* and, by God, I shall....Our strange and stubborn refusal to recognize the existence of Sufis is not only getting us into severe trouble, we might just as well give up the ghost. It is not communist infiltration which is destroying us, it is American non-infiltration. Our strange delusion that we can combine democracy and a superiority complex is going to ruin our country.

October 11

Snafu and then some. The Indian High Commissioner has not sent my visa and I sent a tracer to the Embassy, only to find the man has been transferred. So I am sending another tracer. This means I am off-beat and off-schedule....My return is complicated by this Khalandar-Major Sadiq deal. They both want me to collaborate and travel with them. They both have Rupees. I had hoped they would get together.

October 13   *Lahore*

I visited the tomb of the saint Mian Mir. I got stopped several times by people who knew me in Abbottabad or heard of me here. Everybody wants my blessing— except for the bakshish-wallahs, who want bakshish. At the tomb, I was accosted by some commies who wanted to know why the tomb guardians should permit a foreigner to trespass on holy grounds. But between my bakshish and my prayers and explanations, the tomb guardians have been on my side.

Then I went to another saint's tomb. This one has been written off, because the saint did not reveal himself to the commies. It is unfair for saints to take sides in the cold war or any war— except, of course, when they are "on our side." Saints are supposed to serve Allah, and who gives the orders to Allah? When I went to the saint, known as Data Gang Baksh (or Al-Hujwiri), I got in another grand game of hand-shaking, embracing and blessing. I now have the unamalgamated union of saints, seers, sages, Sufis, sadhus and psychometrists working for me. They say that on my birthday I will have more luck.

October 18

This is my birthday, and under other circumstances I should be the "happiest man in the world." Actually, it is a comedy of errors with comedy beating the errors all over. The Indian officials have held up my visa and I am sitting without a passport.

While I did not meet President Ayub, over the phone he expressed his wish that I assist in introducing the culture of this country into the U.S. I am throwing the ball back to his Excellency, and according to his personal or official decision my future may go up and up....

I have seen enough sages and mystics to know that we have not studied the "rare earth" types or the radioactive types among human beings. We talk about anti-Aristotelianism but are bound by the same time and space psychologically. There may be many kinds of fourth-dimensional consciousness. The possibility and probability of unusual types coming to America may set off some commotion. We shall, of course, try to "normalize" them. We cannot have world understanding as long as we wish to remain ourselves the measuring sticks, the calipers, the micrometers.

October 22

Malik Abdul Hamid Khan has plenty of plenty. He and the Major are my hosts. We have invited the American legation, the American Friends of the Middle East, the Asia Foundation and others to a tea Sunday to discuss real two-way cultural exchange. I do not know how many will come. The Malik will provide the food and everything but the ideas. The Americans may offer ideas. This is not done, you know, but we doo'd it.

Between the Major and the Malik I have had two mass meetings, one of 20,000 disciples in "non-existent" Sufism; the other 10,000 of Shias and Sunnis. You should have been with me today. Nothing but lovelies, a whole college of them and I the speaker and only one other man there. Did I get an ovation. I was in wonderful form, too; with the abating of the heat, my health has reached perfection.... But when the Malik put his stuff to me the other day—my birthday, too—I nearly fell over. He has offered so much in the financial way, but gives two years to work out the program.

Next week I have been informed will be my investiture as a Sufi Murshid. This is going hard on my erstwhile personal enemies in the SF Bay area.

I entered one of the local Sufi centers and found it occupied by commies. Why not? According to the European professors who give us the degrees, these people don't exist or are knaves and fools, so what better place for a hide-out and for plotting against the Peace Corps. Well, Lewises rush in where knaves and fools fear to tread. The commies attacked me; the non-existent Sufis gave me a feast; they attacked me some more, the non-existent Sufis gave me a party. The attacks continued and the Sufis gave me a mass meeting. And so on.

283

And now the possibility of financial support comes up. Well, I'll do the praying and we shall see. But at 65 or not, give me another college of lovelies. . . .

November 1

I am still in Lahore. My passport she is, but where she is two Embassies, one Consulate and one High Commissioner cannot say.

Last night the commies were at least partially successful in sabotaging a third mass meeting, so that the audience was much smaller and the ceremonial was definitely and deliberately interfered with. Then the Sufi teacher went back to Dacca, coincidentally at the same time as the Peace Corps. As the conspiracy, if so it can be called, was against them and not particularly against me, we shall see what we shall see, and I am either mud or made.

My physical health has been fine partly due to better weather, but emotionally and psychically I am hard put. Because of no mail, I also have the enigma of not knowing whether my mother is alive or dead, and if dead whether I am summoned home.

November 9

My dear Harry:

I am back to certain diary entries, but if you think there is anything placid, forget it. Today a man was arrested. It may never get in the papers, it won't go down in history. He is one of the ringleaders of the commies who have been after me, because I have spoiled their show. If any American newspapers or government agencies have accepted a single report of mine, I am still to learn.

November 12

Dear Professor Cutright:

You will pardon me, perhaps, for saying I am a firm believer in

Providence and that I do not believe there will be a third world war, in the usual sense. Rather I feel the danger of fall-out, biological and other equilibria being upset.

Long ago I wrote to my friend Harry Nelson that there were conferences to fight the locust plagues but the locusts had not been invited. Now this country is facing the worst plague of its existence at a time when it cannot afford to do so. The salinity problem is overwhelming in itself. The Afghan border is closed, causing financial losses to that country and so great an absence of fruit here that one pays American prices. This I can afford, but with a country suffering from malnutrition, it seems politics must still go on.

Although this country is "Islamic" and not Indian, there is far more caste here than anywhere else. It is deeply ingrained in the people. When the Indus was in flood, only the army could carry sandbags. So with the locusts all over, they are crying because they don't have enough airplanes! Yet every time an airplane is used to dust, the sugar people are in jeopardy.

The idea of most people here seems to be to get a desk job. Karachi is the victim of the plague, and Karachi is full of unemployed. But does anybody gather the beggars, unemployed, etc. and take them around spraying, dusting or poisoning? This would hurt their pride, and rather than do that, one of the largest cities on the continent is now facing mass starvation.

If you, as an agriculture man, were to come here, you would have to have at least one secretary, a staff, and a telephone which nobody could use without your permission. You would have to fill out forms on what you were doing, how you were doing, why you were doing. The Washington State staff go back and forth spending time and money in station wagons, petrol and so forth. There is very little time to be "down on the farm," and none to mingle with the nationals. The Colorado men are placed in their milieu and, like Shah Jehan in his last days, they look at their Taj and weep. I have not met a single American outside of the diplomatic circles who is not thoroughly efficient, capable, wise, far-seeing and bound up with red-tape and protocol.

November 15

Anything resembling sanity or sense here is quite coincidental. Too many cloaks, too many daggers. Since stepping in the communist cell here, there has been surveillance, and whether causal or not, I have had a tough time getting mail, a tougher time tracing my money and no success whatever as to my passport. I have yet to get one reply properly directed since my run-in with the communists. Either my mail has been intercepted or we are worse fools than I thought. This is my fourth come-uppance and I am tired.

November 15

They had a Tree Planting Week here—parades and parades. In Japan, the Emperor goes out and starts planting. In China, Mao Tse-tung does that. In America, every mayor and Rotary Club would be out planting trees. Here the Rotary Club would have a speaker on tree planting. This is the Garden City of the world— nothing but parks and gardens—and I never saw one person plant one tree during Tree Planting Week. I do not know whether you can realize this psychology or what we are up against. But with it, the locusts have a free hand and the papers are yelling against Nehru. It is just like poison gas being blown the wrong way.

Now the Peace Corps is coming and has no intimation, either of this psychology or what passes for religion or of the social antipathy to labor or the type of accommodations they will get in huts. In East Pakistan there is practically no drainage and sanitary problems are rife, in addition to poverty, lethargy and fatalism. Behind that is long ages of malnutrition—mono-diet on white rice, tempered by spices, not by the greenery found all around. The Indonesians, under similar conditions, studied all the edible weeds and greenery—they even cook Water Hyacinths— but not in East Pakistan.

Add to that the communists waiting for them, disguised as Muslims and I am not very happy.

286

December 1

The Consulate has become more concerned. Even the experimental letters sent out have not brought answers. The saints and seers all say I shall be going to India, a matter made more difficult because I have been receiving invitations from that end. Pakistanis have no trouble in going to India, provided they have not been mixed in politics.

I met one Hashimi, a saint who lives in a town called Sheikapura, which is about 25 miles from here. He has been going around making wonderful predictions about me. He has a strange way of working. He does not tell you about yourself, he tells you about your friends. So I have heard through others. He has confirmed what the other saints and seers say—which is still in the stage of prediction.

I also have a plan for my host, Major Sadiq, to start an herb and medicinal garden. They do not have one here, and as there are so many schools of medicine, it should be not only an experimental station but a valuable commercial venture.

I am also beseeched to function as a Sufi teacher. I had so much trouble in America that I hesitate. But I took four disciples— dogs. The result has been that the crows and birds all join in, anybody but the chipmunks. So far they have not come, but you can never tell. I was at the celebrated Faletti's hotel yesterday, and the cat came and joined, right off. I may not have sex appeal, but between you and me, we have it with the birds. Psychologists, please explain. . . .

The university wants me to speak again tomorrow. The schools want me. The kids want me. I could be set up for life here, but "I wanna go home."

December 4   *Lahore*

I am not sending out Christmas greetings until and unless I can get mail—either regarding proceeding to India or otherwise. . . . My

287

main difficulty is an emotional strain. Indeed, I half write to blow off
steam. . . .

It is the next morning, and I feel fine. But when I look at the pile
of unsettled matters—papers not complete, letters not answered and
the terrific impact of not having heard from India, Ceylon, my travel
agent, the State Department, I cannot proceed. And when I look at
the people here who fill me with delightful social engagements or
just steal my time, I am stumped. I have heard so many say everything will clear up; they say it, and their insistence that everything
will clear up when things don't clear up makes it far worse. Each sees
his own problem.

December 12

A woman has come into my life. She is absolutely against protocol,
and that's how she got there. She mingles with Asians and is against
even my own protocol—she is a member of the Fourth Estate. You
see, in my endless war against protocol, I have my own protocol of
always being agin' the press. And so it is that the best friends I have
here among Americans are ye presse, so help me Allah and
Mammon.

On top of that she is a Paul Brunton-type, that is, a news-*wallah*
who wants Yoga. She spent one and a half years in India getting Yoga.
However, shortly after our first meeting I gave her more Yoga than
she got in India—no European professors of Oriental Philosophy being present. She did not believe it until I brought around two Sufis
who confirmed what I said. . . .

There is a rumor going around that I am mad and I answer: "Of
course I am mad, but my madness is the same yesterday, today and
tomorrow. Other people have Sanity No. 1 on Monday, Sanity No. 2
on Tuesday, Sanity No. 3 on Wednesday and another Sanity next
week. Of course, I cannot accept that kind of Sanity." Inasmuch as
I proved to be informed, my position is not easily overthrown.

December 26

This is the news, and any resemblance is not. I got tired of the Indian situation and so I did the inconceivable — wrote to Nehru telling him who and what I was. Pronto I received a letter from his private secretary saying that the High Commissioner was to give me a visa P.D.Q. and then some. Now I know why he is called the "High Commissioner" and not Minister. Simple — the high commissions.

I was planning to go to Karachi to pick up the visa when the American Embassy wrote me a letter on the cuff: send my passport to them. They trust the H.C. like I do. They would take care of it, but the H.C. wants a high commission of 18 rupees for things which he did not do. He is trying to say now that he wired New Delhi, as if I had to pay for official business. So I shall, but I will go through the Embassy anyhow, because otherwise somebody would blow a fuse.

I have a sore mouth and so did not go out and spend money for a Christmas dinner. The other night, Julie [Medlock] went with me to the Forman Christian College, where an American choir sang carols, and the next day to church, but the Americans who attend church are mostly teachers; the officials are "high" Episcopal.

Anyhow, last night it was a combination of the birthdays of Jesus Christ, Ali (son-in-law of Mohammed) and Jinnah, founder of Pakistan. So there was a big celebration in the Cantonment. The music was all spiritual.

The saint of Sheikapura was here, and he spent some time with Julie, the first time another American has ever bothered, and she a newspaperwoman to boot. They told me she was more interested in spiritualism than religion and more in phenomena (occultism) than spiritualism, so they gave her the "mageek" formula. Me? I make my own formulas now, though they don't heal my mouth. I am not a healer, although the other day I tried the formula on a crying baby and healed his mouth.

Julie also went to to Sheikapura with me and was a guest of honor.

Major Sadiq healed a blind man before our eyes. Even the Major was surprised, because he does not make claims.

I now have 4 dogs, 4 chickens, 40 crows, 100 sparrows, 50 birds of native vintage as my disciples—and one chipmunk. Whenever I go, they sing: "Praise the Lord and pass the _____." I supply the edible, then the crows howl, the other birds sing and the dogs fight each other. The chickens chase the crows away and the crows chase the other birds, but the chickens don't chase the sparrows away, so I have not learned the avian protocol yet. I let the crumbs fall where they may, so they rightly call me "The Big Crumb."

No mail today, so I may know my P's and Q's but not my $'s and £'s. Had my overcoat try-on today—need it whether I go to Karachi or Delhi. Next must check for shots and also see about the trips through American Express. The Indians are to give me a six-month visa, but I want out as soon as possible. This will depend almost entirely on when Major Sadiq gets what job. The saint gave me the same prediction as the Khalandars. The other trouble is that they predict marriage.

I surrender, dear. Interrupted by a letter from the Tourist Bureau. They could not lick me, so they have joined me. Now what am I to do? I said, if it were normal, it would not happen to me.

CHAPTER FORTY-ONE

Excerpts from Letters-Diaries:

India,
Winter–Spring, 1962

January 23, 1962   *New Delhi*

My dear Leonora!

Sh! Sh! The door is closed and the curtains are down. Have to be careful. The Polyankas have arrived. A whole busload, and I am a lone wolf or lamb or tiger or skunk. What to do? They might take me for spy. Me, the innocent, childlike—well, I can't keep any secrets from you so I'll answer your letter.

What a time I had getting here. It was on again, off again. But "Ah Yaint, a Saint" came through and we hid in his cloak of invisibility. What a send-off, what a welcome! In Delhi, we started out by calling on the saints. This caused a commotion: half the attendants put their hands out for baksheesh and the other half for baraka (blessings). You can bet with this skinflint who won out.

I took some of my poetry to Swami Ranganathananda. I am not bragging, just trying to see if I can type his name fast. He is the Vedantist. Then we telephoned my friend S. K. Bannerji, Chief of Protocol. "Is that you, Puck? I have cancelled all engagements for tomorrow morning. See you pronto." Then we got more confident and telephoned Dr. Radhakrishnan and got a prompt: "Don't hang up, the Vice President who is going to be President wants to see you." No wonder the Polyankas are on my trail. . . .

New Year's started off with a bang with everything happening right. But the stories of my meeting Sufis and saints are so fantastic, I wonder if and how they can be written. My trip to Karachi was totally successful at every level. One of the most important events was the meeting with Khawar Khan, whom I shall be calling Saadia. She is a beautiful teacher at the College of Domestic Art and Science. We collaborated on a paper presented at an international gathering of philosophers. It won first prize, she was acclaimed, the paper was sent to Ayub and is being published.

When I return I am also going to dedicate a Garden of Allah for the growing of medicinal and scented herbs. This may be started in the winter of '64-'65 if my program works out right. I plan to return home and start another war, now that all my former wars are won:

A. Against Arthur Koestler and his *The Lotus and the Robot* in which I shall insist that Dr. Radhakrishnan and others are real people.

B. Against Captain Lederer on how to beautify ugly Americans. As I told the foreign service, if you write fiction, everybody will read, but if you bring facts, nobody cares. . . .

(Later.) Gott in Himmel, Leonora, Samuel—among the prophets. Wowie and zowie. They *are* Polyankas! A troupe of Russian Folk Dancers come here to take part in Independence Day Festival this Friday. What to do? Shall I take out my castanets? Shall I hum? I hope they will sing a little before the week is out. They went to bed and I let the Indian staff in on a secret. You see, my nickname (one of the 57 varieties) is "Naj-karoji," which means "Mr. Dancer." So tommorow I may take out my castanets and put on my gall and *karoji* and maybe the Polyankas will unfold. "Aren't we devils!"

(The next day.) Well, the Polyankas did not unfold—to the Indian staff. Instead, they had a vodka-drinking contest and that just about did it. So this damn fool danced for the staff and won their affections: my private war against protocol goes on. . . .

After this next hiatus, I will return to New Delhi to see Bannerji again as well as Dr. Radhakrishnan. My job with him is to bring the Integralists of the East and West together.

February 15 *Bombay*

[Norman McGhee was one of Samuel Lewis' godchildren.—ed.]

My dear Norman:

Between warm weather and successes, there is little time for rest. I leave early in the morning for Cochin and then for Anandashram for what may be a relaxing period. I hope to go further into my Indian sadhana and tapas as has already been achieved in Sufism.

Regardless of S.F., I am now regarded as an important person in both Sufism and soil-and-food problems. The agricultural work started here with Satya Agrawal has progressed by leaps and bounds. I do not get turned down either in seeking appointments or in getting ideas over. This year, so far, nobody—Pakistani, American or Indian—has turned down a single item. . . .

February 20

Your letter of the 8th found me in a Yoga Ashram. It is not what the average American calls "Yoga," which consists mostly of "making it like a fish, making it like a crocodile, making it like a stork, making it like a tree, but like a human—no making it." I leave the postures to others. There are three basic types of Yoga: work, love and calming the mind.

Anandashram gives me a place to be quiet. For two years now I have been moving incessantly and generally successfully. . . .

When I was in India before, I met one Ali Mirza during one of my "madventures" that had to do with a conflict with the communists. At the time, Ali Mirza showed up miraculously; also his brother and I are spiritual brothers in being dervishes. I called on Mirza Sahib again. He has four children, three of whom are destined to come to the US for further education. I began to plot how they might collect a few American ducats when they came, and between art goods and saris, the chances are bright. . . .

I had to go to Poona and there worked out my thesis: "How California Can Help the Orient." This will go to the University of California, but the paper will emphasize food and soil problems. In 1955 when Mr. Dulles asked for peaceful means to bring nations together, I chose horticulture. It is not "exciting." However, after a long struggle, even magazine editors accept my reports. Some commentators may wonder why, just before Independence Day when they were not granting interviews, I got in with the Chief of Protocol and Vice President and both promised further and more extended talks. There are no "experts" on Asia, but I am getting a fine all-around picture, which entitles me to write books and give lectures.... I have had to take some ironies and tragedies in my "love life." Now the augurs and soothsayers are unanimous that despite my superannuated torso, I may still go to the altar. Only this time the romance is promised for America, not the Orient. The only thing is that now I have three careers in front of me and have made progress on all.

There is another side of Yoga, and this can be associated with the word "Shangri-La." What ever has happened to me — and plenty has — this *corpus* does not seem anywhere near *delicti*. I am, if anything, more sprightly and have danced before thousands of children. I bet I have embraced and been embraced by more people than any other *genus homo*! This besides hand-shaking — Harding was an amateur.

I am hoping to return in May, but am not sure — terrible conflict within myself between Northern and Southern California.

I carry my castanets with me and subscribed to *Let's Dance* for the American-Pakistani League. As usual, every folk dance festival I have expected to attend here has been called off by rain. And it is now raining around my next destination: Bangalore.

(From "Genuine Mystical Experience Versus Pseudo-Mystical Experience":)

In 1962, at my revisit to Anandashram, home of Swami Ram Das in South India, I woke up three mornings to find myself not Sam Lewis but Ram Das.

"It is time to go," I said.

"Yes, it is time to go," he replied.

But who comes and who goes? Anandashram was a veritable Shangri-La. Because our metaphysical friends always want to place Shangri-La elsewhere, we often don't realize that the Kingdom of God not only can be on earth, but *is* on earth. It is our eyes and senses that are blind—*there is no unsolvable problem.*

March 21   *Agra*

Dear Leonora,

Typewriter in the hospital and ink supply low. I am now a saint. Of course, you have known it all along, but now it is official. It is HOLI week, which is the Indian Holy Week and Carnival and Halloween all together. The roads are blocked and everybody is baptising everybody else with colored holi-water. So I won't leave until tomorrow and will have to miss Brindaban this time around.

"Ah Yaint, A Saint" went to Fathepur Sikri. Rushed to the tomb of Saint Selim Chisti and did the usual bowing and everything including baksheesh *[Hindi term denoting a cross between a "tip" and an "alm"—ed.]*. Then I had the guide take me to the local saint. No Americans call on local saints, but Ah Yaint, A Saint did. We greeted and embraced and I gained in holiness—boy! When we returned to the shrine, my friends the Sufi qawwalis came and sang, and I danced and danced—real dervish stuff. A crowd gathered, and when I got tired, I sang and the qawwalis answered. Then the leader got up and asked the crowd for baksheesh to watch the American saint!

I later made a courtesy visit to the Hotel Imperial where I had stayed before. I was recognized: "Oh, the Saint!" So now you are not the only one who knows. Please interpret! If the Russians ever have a saint, all our papers will report it, but any American who does this and goes native is a "squaw man."

After that, I met nothing but crazy Englishmen and Englishwomen. They go for adventure—yogis, native places, wild places.

They outnumber the "tourists" 10-1, but nobody pays any attention to them, especially in these days of "social democracy." They are mad like me, and I love them. They are all over the place seeing the Taj by dawn, Taj by day, Taj by dusk and Taj by moonlight. Also TAJ.

Meanwhile, *our* top authority on Islam, who of course is neither a Muslim nor an Asian and of course not an American is very sorry he has hurt my feelings by insisting there are no Sufis. And there is going to be a big Sufi gathering in Delhi with this Yam-Dankee the guest of honor.

CHAPTER FORTY-TWO

Book Excerpt:

Pir Dewal Shereef
(from *The Lotus and the Universe*)

AT THE BEGINNING OF 1962, ONE FELT ENTIRELY SATISFIED, AND yet in a strange position with a spiritual teacher of each of the great faiths of Asia. Sufi Barkat Ali seemed to dominate everything in my "occult" life. The practice of *tassawuri*, which is to keep in tune with the Murshid—in thought, breath and vision— manifested in some delightful episodes.

The departure from Pakistan, the welcome to India and the departure from India were all marked by incidents which do not fall within our accepted modes of "realism" or diplomacy.

At the tomb of Amir Khusrau within the compound of Nizam-ud-din Auliya in Delhi, I saw myself invested with a robe. I described it to the sons of Hasan Nizami at the time. Upon my return to Pakistan, I found Sufi Barkat Ali and my Sufi brethren ready with that very robe at a public gathering and henceforth I became known as "Sufi Ahmed Murad Chisti."

But self-satisfaction has nothing to do with the spiritual life. *Riza* means satisfaction with the Deity Who is Compassionate, Compassionator and Compassionated.

When I had been with Major Sadiq in Dacca in 1956, we had been invited to dinner by his chief, Brigadier Ghulam Mohammed Khan. The general was very careful not to throw rank at us in spiritual matters, but told us anyway that sooner or later we would both come to recognize his spiritual teacher. Having then entered into bonds with Maulana Abdul Ghaffoor and later with Pir Barkat Ali, we believed we had come to the place where we could and would progress without any further "aid." But it was not to be.

Pir Abdul Majid Khizri, commonly known as Pir Dewal Shereef, had his *khankah* or headquarters at Islamabad, just north of Rawalpindi. The Brigadier, now retired, had his home nearby. The Pir appeared to be cold both to the Major and myself, but this proved to be a facade.

Pir Dewal Shereef claimed to have received his spiritual illumination through Khizr, that semi-legendary figure who, together with Elijah, remains as one of the two "guardian spirits" of this world and the next. Those to whom Khizr appears are supposed to be specially blessed.

From the moment I had reached Pakistan in 1961, wherever I settled a young emissary of the Pir appeared. It did not matter where. First it was in Abbottabad, my original "home" in Pakistan. A few devotees in *tassawuf* would gather at the home of Chief of Police Ghani, and he came and "tapped" me for his Pir. This happened over and over again at Lahore, Rawalpindi and other places. And when I doubled in my tracks, so did the Pir, over and over.

So Major Sadiq and I determined independently to place our cards on the table. It was a case with each of us of absolute, unconditional surrender. The strong, the self-willed, the adamant became like babes — and later I was to see other persons go through even more dramatic performances. There was *bayat* (pledge of initiation) on sight, regardless of earlier commitments.

Later I spent some days with the Pir at Murree, his Himalayan retreat. As with Paul Brunton, it was not necessary to use words or the ordinary means of communication. As the heart becomes more alive, this method becomes easy and effective. . Our bodies may occupy different portions of "material" space; but in the heart-world, there is a totally different sort of arrangement. Attunement is of prime importance.

Pir Dewal Shereef is now superintending the construction of Islamabad University on the site of the new capital of Pakistan. He has been successful in obtaining funds for this new institution, even beyond his own original scheme. The university plans to coordinate the ancient and the modern, to preserve religious and spiritual traditions, to incorporate all aspects of modern knowledge and methodologies, but in particular those arts and crafts which require some use of the hands.

Pir Sahib realizes the weaknesses of Pakistanis: their unconscious Indian heritages of caste and class, their low regard for certain types of labor and their complete ignorance of the personal habits of Mohammed and his immediate successors.

Pir Sahib may even, in a certain sense, be regarded as the spiritual teacher of President Ayub Khan. The President cooperated in several of his ventures and is open to guidance in ways we of the Western world either do not understand or do not accept.

The Grand Sheikh of the Khalandars visited him while I was at Murree. It was a strange sight. The old man, then 115 years of age, acted more like a youth in love. Excepting for his wrinkled skin, he showed no sign of age. It was even more remarkable to find the spiritual leader of one school paying such obeisance to the Pir of another Order.

Even more amazing, to me, was the absolute surrender of Sheikh Mahdudi, who had been regarded as the leader of those Muslims who wish to be conservative in their religion but "march with the times." The two men had held profoundly different opinions and each seemed rather adamant. Each had a large following and there seemed some uneasiness in Pakistan as to the exact nature of "Islam."

They debated for two hours. At the end of that time Sheikh Mahdudi came from the classroom and sat down on a bench with me (we had not met before). He said: "My whole life is ruined. I have been wrong in everything. All my writings are wrong. All my teachings and contentions are wrong. I have been mistaken in everything. I am ruined." He burst into tears — this from a once proud and self-reliant man.

"Nothing is wrong, nobody has been ruined," I replied. "Allah is the Most Merciful and Compassionate, the All-Wise and All-Loving. You have been calling yourself a 'Muslim,' but you did not know how to surrender in anything. You demanded, you did not concede, you did not surrender. You have until this moment not had the slightest idea what peace is or means. Now you have surrendered for the first time and yourself become a 'submissive one,' you have become a *Muslim. Alhamdulillah!* (Praise to God!)"

CHAPTER FORTY-THREE

Excerpts from Letters-Diaries:

Pakistan, Spring–Summer 1962

April 11, 1962 *Lahore*

Perfidious Puck rides again, but soon he may be walking. In the next few days or even hours we shall be concentrating on a final effort which will either end in a hoopla or an humble return, though it does not matter. Indeed, the chief difference will be whether we are to make money or make history and the *ides, nones* and *kalends* seem inclinded to the former without negating the latter. . . .

The Pakistani-American League in Karachi now has a folk-dance class on Fridays, and I hope to visit them before I leave. Boy, are there things to do. And you can't do them. Go out? "Where are you going?" "Why?" And between Puck, Sam Lewis and Ah Yaint—a Saint, everybody stops one for any or no reason. It will be good to get home and be anonymous—or will it and do I want it? "'You don't know Nellie as I do,' said the naughty little bird on Nellie's hat."

May 1 *Rawalpindi*

Happy International Day. In a few hours we will know about meeting Ayub.

Nothing but an endless series of fictional events. On the bad side, I've been robbed and also lost money. The robber is known, but if I prosecute, I lose face. It is actually a rollicking horrible mess of folklore, some of which passes as religion.

The most serious part of my life is S.A.M., Sufi Ahmed Murad. I am meeting all kinds of strange and mysterious personages. It is simply unbelievable that a series of events kept me away from "Yogi Nehru" and seems to be drawing me to Ayub. At the moment, it looks as if I were near my heart's desire and greatest hopes. If successful, I may be too busy to write again. All my life's efforts synthesized and integated and put out in practical form.

My host, Major Sadiq took me to his property and we planned a home and garden. But I am hoping he gets both an appointment and permission to come to the US and soon. Moi aussi (Me too). I was never more tired and yet more alert—and both at the same time.

May 14   *Lahore*

My dear Norman:

My horticultural and soil reports have been accepted by top officials, but they have not given me a letter which I am asking for. Neither did I contact the President or Secretary Shahab. I got the run-around and then a "No," but I was told the "no" did not mean "no," because Shaokat (Ayub's son) said "yes." This is what happened—quit reading fiction, please.

I then met again with Pir Dewal Shereef. I am to be his representative and of Islamabad University in America. He wants me to introduce Sufism with spiritual philosophy and healing. He has been most successful in collecting funds for Islamabad University; I have already written Berkeley for reciprocal relations. He is also the Pir of none other than Ayub Khan and visited him twice last week. He refuses the refusal I received, sent me back to Lahore and told me to arrange another visit both to him and the President. He will take care of things, inshallah. What we are concerned with is the official recognition of either Major Sadiq or myself or both.

Meanwhile, the Major has extended leave and we are moving. I hope to see him tomorrow and will inquire about my mail. But without word about his business venture in Texas or confirmation at Rawalpindi, we are both stuck. The appointment of me grapevined around and now the whole host of Sufis is pulling for me. Besides, I have seen both Dewal Shereef and the Major perform some miracles—the Pir causing the dumb to speak and the Major the blind to see. The question is: when shall we get the money and recognition promised us?

To make things more opaque, the Khalandar crossed my path twice recently. Unfortunately, he is now immersed in politics and I could get nothing out of him. . . .God moves Himself in mysterious ways, His wonders and His unwonders to perform. After using all the official channels to trace my missing mail, I went to the USIA office and they had it. It was a mystery as to how they got it and why, but they did.

I am living near Shalimar Gardens where we had to move and have few comforts or privacy. All these pressures counterbalance with the best inspirations of my life—and in the heat. "I wanna go home" and can't.

Well, Major Sadiq heals cancer and blindness—you would think the authorities would subsidize him to come to America and tell about certain aspects of this land. . . .I am successful, too much so, in talking to college students. I don't want the success. I want out and I want to help you out.

May 29

My dear Norman:

Guaranteed to keep you in suspense—and in 110 degree weather. I saw Barkat Ali again and told him one does not mind good news, one does not mind bad news, one does not mind in the least having bad things foretold and having bad things happen, but the constant series of good "fortunes" accompanied either by an impasse or by bad events was over-trying.

On the brighter side, I spent yesterday with Khawar Khan, who is slated to be my chief disciple, and with her beautiful and brilliant chum. She now has ownership of the property that was Gandhi's here, and we are planning a big celebration to open it for my spiritual work. While this is a minor facet of my work, it will establish the seed for my future ventures here—the spiritual half—when I return. The scientific half is already established. And the poetry gets its final review next week.

Now I am going to ask you a favor. My last dancing partner, Leonora, and I were and still are good friends. I would like the Major to come and help clear the slight deafness she suffers from. She lost all her men friends in a short period by death, excepting me who was far away, and on account of my Asian propinquities, there was no romance. She then married a mulatto and has since been involved in some social melees. Now being far away and otherwise involved, I may seem to be apathetic. So I wish you would go sometime to her laundry on Webster St. If you introduce yourself, this will do me a world of good. It is all right to write endearing letters, but a few hard facts would serve better. Actually, I may even join Martin Luther King's movement when I return. I see no reason why not and you can tell them this, too. Only my "work" ostensibly is in Asia.

June 28

My dear Norman:

Life is anything but what we like to think it is. One part of me feels like a heal—and the other part is a heel or will be. I did not see the President and all efforts to have Major Sadiq given an appointment have failed (?)—because nothing is final here. The National Assembly is meeting, and many delegates have criticized the government strongly on just the points for which I wished a conference. There is a terrible glamour here on behalf of something called "Islam," which has no relation whatever to Mohammed and Quran and covers every type of human selfishness.

The story of Major Sadiq is so complicated, so full of pathos, success and frustration, that I cannot say anything. He has been stationed at Kohat unwillingly and is mostly not there. There has been

304

an invasion of Pathans who come for his spiritual healing on such a grand scale that the General of his sector wants to remove him. And Pir Dewal Sheref also wants him to come to America for his healing. The Major also wants to come to put through a very large commercial deal. However, he was in an auto accident (only the car was hurt) and so missed me at both Lahore and Rawalpindi. His wife has been elsewhere, the house is locked up with my possessions and communication bizarre to say the least, that is, snafu.

I am booking to return from Karachi tentatively on August 2.

Well, Norman, you can see from this my life is mysterious and not yet clear. Every time I think I may hit the jackpot, I get a snag, and every time I think I have overshot, something unexpected turns up. No doubt, at the moment it looks like a personal success, but that is not what I wanted or aimed at. But the growing optimism of all the saints, seers, soothsayers, Sufis, psychics and such makes me hesitate to make any conclusion. The great point here is the almost unanimous agreement between and among them, people who have no visible means of common contact. This does not help you, and at times I feel like a bloated ass....

July 4

My dear Norman:

Salute to Flag. Attention. Hup. From that point you can be sure(?) of anything(?). My Abbottabad-San Francisco colleague, Felix Knauth should be back in September and we may lecture on "Frustration-istan." If I say it is bad, it will reverse, and if I say it is good, it will reverse, and "The Comedy of Terrors" is not over, with me being the stooge.

Major Sadiq: I am leaving for Rawalpindi trying to locate him. His constant changes of movements are due to a combination of army and legal matters. You are not a good Muslim if you don't have at least two lawsuits on. This family has just three and the retainer is kept busy all the time.

Roving Envoy: My ideas have been turned down cold(?). I have heard of no less than three persons planning to come to the S.F. area alone, and I shall meet more, no doubt, scheduled to come to America. All former ideas are still just that, and the only thing you can count on are uncertainties, possibilities, plausibilities and frustration.

My Own Future: I am very optimistic between Islamabad University and Sufism. I am going to write two books, at least. One against Koestler and the other on "How California Can Help Asia." If anybody gives me a grant for that, you as my godson get the grant. I'll need you, so pray.

July 23

My dear Leonora:

Dear Sir or Madam, We have an assortment of Pukhtunistan cloaks (we've taken care of the daggers) that need cleaning. They are all Afghan bordered and have Kashmiri trimmings. We keep them in India Rubber to keep the Indians from rubbering. Please give them careful attention.

My ticket ends in San Diego. I can fly there cheap buying it here. I don't know who is meeting me or where I shall go, but my "son" Norman says he will take care of that. I am glad he called on you; he is as anxious to help you as I am to help him. . . .

Two and a half years—the zest of my life! I'll be glad to get back after 80–105 degree weather and sometimes hotter interminably. . . .

(To Norman:) The financial prospects with Major Sadiq, Malik Hamid and the Khalandar seem to have left us holding the bag. . . . I doubt now whether I can get back before August 4. This has become a universal "Do It Yourself." I have the complete good will of the staffs of both the American and Pakistani foreign offices in Peshawar. The monsoons have come and the heat has abated. But I still have to face oodles of red tape.

There is one thing omitted here, and it is stronger and more

important than anything and everything else: UNIVERSAL LOVE
AND BROTHERHOOD. God bless you.

— SAM, Sufi Ahmed Murad, Samuel L. Lewis

April 1968: In front of home in San Francisco with Moineddin Jablonski.

Ruth St. Denis. Inscriptions reads: "To Samuel L. Lewis with the blessings of Kwan Yin July 7, 66" (photo: Marcus Blechman).

VI. HOMECOMING

At Lama Foundation, 1970 (photo: Saul Barodofsky).

CHAPTER FORTY-FOUR

Editor's Note:

Return to Family

Joseph Campbell in The Hero With a Thousand Faces *proposes that all mythological hero stories have their basic elements in common: a call to adventure, finding helpers, crossing the threshold of adventure, tests and trials, some form of sacred marriage, apotheosis or elixir theft, then a return across the threshold with the elixir or fruits of the labor.*

In Samuel Lewis's life, his journeys to the East saw him pass the tests and integrate all of his past history and trials to win a new realization. His work life had been fulfilled. He had yet to find a family with which to share the elixir of his hard-won realization. This occurred in the last 5 years of his life when he was found by the young people whose hearts were open enough to accept him, many of whom had also been rejected by their families, and who were willing to receive the baraka *or Sufi blessing-magnetism that Murshid Samuel Lewis offered. This expression of a grateful family is witnessed in the collection of his writings and remembrances about him entitled* In the Garden.

That this baraka *was received is evidenced by the fact that the work he began in bringing peace through the arts, especially music and dance, has prospered tremendously. The Dances of Universal Peace, which began to come through Samuel Lewis at this time (circa 1966), have grown and expanded around the world to many gatherings which may never have heard the name of Sufi Ahmed Murad Chisti. In addition, in a much more subtle way, the people that Murshid S.A.M. touched (or were touched by those he touched) have carried some of this elixir of divine love into whatever their occupation or situation might be. As Samuel Lewis wrote in an unpublished book called "The Bestowal of Blessing."*

"The great work of the initiates henceforth will be to spread baraka. By so doing, they will purify the general atmosphere, and by that the Message which belongs to the sphere itself will gradually touch the hearts and minds of all who pass through it, who breathe the air or go to the places where the seeds of baraka have been sown. This is the selfless propagation of the Message."

On December 28, 1970, in the early morning, Murshid Samuel Lewis fell down the front stairs of the Mentorgarten and suffered a concussion. He was taken to the hospital and died 18 days later. During the interim, he came into consciousness at various times and dictated the "last letter" included here. The closing piece, entitled "Peace" is both a coda to The Lotus and the Universe *and his accomplishment as a Sufi.*

With family, 1970, leading Dances of Universal Peace.

CHAPTER FORTY-FIVE

Excerpts from Letters-Diaries:

1963–68

September 26, 1962   *Hollywood*

My dear Norman:

Few people here understand that I am dealing with big problems. The problems are too big for them to comprehend, and besides this they deny to me, as an individual, capacity therefor. This becomes silly, because everywhere I have become the companion of the top scientists dealing with food problems, and I am not concerned with public reactions.

When I saw 600,000 homeless in Karachi, I went almost mad (or maybe it was becoming sane)—what to do! The events leading to mass hysteria and migrations still go on and will go on, undisturbed by any and all political philosophies of whomsoever. An editorial never saved anybody's life, and editorials have led to wars and massacres.

Metaphysical people in general can not envision mass suffering and mostly they don't care anyhow. The stuff going out as "Zen" by a lot of comfortable — call them bourgeois if you want—has nothing to do with the Buddha's great concern with mass poverty, illness and want. He even deserted his wife and family and came up at least with an answer. More important than the answer was his concern. Few are actually concerned with mass suffering. Engels was and Marxists are not, etc.

The spiritual measure of a man is his horizon—how far do his sympathies extend. Nothing else. Spiritual awakening and suffering are the two things that enlarge us.

The other side is that I am doubly tied up with Nkrumah. Nobody here really knows about the Sufis. It is ridiculous. I have the same spiritual teacher as Ayub, and I have just written to the new Vice President of India who is also a disciple in Sufism. We represent God-in-action. Most people either deny the existence of God (and why not, I see nothing wrong here?) or else they make of Him everything else — a policeman, grandfather, boogabboo, Justice of the Supreme Court, scales operator, etc. There is no serious consideration of God in and with His actual attributes. These attributes manifest in human operations.

(From an undated 1963 letter:)

On March 7, this person will make his public career known as a Sufi, but he is not going around establishing meditation or any centers, and he is certainly not competing with those that do — they are too busy competing with each other.

Now you have the fire and the power and the bliss, and this will be believed when it manifests in somebody else. My first mureed in Pakistan was an old, old man. Abu Latif was one of the ugliest and most unkempt persons I have ever met, but my belief is that he was an "angel in disguise" sent to test me:

"Why aren't you a Murshid?" he asked.

"I am no Murshid."

"Why aren't you a Murshid?"

"I am no Murshid."

"Why aren't you a Murshid?"

"All right, I am a Murshid and you are my first mureed."

I sent him to a holy place, and the next day he came back dancing: "I have a Murshid. I have a real Murshid." It was nothing I said, it was the realization that came to him. And so it went until an important public person received the bayat (initiation) and had the realization. That is fine in the Orient. Here one puts on a cloak and acts in a different character and does not waste any more time trying to convince or even tell.

I waited a long time before daring to try to be a spiritual teacher, public or otherwise, feeling that any failure on the part of anybody coming to me was my failure. So I have few disciples and *no failures.* But I do have people calling me their spiritual teacher to whom I have given no esoteric instructions.

Externals count for nothing in the eyes of God, but all internals count for something in the heart of God.

January 31, 1963

Here I am writing *The Lotus and the Universe.* Just as in previous years, Pir-O-Murshid manifested and said, "Be a Flute," and opened the doors to the cosmic universe, God—so to speak—manifested and said: "Be a Lotus. You fool, you can't both write *The Lotus and the Universe* and accuse Koestler and not be a Lotus. Be a Lotus and be blessed." So here I am, writing now from the "lotus point of view" against the "robot point of view," and it is transforming the manuscript. This will require, no doubt, extra revisions, but at least there is inner satisfaction and joy.

March 17, 1963

To Shemseddin Ahmed,
Lahore, Pakistan
My dear Friend and Brother:
As-salaam aleikum. You may understand now why I do not call myself a Muslim but an "inshallahist" [*Inshallah* means "God willing"—ed.] While originally a Muslim meant one who surrendered to God, it later came to mean mostly those who accepted *Shariah* [the outward religious rules, the external practice of Mohammed] and finally those who followed openly or blindly an *Ijma* [body of traditional customs], the source of which is not only unclear, but often has nothing whatever to do with revelation. . . .

The translation of *Rahman* and *Rahim* [From the opening words of each chapter of Quran: "In the name of Allah, who is *Rahman* and

Rahim"—ed.] into other languages has resulted in the use of terms quite unrelated to each other whereas it is obvious that the root Rahm [womb—ed.] is common to these two words and they must have some related function. Off hand, I call them "the Compassionator" and "the Compassionating" without holding too fast to these words. To explain further:

I call Mohammed the example of *Rahman* and Isa (Jesus) the example of *Rahim*. It comes out in their prayers that Mohammed begins with praise toward God and the concern is with Allah, while Isa is concerned with mankind and says: "Give us this day our daily bread and forgive our debts."

Or, in the practical life I am called upon to bring man to a greater spiritual realization following Mohammed; and also trying to increase the world's food supplies, following Isa. There is no contradiction, but this takes *Rahman* and *Rahim* out of the realm of the abstract into the concrete and practical. Therefore any problems or questions which have no relation to *Fatiha* [the first "Sura" or chapter of the Quran] or the Lord's Prayer are outside my duties in life.

September 23, 1963

When I was at Virginia Beach, I behaved so properly that people thought I was a monk or saint—or trying to be. One day, a young seeress came, and she was too tired to talk, so I went up and kissed her full, a type of kiss which would not be understood by many, because it was a three-body kiss. Here they understand the physical kiss, the subtle kiss and, of course, the sex kiss; but this was a karuna or heart-kiss, expressed like you see the pictures of angels. Jesus Christ has said that when you drink of the waters-of-life, you will not thirst again. And when you give this kiss, it must be the communion or you don't do it....The Western world cannot accept that you must be like a little child. They will even accept the miracles before they will accept that childlikeness. Most of those who have seen my diaries think I am very conceited and self-centered. I write what happens.

October 21, 1963

Ever since I was a child I have been moved by the Biblical passage: "My house shall be a house of prayer for all peoples." It seemed to me at an early age that some Jewish people were destined to return to Palestine. But the history of "Lawrence of Arabia," the blind following of Baal Peor (Balfour) instead of Moses, the repudiation of tradition for political zealousness shows that we are still in a world which confuses words with things, and clinging to words has replaced the attainment of an ideal.

October 16, 1964

Since your Murshid's return here, people have been kind, courteous, friendly, gracious, graceful, but never have they let your Murshid tell of his travels, exploits or anything about *tassawuf* [Sufism]. Even some of your Murshid's longest and best friends know nothing of his career, its significance or anything of the sort.

About two weeks ago, when a lady who has been most friendly and is of wonderful character, broke an engagement for a number of weeks standing—always an excuse—your Murshid said, "This is the end." He hung up the phone and heard the Divine Voice saying: "Samuel, I need you." And as he turned to leave the room the telephone rang, an emergency call.

This was the first of several such emergencies, people in dire troubles, seeking spiritual or psychological solutions and trusting your Murshid. This is one of his real functions, and it seems only great pain or difficulties cause people to turn that way. But this Sunday also, he is having a meeting, the first meeting in response to the cry of those who are in deep pain or difficulties caused always by so-called "spiritual colleagues" who are mostly so concerned with their spirituality that they have lost all humanity. This means a new direction, one in answer to problems of pain, suffering, illness—for which your Murshid was especially trained.

Professor Shad is a teacher of Urdu [at the University of California] and also a friend of many saints in India who have been the closest friends of your Murshid. The professor had asked "the secret questions" which, if asked, free your Murshid from the false covers which he is compelled to wear publicly and privately. So long as people see only the covers, he cannot be himself and they see only the covers—the clothing, the mannerisms, the behavior patterns, the niceties or their absence—none of which have anything to do with anything but *nafs* [the ego or thought-form of self].

Even praise or blame do not affect your Murshid, but when the proper questions are asked, then he is transformed or transforms himself. Here again, there is a large sector of your Murshid's history in Cairo which looks like it came out of something more bizarre than the Arabian Nights. For behind Sufism and the Sufi Orders there is that Hierarchy which controls the destinies of the world. Only this Hierarchy is not only manifesting through Islam, it manifests above and beyond all religions.

February 1, 1965

It does not make any difference whether one calls himself Christian, Buddhist, Yogi or what not. Any and all are still so egocentric they cannot see the light in their own neighbors. "Love thy neighbor as thyself" is back, for the hero or heroine is always somebody who comes from a distance, about whom one does not know too much, and who passes certain social and what is more Freudian tests which you did not pass, so you can't "possibly" be what you evidently are. . . .

The secret is that nobody has the dharma-transmission. It is only when a person surrenders that that produces the circumstances of the transmission which is *sanghic* [based on the spiritual community] and not personal, and thus one seems to be the teacher and one seems to be the pupil.

March 16, 1965

It is certain now, after 40 years, that the instructions of Pir-O-Murshid are coming into objective manifestation and they are coming not because he established any organic body called "Sufi Movement" but because, as he said, "The Message is in the Sphere...."
If one were to tell of his personal woes or other woes and pile them on, this would be simple compared to trying to get people to observe the truth of resurrection in the body. This has been the most difficult lesson to present and when one shows and glows, he is regarded as a performer and not as a saint. It is my saddest story—not that of crucifixion and public ignominy, but the total rejection of the truth of resurrection as vital, virile, demonstrative in everybody.

March 22, 1965

Inner: This is the real Peace. Words are not peace. Thoughts are not peace. Plans are not peace. Programs are not peace. Peace is fundamental. It is easy to prove it in the sciences, and the real Masters who are here are teaching it. It is hard to appreciate, hard to experience, hard to realize. It is fundamental to all faiths, all religions, all spirituality. It is from this that everything was, or let us say: *In the Beginning was Peace and the Peace was with God and the Peace was God, and out of this Peace has everything been made that was made.*
The difference between this Logos-Peace and what we generally call "Peace" is that the latter is a vacuum, a zero, a nothing, a blank, a negative to the extreme. The Logos-Peace is fullness, is all-inclusive, is brotherhood. The human body is a society of myriads of cell units working together. The total of humanity (Adam) is a society of myriads of personalities which must work together in and with and under God. Only this must be experiences and not syllogisms, truth and not truism. Every transcendentalist poet of America knew it, every newsman seems to work against it—we must have *excitement.*

Excitement is the death of peace. I have my poetry, and the Dance of Universal Peace. . . .

February 27, 1966

Ruth St. Denis has the faculty of drawing music and dances right out of the cosmos, out of the heart-of-God. She has taught me this faculty. Not many people can do this, but with the "coming race" appearing, more and more are coming into incarnation. They have a hard time, because the people who say they believe in reincarnation and the "coming race" wish to teach, they do not wish to learn from the advanced souls. And the advanced souls, being advanced, have more to teach and less to learn than the cult leaders.

On my next trip south, I am to see, God willing, Ruth St. Denis, to present to her the "Dance of Universal Peace." This has been accepted by world leaders of religion and been rejected by cult leaders. As Miss Ruth and I commune, it is not necessary to say much. She wanted to tell me her philosophy, and I said: "All right, you speak and I'll dance." That made her very happy.

March 6, 1966

There are no persons harder to face than the self-righteous who ascribe all sorts of virtues to themselves and all sorts of faults to others. Shams-i-Tabriz taught that hypocrisy was the only sin, and while one does not present a life of anything near to perfection, all efforts are made never to be guilty of hypocrisy.

June 11, 1966

Joy to the World! Next week one goes to the Psychedelic Conference with the theme "Joy without Drugs." One has already presented this theme to the young and they are accepting it. The old, the power hungry people, the samskara [impression]-collectors are different. They will not accept "In Joy we live and move and have our being."

July 28, 1966

One way to stop turmoil is to stop samskaras [reactive-impressions]. In my forthcoming talk on "Peace," this will be Peace-as-experience and most certainly not Peace-as-idea. And so long as we are "thrilled" by orators, we are not going to have peace. For instance, I told one of India's top savants that the greatest obstacle to peace was the repetition of a sound-noise, any sound-noise, and that even words like "peace," "salaam," and "shanti" were obstacles for they disturbed the Universal Peace just as much as any other sound-noise. I lost the debate and India had two fighting wars after that.

February 6, 1967

No man is a "brotherhood." That is nonsense, but it is the type of nonsense acceptable to metaphysical people who shun realities. Even less is a single person Hierarchy.... But metaphysical people do not learn from this and parade themselves as if each of them were a "brotherhood" or a "hierarchy." And thus they separate themselves.

Mohammed, who was a Messenger of God, said, "I am not different from you." And he meant it, and our mis-leaders do not. The more different they are, the more some people think they are spiritually advanced.

June 3, 1967

I shall continue in Desert Reclamation Research, knowing that sooner or later Israelis and Arabs will both have to drink from the same well.

321

October 7, 1967

It is a mistake to assume there is any "teacher." The teacher is the positive pole of a cell and as the pupil or pupils — the negative pole — show more aptitude, the EMF [electro-magnetic field] of the cell increases and knowledge comes through the teacher which would have otherwise been impossible. . . .

In the real samadhi, one has not only union-with-God but with all humanity; when one is helping others, he is helping himself, and when one is really helping himself, he is helping others.

December 1, 1967

The Sufi not only prays to God, he represents God. By this I mean that he not only asks for Love and Wisdom and Joy and Peace, he does everything possible to awaken Love and Light and Wisdom and Joy and Peace in others.

April 18, 1968

Divine truth does not belong to any organization. If I organize here, it will be organized under the title of "Islamia Ruhaniat Society," that is, the complete teachings of spiritual sciences which lead to realization of *peace*. As I'm working with my colleagues in other faiths, this will demonstrate this. We're not going to be called "Sufis" to distinguish ourselves from somebody else.

July 3, 1968

The essential of all knowledge, wisdom and morality is God (whom I prefer to call either *Allah* or *Ram*). Inayat Khan said, "God is the only Teacher, we all learn from Him."

October 2, 1968

I went to Dr. Blanche Baker, a psychiatrist, and I said to her, "I'll give you $200 unless my case is the worst case you ever had. And if it is, I'm going to ask you to treat me free, but first I have to prove that it's the worst case you ever had." I got it free. . . .

I had trouble with my eyes earlier in life due to physical injuries. Dr. Baker, who was part psychiatrist, and part drugless physician, retrogressed me right to birth for the purpose of healing this. I found I was a seven-month baby—premature. Astrologically, this is funny, because I'm a mercury-type: in a hurry. . . .

At one point in my life, I became totally and absolutely pessimistic to the point that I was a sort of left-handed masochist—I began expecting pain. My life readings have all been consistent. During one of them I finally began to see my whole karma, the justices in the injustice. If you take a single life, there's always injustice, but if you take a whole series, it all balances out. This has given me a much greater capacity for pain than almost anybody I meet. If I have a sort of composure, it isn't a real composure, it's a composure of having gone through such a tremendous quantity of pain that other things don't, by comparison, bother me. Perhaps, in the end, that's wisdom.

When we had a group therapy at Dr. Baker's and it was my turn, I said, "My problem is that I don't feel pain. I don't know whether that's a problem or not, but things that used to scare me have been scared out of me, and I don't think that's good at all. If you were to look at my body, half the time you'd find cuts and scars—I don't feel them." I asked them in this group therapy what was wrong, that I didn't feel pain and I didn't have fear and I wasn't comfortable about it. Maybe it's a compensation or an overbalance, not a mastery. Most of them thought it was a compensation, but they didn't have any clear answer. This is not necessarily good, because pain is a warning. When you don't get it, you don't get warned. . . .

Last year, for the first time in my life, I landed in the hospital. When I was flat on my back, unable to move, God came to me and said, "I make you spiritual teacher for the hippies." At that time, I had six disciples. At the end of the year, I had 30. A spiritual brother came, and the 30 became 60. And I think I'm ready for the next step, which I don't know. . . .

I'm involved in two revolutions. One of them was when I told Ruth St. Denis:

"Mother, I'm going to start a revolution."

"What is it?"

"I'm going to teach little children how to walk."

"You have it! You have it! You have it!"

The second revolution is to say the Lord's Prayer in Aramaic. . . .

I was staying in the home of Roderick White in Santa Barbara. He always used to invite me to his house, and every time he'd invite me, Krishnamurti was in trouble, and he had to go out and see Krishnamurti. So he left me alone in the house. Each time this happened, the doors opened—the doors to the next world. One time, Mohammed came and began to dictate "Saladin." He'd dictate something, and I'd say, "I don't believe that." And he'd say, "I didn't ask you what you believe, you either take it down willingly or unwillingly." He's not the only one who did that.

One time, Khuthumi came. The last time, L. Adams Beck came [author of *The Garden of Vision* and other mystical novels of the 1920s; also *The Splendour of Asia*, an excellent retelling of the story of Lord Buddha—ed.]. She said, "I have come to restore to you the memory of former lives." I said, "I don't believe in reincarnation." She said, "I'm not here to discuss philosophy with you. Do you want to have this faculty willingly or unwillingly? You can't avoid it. Now which will it be?" She dictated a manuscript which I still have. After that, the memories started to come back.

December 1, 1968

The book of bitterness is closed. A new cycle has definitely begun.

It is obvious that there is a huge integrative movement going on. This may be indicative of the Aquarian Age, for something like this is certainly happening. The group has displaced the individual, but it is a dynamic, organic group, demonstrating "I am the vine and ye are the branches thereof."

1970, walking with children.

CHAPTER FORTY-SIX

Excerpts from Letters-Diaries:

1969–71

January 27, 1969

I am addressing about a hundred young people every week, but the signs are of breaking out. My colleague, the Rev. Earl Blighton [Father Paul of the Holy Order of MANS], who went through the Valley of the Shadow of Death with me (or I with him), has also jumped from three to a hundred disciples in a very short time and has three centers, three outposts and cannot handle it. As the psychotherapists said, the young seek love and peace and all their elders give them is "excitement." The quest for "excitement" is the only quest today. Or is it?

The giving out of moral instruction by Dancing and Psychic Sciences is in some ways a departure. That is why I have to give so much time to Hazrat Inayat Khan's teachings. In this, and in a few other mostly unpublished Sufi manuscripts, seem to be the keys to everything. Today it is necessary to start many new ventures. Advice is easy, suggestions are easy, but I am not the Universe. I have a little secretarial help, far less than is needed to attend to the wants of a growing number of disciples. But now the young believe — in contradiction to their elders not believing — and sometimes for that very reason.

February 12, 1969

So many go around claiming God-experience, and when they ask Sam, he always says: "Never mind their claims. Show me their disciples." And we hear stories of the rise and fall of this great personality and that, but never a sign of any great disciple. So many churches and so many cults, but only the young experience God, so we shall have a "New Age" in which the God-people may be separate, in a sense, from the Church people.

February 16, 1969

As-salaam aleikum [Peace be with you]. We may keep a phrase as a motto or we may weave it into our lives. Religion has failed, because sacred words have been turned into mottos, often in self-defense or otherwise and have not become the measurements of our beings.

February 16, 1969

While a Murshid does not like to point out the errors and sins unless they are big and important, you have been more concerned with your possible short-comings than with the Glories of Allah. My own work especially with *wazifas* (sacred phrases) and their repetition in the Dance is on the Glories of Allah, not the short-comings of mankind.

March 7, 1969

I am at the moment in an awkward position. There has been a constant increment of both attendance and financial income, and yet I am in debt. It may require a complete house-cleaning. I have refused to accept the tragic deaths of Hazrat Inayat Khan, Robert Clifton and Dwight Goddard as an example and either will avoid a tragic death (some success here) or it will be of a different kind.

March 20, 1969

I am to take a day off next week. This is a rarity. It is not yet 6 a.m. I am like the director of a gigantic psychiatric hospital. You may not be able to understand it, but a Sufi is one who sees from the viewpoint of another as well as of himself. It was necessary to call one group to account after another, and I boldly insisted that there were to be no more requests for questions and interviews after meetings. This has been the bane, and yet when Fudo came out I think it worked. True, there were more interviews and questions than ever before.

May 10, 1969

Every time a group comes, Allah bestows a blessing. The other night one had the disciples get up and do another dance — these dances are always coming. It is based on nothing but *Bismillah Er-Rahman Er-Rahim* [We begin in the name of Allah, who is Mercy and Compassion]. It is real, it is effective. It is based on the knowledge of psychic and mystical law, which pretenders and proclaimers do not know. These dances are pouring out of one.

May 27, 1969

Pir Vilayat wishes to organize, and I am at my wit's end now, because one cannot hold more than a hundred individuals close to one, look after their spiritual, psychological and social needs, etc. And so one has to "institutionalize." And my now scattered disciples also want the Dance, and so far I have failed to obtain a proper secretary, but must start all over. My senior friends have plenty of suggestions, but direct help is a rare thing to get, and I am not demanding it.

June 4, 1969

With all the love and apparent harmony around, there are some fierce obstacles to face. We came here to establish a spiritual cooperative and then made an entity of the place — it is called *The Garden of Inayat.* But the name does not matter. To too many of the so-called

"New Age" people, the name of the commune is *Santa Claus,* no matter what they call it and Santa Claus (or God) is supposed to provide while others sit back. It is not only others that sit back, but there is a certain degree of "baksheesh" [Hindi slang for begging] on top of it.

September 2, 1969

When Phillip Kapleau wrote *The Three Pillars of Zen* I knew a new age had come, that the world sooner or later would have an impartial, objective view of mystics and mystical experiences, as it has had to have with regard to scientific endeavors.

September 2, 1969

The first lesson taught here is *Allah* and also the last. The sins of Americans are not the sins of the Arabs "in times of ignorance" and have to be approached differently. There is more and more a tendency toward universality. The Dance of Universal Peace, first presented before the tomb of Selim Chisti at Fathepur Sikri [near Agra, India] was fully blessed by my late "Fairy Godmother," Miss Ruth St. Denis. It has expanded into all sorts of dances, beginning with Dervish Dances. Of course, the "good Muslims" object to anything that their grandfathers did not know. And the first step was merely to integrate the efforts of the Rufais, Bedawis, Chistis, Mevlevis, etc. Then it expanded. . . .

I have returned from New Mexico where a summer school is being provided. There are more and more young Americans who seek spiritual perfection. The demise of the Parsi Meher Baba left a vacuum and people see a need for a universal approach to universals. Why, I even had to give a "Mountain Climbing Yoga" practice which enabled people half or less than half my age to climb high in the Rocky Mountains along with me. But I assure you it was a Sufic and not an Indian practice. And it worked. Some day we shall accept that

Akhlak Allah works [practice of free movement as if in the presence of God].

October 21, 1969

An old friend has shown up, and it is possible, inshallah [God willing], that he will take over. One now has, praise to Allah, sufficient funds to handle such emergencies. There are a growing number of young disciples, and they say they love Murshid and would like to work for him, but they are so unsettled as to where they live and how they live. There have been both necessary and unnecessary moving about, and in this so much concern with the ego-self; it is a touchy problem, but there could be worse ones.

November 9, 1969

I do not believe you have to become a Sufi devotee to become perfect. I find perfection in devotees of many paths. I am not talking junk-theory or emotions. My friends include many realized souls of many faiths, and I can substantiate this with facts, not emotions.

November 11, 1969

We have gone through the phases of simple art and concentration practices.... But a higher dimension has intervened in the form of Dance, ritual and pageant. One could hardly imagine the effects of three- and four- dimensional application of the Gatha studies [the esoteric study papers of Hazrat Inayat Khan]. This is what is being taken up today.

This will mean the reproduction of the eternal Mysteries to the human race. These dances first come in visions at night with no explanations. It generally takes three nights before they are clear mentally. The vision comes with no explanations. It proves later to be totally rational.

November 19, 1969

It was during the War that when it was said that Hitler was going to call in psychic powers, I asked God what to do and He said: "Go upstairs!"

December 24, 1969

There is a great resonance which takes place in singing Ram Nam [Om Sri Ram Jai Ram Jai Jai Ram—ed.] using the head as a dome. Now the resonance has become complete, using and vibrating the whole body, demonstrating what is taught but not studied in the Christian Bible: "The human body is the temple of the Holy Spirit."

January 1970

I am teaching "Dances of Universal Peace." I led one thousand young people in a version of this in Golden Gate Park just before leaving San Francisco. The idea of "Peace through the arts" came to me years ago when the old Roerich Museum was functioning during the lifetime of that once celebrated, but now forgotten artist. Unlike Nicholas Roerich, I am appealing to the young and not to the "les fameuses."

January 18, 1970

Sam has just been reading the Sufi saint, Shah Latif ibn Sind, and gave the following short talk: "Allah is not your jailer, He is your Lover."

February 13, 1970

With the Sufis in particular, love is regarded as most important— love that is living, communicable and able to be shared. As the Bible teaches us, although it is not part of religion at all: how can we love the God whom we have not seen, when we do not love ourselves and our fellowmen whom we have seen?

March 6, 1970

I shall be leaving here toward the end of this month for Geneva to attend a conference of The Temple of Understanding with the ambitious program of peace through religion. I have been in this field for many, many, many years without any reports ever being accepted by persons or bodies *verbally* interested. But now action of some sort is necessary. The failure of important persons to study history, or to be aware of what their fellows are doing is as much an obstacle to peace and understanding as are all the connivances and machinations of the presumably powerful. Besides, it is so easy to blame others.

A few years ago, when the Jewish peoples, however defined, were in many respects the unfortunate victims of intolerance and persecution, a great deal was heard of Boccaccio's story of the three rings and the sequel of "Nathan the Wise" written by the German philosopher Lessing. But now no more. Why?

I hope to present a "three-ring" approach to the complex of Palestine, but I shall not favor any "resolutions" whatsoever. Resolutions are invariably followed by wars and conflicts even worse than those of a previous era. If religion will not accept its own Living God, if religions do not accept the promises of their own Scriptures, we must look for something new or something destructive.

For the first time, youth — and not apologists for youth — is going to be given every opportunity to express itself, and this alone will help toward peace and understanding. It is the acceptance of God, not the acceptance of words, which will bring peace.

March 11, 1970

Sam was influenced to maintain a diary after reading the words of

Thomas Jefferson, Ralph Waldo Emerson and Papa Ramdas. But, in retrospect, it must be said that the more one considers it, there is no diary. There is only the fulfillment of the divine life in and through what would appear to be an ego-personality which is nothing but a mode of God Himself expressing Himself outwardly. And daily Sam seems to find that there is really nothing else but this divine life.

March 11, 1970

No doubt there is a time for all things. And now, instead of lapsing into the presumable securities of old age, Sam's life is becoming more and more public. No doubt it requires considerable patience when one's theme, so to speak, is "The stone that is rejected is become the cornerstone."

March 22, 1970

The day has gone when audiences are impressed by lofty emotions apart from direct experience. The young want direct experience; they are getting the direct experience; they love the direct experience. They mount the ladder of *Ananda* [bliss], which in a certain sense is the same as Jacob's Ladder in the Hebrew Bible.

My friends, it is a New Age. It is an age of warm delight in the Divine Presence. There is hope for the world when it accepts the evidence of spirituality not only as presented by, let us say, a guru, but when it is reflected in the awakening of hearts, in the brilliancy of faces, in the manifest joy and delight.

The second lesson Sam has learned is that of and from pain. To him, this means the wiping out of samskaras [impressions on the reactive mind]. It is in no sense an evil. The wiping out of samskaras helps free the spirit, helps one to appreciate joy.

A series of reports have shown that the harm done by alcohol is 40 times as great as all problems — moral, legal and otherwise — due to partaking of psychedelics. Sam never used psychedelics, because he felt the superiority of the mantram to begin with—not the philosophy of the mantram, but its recitation.

April 1970

[At the conference in Geneva] it was the top intellectuals themselves who labored to see that love and devotion, not exhortation and emotion dominated. And it was so. The dominant figure was our very good friend, Swami Ranganathananda of the Ramakrishna Mission. Sam has always called him the Vivekananda of the age. He has immersed his whole life in Vivekananda, but now he has functioned as Vivekananda. He was probably without peer. He was so recognized chiefly by Dr. Seyyed Hussein Nasr of Tehran, Iran, who represented spiritual Islam (and so Sufism). When the supreme personalities of different religions meet in amity and devotion, a certain goal has been reached. . . .

I put on a little show that I was an incarnation of Lessing's "Nathan the Wise." Nathan the Wise was a grand hero during the rise of Hitlerism. But today nobody refers to him. I have written three epic poems, the themes of which are respectively the Jewish, Christian and Islamic divine aspects of Palestine. They were shunned by the different religionists, but recently have evoked such wonderful response that I can see that today there are persons and forces who are really concerned with peace. [The names of these poems are respectively "The Day of the Lord Cometh," "What Christ, What Peace?" and "Saladin." They are contained in *The Jerusalem Trilogy*—ed.]

June 2, 1970

Then we came to Lama [Foundation, near Taos, New Mexico], which may well become the center of a sort of American Lama-ism. While I am here to present Sufism, it becomes obvious that something more is in the wind. Both Sufism and Mahayana Buddhism teach the transcendental intuition (kashf or prajna, and no nonsense). It is operational and it has made me bang down hard on rump-ritualism called "Zen," which ignores the fact that Zen is *prajna* (insight or wisdom) and not *dhyana* (meditation).

The Quran teaches that the Divine Light is neither of the East nor West, and I presented that therefore the Rockies were as Holy as the Himalayas, and that this was the place to present the Maha Mudra Meditation.

June 17, 1970

Pir Dewwal Shereef
University of Islamabad
Islamabad, West Pakistan
Beloved Pir:
As-salaam Aleikum! It is a long time since one has attempted to write. The experiences, favorable and unfavorable, which have occurred in the last nearly seven years are now resolving themselves into a grand symphony. No doubt everything has happened, is happening as Allah wishes. One finds oneself in a rather strange universe in which neither orthodoxy nor heterodoxy seem to matter very much, but there is a more and more constant *Akhlak Allah* [acting as if in the presence of God], and this Akhlak Allah becomes even more natural than necessary.

The first part of the life, which lasted almost five years, was like a sojourn in The Cave: whatever one's intentions, whatever one's commissions, whatever one's wishes and ambitions, they neither failed nor succeeded. It is easy to presume that one can go into another land and by his mere presence convert a lot of people to whatever he wishes. It is easy to dream of the ignorant converting the intelligent, but this is nonsense. It requires intelligence to convert the intelligent.

About five years ago, one reversed one's habit of peacefulness and non-violence and brought suit against a member of one's family. The suit was never terminated; not only was it settled out of court, but it has resulted at the lowest level in a much larger income which keeps on increasing, until at this day it is about four times as great as it was when one was in Pakistan, Alhamdu Lillah [Praise God]!

Just before this change, one suffered from an infection, ptomaine poisoning to be exact, and when one was flat on his back in the hospital, the voice of Allah appeared and said, "I make you spiritual teacher of the hippies." One may surrender to Allah willingly or unwillingly, or one may refuse to surrender to Allah; but when one is flat on one's back, one has not even a choice.

This was followed immediately by a series of visions; every one of those visions has now come into outward manifestation, down to tiny details. Now this is in harmony with the predictions or commissions of several Pirs and holy men that one was to get 50,000 Americans to say and repeat "Allah" and believe in Him. This of itself looked immense, and when one considers in the past that this person was a recluse and an outcast, it looks even more ridiculous. But so did the outlook, no doubt, of Siddiq when he was in The Cave with the Blessed Messenger.

One began teaching spirituality through the *Walk*. This was a grand adventure during which three of the original six disciples deserted this Murshid; but it was remarkable that one has not had three desertions since. This method was blessed by the late Miss Ruth St. Denis, a very spiritual dancing teacher who knew how to receive inspiration from the very space itself.

The Walk developed in two directions: extentionally and intentionally; in the extentional walk, disciples learned to climb hills and mountains and walk long distances. The sacred phrases needed for these are comparatively few. But then the question arose: if the *Sifat-i-Allah* [Divine Attributes] and Hadiths [Traditions of Prophet Mohammed] can be used to help one walk long distances, climb mountains and work without fatigue, couldn't they and other *Wazifas* [sacred phrases] be used to help humanity in its greater education, purification and development? So now we use many of the sacred phrases in psychic and moral procedures. These take on two entirely different aspects:

*Moral Development.*By applying the divine qualities to humanity one helps to remove the evils, the shortcomings, the impediments and all the grosser aspects of being. A sacred phrase is better than a chastisement. A chastisement is a reliance on man; a prayer or devotion is a reliance on Allah. All theories, doctrines and orthodoxies aside, the simple fact is that these methods work.

When I told Muslims what I was doing, they said, "Muslims will not approve of this." I answered, "It is not a question of whether Muslims will approve of this, it is a question of 'Does Allah approve of this?'" I live in a district where there are some Jordanians and Palestinians, and they are amazed and approve.

The next phase seems to be coming—that these methods can be extended to deal with psychological problems. Without going into details, there were two such instances just before I left San Francisco about a month ago and both turned out successfully, Alhamdu Lillah!

Psychic Purification. The great pseudo-problem—it is a pseudo-problem and not a real problem—is that the young people in this part of the world and others are resorting to the use of products of the vegetable world to open themselves up or to be opened up to what might be called the subtle world (following an Indian term) or possibly to *malakut* [Sufi term for one of the "heavens," the realm of ideas and ideals, the mental plane—ed.]. The simple fact is that this is so. The soul of man knows very well that the material world (*nasut*) is only one of several planes of existence. All the common or uncommon sense cannot change this. In the last days of his life, Aldous Huxley concluded that this hidden world was real. It was also known as *faerie* by the Celtic people. It was considered variously immoral, illegal, insane and perverse to have any dealings with it. People diatribe against materialism but keep themselves bound in it just the same.

There have been many predictions supporting the principles of psychic and spiritual evolution. One began with the theme "Joy Without Drugs." It is so easy to have a formula, words. Then the question came: how to implement these words with actualities?

It is one thing to *say* "La Il La Ha El Il Allah" [There is no reality but the One]. It is beautiful to say, "As man takes one step toward Allah, Allah takes ten steps toward man," but how about the actualities? This is exactly what has happened.

Now one is daring two tremendous things: the first is based on a Hadith: "In that day will the sun rise in the West and all men seeing will believe." It is true that the Blessed Messenger said, "Seek wisdom even unto China." But try it. You will have down on you almost all the Islamic world except the most advanced sages and seers. Well, the voice of Allah came to me and presented more visions of Dervish Dances. These dances are based only slightly on the methods of the Mevlevi School. They also have in them elements of the Rufai and Bedawi Schools. And along with them the operative aspects of *kashf* [insight].

So we began Dervish Dances and everything has followed exactly to details of what Allah showed in vision: the growth from 6 to 30 disciples, from 30 to 60, from 60 to 100 and then the aureole burst into another dimension. I have not yet organized to that dimension. One felt his participation was entirely satisfactory in a conference of the world's religions where Sufism, so to speak, was represented by our good friend Dr. Seyyed Hussein Nasr. After that, one was entirely successful in communicating the Sufi dances to the young in London, Boston and now in the Southwest.

Then the question arose of this body and other bodies being overworked, whereupon the wise Allah intervened and gave the commission that Sufi Ahmed Murad Chisti would be called upon, inshallah, to play a role in the United States similar to that of Saint Moin-ed-din Chisti in India [who brought Sufism there from the Mideast, through music — ed.]. Although the vision was clear, it was so daring that one could not face it, but instead surrendered himself entirely to Allah and from that moment a new type of *Qawwal* [sacred song] was born.

So during the dancing classes we intersperse the rest periods with chanting. The next thing is the revolution going on in the Western

338

music, and the inspirations from Allah seem to blend in these modes with the chantings of sacred phrases.

One has, so to speak, several missions and commissions from Allah about which one does not wish to speak here. One sees the need of a return to Pakistan, inshallah, in 1972 or '73 (unless Allah directs sooner and money is forthcoming) and of bringing a group there, especially to the Universities of Islamabad and Punjab and presenting this material. This would not only improve American/Asian relations, but would do much to raise the consciousness of the young so that they would realize that whatever experiences are derived from so-called drugs, these are very little when contrasted to the experiences of *kashf* and *shahud* [insight and inner experience, respectively—ed.].

Upon my return to San Francisco, I am commissioned to write on the coalescence of the moral teachings of my first Pir-O-Murshid, Hazrat Inayat Khan, with the Hadiths. This will be in part a labor of love and joy, and in another a directive to the very questionable situations in the world today. Fortunately, I have three wonderful secretaries who are very devoted. I also have two remarkable young men serving as Khalifs, and at least one young man and young woman almost as advanced. Their dreams, their visions, their outlooks, their high standards almost cause one to weep.

This is written high in the Rocky Mountains in a place more comparable to Natha Galli than Murree [where Pir Dewwal Shereef lived], some 9,000 feet up. I shall be returning to San Francisco at the end of the month. One must fulfill the commissions given to one by Allah and the Pirs who represent Him on earth. Although well on in years from the worldly standpoint, the mind is such that this letter was dictated without pause and the body also is remarkably active, Alhamdu Lillah!

> Love, Blessings and Respects,
> Sufi Ahmed Murad Chisti

June 24, 1970

The difference between the emotionalist and the mystic is vast. The emotionalist meets somebody and has what, for him, is a transcending experience — and it usually is. But when it is all over, he has *hal* and not *makam* [a state, not a station]; he does not grow and he thinks others are his inferiors and that he has a "world message" for them. In general, the leaders whom the divided emotionalists support have laid aside Christ's "Sermon on the Mount." They are so superior they can dispense with the moral order, and often do. But few know the depths of any Oriental Wisdom.

July 19, 1970

I am very optimistic, because I believe the young will live longer than the old. That is all. The young have the ability to *think through* the problems of pollution, soil preservation and reclamation, even slum clearance, because they have simple capacities, simple natural capacities totally outside the "realisms" current in America and the Communist countries.

July 28, 1970

My fairy godmother, so to speak, Ruth St. Denis, approved of all my plans, and before she left the world I had begun my "Dances of Universal Peace." I started out with Dervish Dances, then Indian ones. Now I am ready to restore or start Christian mystical dances. These dances are dedicated to The Temple of Understanding of Washington, D.C., which is endeavoring to take to heart the psalmist's words, "My house shall be a house of prayer for all peoples."

July 28, 1970

Some time ago, a young man thought he would see a battle royal

340

by introducing me to the Hassidic Rabbi Shlomo Carlebach. We took one look at each other and there was a love-embrace. I have had such love-embraces from a Greek Metropolitan, Franciscan Fathers, a Vietnamese Thien, some Chinese Buddhist masters and innumerable Muslims and Hindus.

July 31, 1970

This is really my diary entry. Qualitatively, things were never so good. Quantitatively, I am in a quandary, and perhaps this is for the good of my soul. Today, I must telephone my attorney about organizing legally. I understand this is what Vilayat wants, but I have not seen the official report of the meeting. Vilayat and I have a tacit agreement that if we are separate, we can both be reaching new audiences. I am thoroughly satisfied with his plans, programs and endeavors. Yet I am not so concerned about planning as in putting the plans into action. I was given the same instructions in Pakistan, and within a short while, we may be *doing.* But today I am trying to get a few hours off. I have had no leisure whatsoever since returning from New Mexico. Nearly everything is proceeding favorably, but nearly too much.

August 31, 1970

My disciples and friends have already successfully programmed joint Israeli-Arab dinners. We have even been successful in getting young Jewish people to recite the *Kalama* [Islamic affirmation of the Only Being] and Arabs to recite the *Shema* [Hebrew affirmation of the Only Being]. As I do not believe in any ethnocentric religion, and as I absolutely believe in theocentrism (and I think Moses did, too), I see no reason why we cannot put into practice, "Love thy neighbor as thyself."

September 6, 1970

In 1928, Dr. Henry Atkinson of the World Church Peace Union came to this city and was so satisfied with our interview that he asked me to continue my studies of the religions of the world. . . .

In fact, the program for the Near East was part of a larger program of "How California Can Help Asia." As part of this program, I know what the graduates of the "Multi-versity" of California have done, and can do, toward the solution of water, desert and soil problems in the Near East. This was particularly true of Professor Paul Keim, who accomplished wonders — actual wonders — in Egypt which are hardly known anywhere. Both Paul Keim and an Iranian professor, separately, worked out methods of low-cost construction of adobe homes with plumbing and sanitation.

In 1930, I proposed that all religious holy places be de-nationalized and de-politicized. After the UN was established, I felt that it, or some co-ordinative or subsidiary group, should in some way be given jurisdiction over the holy places of all religions. The peace plan which I proposed was accepted as wonderful by Mr. Gunnar Jarring and separately by at least three other UN officials. It included at least mutual recognition of all religions by each other and even the establishment of a Papal residency in Palestine.

The welcomes finally received at Geneva from the real leaders of the real world's religions and later receptions from the youth make me feel certain that something will be done.

I am optimistic enough to believe we can have peace in this world on two simple bases:

A. Facts should be considered as more important than subjectivities about them by important persons.

B. Facts should be evaluated not on reactions to personalities presenting them.

I am very much for one world. I have lived in many lands. I have had no trouble with strangers anywhere, no matter how exotic we may claim them to be.

October 4, 1970

We have eaten in a Syrian restaurant, owned and operated by Jews. Although it is impossible to convince "realists" about hard facts, this very institution shows that some human beings would rather make money off of others than kill them. This, as you know, is a feature of our peace plan.

December 21, 1970

Outwardly, Sam's work is through "Dances of Universal Peace." Along with that has been a choral group singing hymns and themes drawn from the real religions of the past, but integrating according to the contemporary types of music, which are becoming universal and international.

The Divine Spirit does not manifest as any thought-form, still less as an orthodoxy. We have done it, or it has been done through us, by Ram.

January 2, 1971

Pir-O-Murshid Sufi Barkat Ali
Lyallpur District, West Pakistan
Praise be to Allah!
This has been a glorious exit, and one which will go down in history, a sign of all the beauty, truth and goodness in the universe.

One has been truly saved from the jaws of death and adversity, and may live on indefinitely as God wills. It is the sign and symbol of all goodness, and the establishment of God's Message in the Western world forever, praise be to Allah.

For I am the first one born in the West to have received the Divine Message, and believe to have representatives in all the purity and goodness of which Allah is capable and which will now be presumed done forever.

CHAPTER FORTY-SEVEN

Book Excerpt:

Peace
(from *The Lotus and the Universe*)

Every ten years a Nobel Peace Prize,
Every five years another war.

"Peace, peace, when there is no peace."

—Jeremiah 6:14

"War and peace are two things too serious to entrust to diplomats and generals."

— Clemenceau

EVERY SOUL LONGS FOR PEACE, AND EVERY MIND—BY ITS nature—brings a disturbance. The snake offered the fruit of knowledge to Adam and Eve, and with it agitation and excitement. So humanity has sought the excitement, it is still seeking the excitement and crying because there is no peace. Everybody blames somebody or something else.

According to the Sufi view, and perhaps this covers all mystics, one must find the peace within and by the *power* gained thereby, radiate one's atmosphere. Thus there is an explanation of *Allaho Akbar* that not only is there "no power or might save in Allah," but that *in peace there is power.*

This age, bent on excitement, no longer recognizes the small print of Newton, that "every body remains in a *state of rest* or. . . ." Nor can it be compelled to accept the words of Jesus Christ in the *Gospel of Thomas:* "the sign of the Father is an activity and a rest."

The saga of Noah and the Flood, not being studied from the four-fold Hebraic PARDES point of view, gives us at best but symbols. [The fourfold consideration of any passage or story—literal, poetic, symbolic, experiential—were said to lead to an experience of PARDES—root of our word *paradise.*—ed.] What is valuable is hidden. *Noah* means either "Mr. Peace" or "Mr. Rest."

The theme here is universal: there is a world of agitation and beneath it a world of rest. Or perhaps they are so intermingled that the universe is a "Razor's Edge." Indeed, we find this in and under all religions. Yet it is also true, as one Oriental sage put it, "I have come to abolish religion—and bring God." Until we find the depths, we are concerned only with words or thoughts. These proceed from peace; peace is their origin, it is not affected by them.

One gains encouragement that the Nobel Peace Prize has been given to a scientist (Linus Pauling) who is something of a Lotus-man himself. Between his being a scientist and a "universalist," he is either anathema or completely misunderstood by C.P. Snow's literati. On the one hand, we have the analysts and speculators, on the other hand the synthesizers and integrators. They stand far apart.

The scientist, the artist, the adventurer and the mystic are alike in that they tend to confine themselves to experience. Therefore, they are often regarded as queer or egocentric by those who rely on analysis and dialectics. Jesus has declared that by taking thought we cannot add to the hairs on our head.

The founders of religions have presented similar programs. Moses went so far as to present a complete political system which could, in a sense, bring peace, equilibrium and prosperity [one feature of this included a year of *rest* every 50 years during which all slaves were to be freed, alienated property returned and the land left untilled (Leviticus 25:8–17)—ed.]. In historical times, the one effort to establish such an order, by Jesuits in South America, came to an end because it interfered with selfish politicians.

Jesus offered the communion, in which each and all would share in the universal life, and so in the lives of each other. This theme is presented again and again in the Christian Scriptures, but unfortunately communion has remained either symbolic or formal. This is not enough.

Peace is not concerned with mere negations. Life only ebbs in the cemetery. The Indian *"neti, neti"* [not this, not that] may bring a form of satisfaction. It does not bring life. For peace is not mere euphoria.

Our LSD experiments make us discover that there is an ocean of consciousness beyond our immediate ken. But we only dip our little toes into it. The practice of meditation in one of its many forms can bring us to the experiences of peace at many levels, until we find we are one with the Grand Consciousness which embraces us all. But so long as dualism persists, we cannot have the peace.

When Mary Pickford wrote, "Why not try God?" it was not always interpreted, "Why not try Peace? Why not try Love?" The mind selects, the mind abstracts. What is not only near at hand but may be the core of our very being can remain outside our knowledge.

St. Paul has said (my own translation): "To each is given the manifestation of the spirit to *universal* benefit. (I Corinthians 12:7). The Greek prefix *sym* corresponding to *universal* comes from the same origin as the *samma* used by the Buddha in his proclamation of the Eightfold Path [usually translated "Right Views, Right Speech, etc."– ed.]. It is the *universality*, the collectivity as against the *each*, the individual.

In these words of St. Paul, we have some pretty good Buddhistic teaching, or some very fine mystical philosophy, or the application of that universality which pervades the words of Jesus Christ and the teachings of the founders of all faiths. So peace is not something to be gained by attacking "erroneous views" as some un-attained among the Buddhists hold. *Samma dhrishti* means to have the universal, the cosmic outlook. Finding the whole universe, finding "the kingdom of heaven" within, one can do something about it.

The greatest lesson received from Nyogen Senzaki was his "Buddha Hridaya" [Buddha Heart]. It was not only the words, but something conveyed with them. Or, as has been put in this age, "Let the mind go, let the heart come."

We again come back to the need to cultivate peace within ourselves, howsoever it be done.

Peace cannot come from a pact. We must alter "foreign aid" into "foreign understanding" without changing policies. Changing policies may bring satisfaction, but not peace. Changing attitudes might be tried.

Without any of the credentials of the scholar, the writer has communed with the trees in the Imperial Gardens in Tokyo as a guest of honor. Without any of the credentials of the diplomat, the writer has communed with the President of India. All this besides meeting the sages and saints and holy men of many faiths. In each case, one became aware of the grand ocean-of-stillness in which we live and move and have our being.

When the United Nations was organized, the United States took its stand with Russia and other atheist countries against a room or house-of-prayer. It is to the thanks of the Muslims that they compelled such an establishment. And it is also to the credit of the Muslims that they presented the history of Mecca—perhaps the only occasion in history where the foes were forgiven in the name of God, and the "sins" of political aberration were totally erased.

Not only do we fail to find the kingdom of God by "lo here! lo there!" We do not find any peace by ascribing its absence to some particular "devil" here or there.

Now a universal man has been awarded the Nobel Peace Prize, a man of good will. This may even be the beginning to real understanding and avoidance of the "tyranny of words." Let us so hope.

Hazrat Inayat Khan taught:

O Thou, Who art the Perfection of Love, Harmony
    and Beauty,
Lord of Heaven and of Earth,
Open our hearts that we may hear Thy Voice
    which constantly cometh from within.

In other words: God is here. This can be practiced, this can be realized, this can be known.

My love and blessings to you all.

OM MANI PADME HUM!

Hail, the Jewel in the Lotus!

Samuel L. Lewis
Sufi Ahmed Murad Chisti

1969, in the garden at Lama Foundation.

APPENDIX

Chronology of Unfoldment:

Dates from the life of Samuel L. Lewis

1896

Born on October 18, at 2:20 a.m. in San Francisco. His father was Vice President of the Levi-Strauss Company and his mother was Harriet Rosenthal, of the international banking family. As a child, Sam recited from the Bible and other scriptures unknown to his family. His family frowned on his spiritual work when they realized it was not Jewish and that he was not interested in business matters. His mother was more sympathetic to his work than his father was. She would tell the story of the Prophet Samuel and then say of her own son, "He is. . . he was. . . born a prophet and he came in the spiritual body first."

1898

Reading before the age of 3 ("Intimations of Immortality").

1902

Completed reading of Old Testament ("Intimations of Immortality").

1906

Shaku Soyen in SF/introduces Mentorgarten.

1911

"Came very definitely, suddenly at first, but often repeated, that I would be a philosopher, although I had but the vaguest idea what the word meant."

1914

Involved in Socialist movement ("Intimations of Immortality"). Begins spiritual studies in comparative theology, theosophy, "Morals and Dogmas of Masonry."

1915

Contacted the Theosophical Society for the first time at its booth at the International Exposition in San Francisco.

1916

Began reading Upanishads. Began studying non-Euclidian geometry and mathematical philosophy under Professor Cassius Keyser of Columbia, who later introduced him to Dr. Alfred Korzybski and thus to general semantics.

1919

Met Murshida Rabia Martin, a student of Sufi Pir-O-Murshid Hazrat Inayat Khan, and began work with her and Sufi group based in San Francisco and Fairfax.

1920

Met and began studying with the Rev. M.T. Kirby (Sogaku Shaku), a disciple of the Rinzai Zen Buddhist Abbot Shaku Soyen. Meets

Beatrice Lane and Nyogen Senzaki also through Kirby. When Kirby assigned to Hawaii, his teaching work continued by Senzaki.

1923

At age 27, following a vision of Hazrat Inayat Khan, is initiated by the Pir-O-Murshid in San Francisco—the first person to "touch his heart." Introduces Senzaki and Hazrat Inayat Khan; they go into samadhi together.

1924

March—Retreat at Kaaba Allah, great visions and blessings of Khidr and all the Messengers, culminating in Mohammed.

1926

Six interviews with Hazrat Inayat Khan in Hollywood, given the title of "Sufi," appointed "Protector of the Message" and assigned commentary work on esoteric writings, brotherhood work to bring world of intellectual and mystic closer together.

First Zendo in US opened by Nyogen Senzaki in San Francisco, aided by Samuel. Introduces Senzaki and Paul Reps. Meets Rev. Ishida at the San Francisco Zendo

1927

Pir-O-Murshid Hazrat Inayat Khan dies in New Delhi. Samuel alternating living between San Francisco and Fairfax (1927-49, off and on) serving as chief assistant (Khalif) of Murshida Rabia Martin; gardener and director (in Rabia Martin's absence) of Kaaba Allah Sufi khankah in Fairfax, California.

1928

Meets Dr. Henry Atkinson of the World Church Peace Union, asked to study lesser known religions. Around this time meets Robert Stuart Clifton (Phra Sumangalo) in San Francisco. Rabia Martin travels to Europe, is rejected as Hazrat Inayat Khan's successor by European Sufi conclave.

1929

Concerned with reconciliation program for Middle East in religion and desert agriculture, continues work for World Church Peace Union.

1930

February: vision of Hazrat Inayat Khan, begins receiving commentaries and other writings from him. September: visit to New York, meets Zen Roshi Sokei-An Sasaki, received Dharma Transmission, his eyes opened to the future for period 1930–45, resulted in auguries in *Book of Cosmic Prophecy.*

1936

Co-authors *Glory Roads: The Psychological State of California* with Luther Whiteman, published by Thomas Y. Crowell, New York.

1937

Met Vera Van Voris at Sufi center on Franklin St. in San Francisco. Studied yoga of Ramana Maharshi with Paul Brunton.

1938

Living in Los Angeles, attending Senzaki's lectures at Zendo (now in LA).

1939

Met Bryn Beorse (Shamcher) in San Francisco, introduced by Luther Whiteman.

1940

Went to meditate at Sufi Rock (Pir Dahan) in Fairfax; told by God if he could sleep through the night London wouldn't be bombed.

1944

Rabia Martin died after turning land and Sufi organization over to Meher Baba, appointing Ivy Duce as her successor. Samuel attempts to continue work within organization, but withdraws two years later.

1945

Awarded citation for work with Army Intelligence (G2) during World War II, probably as researcher and historian. The exact work was never revealed, but included reporting troop movements in North Africa, seen clairvoyantly.

After visiting Baba's Myrtle Beach center, travels to New York to see Sokei-An Sasaki, who died the day he arrived.

1946

In the inner world, Hazrat Inayat Khan turns him over to Prophets

Mohammed and Jesus for guidance. Receipt of name "A. Murad" from Mohammed. Worked in Golden Gate Park, landscaping and collecting refuse.

1947

Receives first letters from Robert Clifton regarding situation in Viet Nam.

1949

Fire at Kaaba Allah in Fairfax destroys upper house of the khankah and most of his writings and library. Predicts that the school would be reclaimed. Attends City College of San Francisco, studies horti-culture/agriculture (A.A. Degree in 1951).

1953

Told by Paul Reps that he ought to meet Swami Papa Ramdas; Ramdas appears to him in vision and predicts meeting in the flesh one year hence.

1954

Corresponds with Dr. Radhakrishnan; living on Harriet St. in SF; meets Swami Ramdas, October 1954

1956

First journey to the East: Japan, Hong Kong, Thailand, Burma, East Pakistan, India, Pakistan.

1957

Upon return from the East, living in Mill Valley (106 Ethel Ave.) Reports his mother is dying. Last conversation with Nyogen Senzaki after coming back from Japan. His friend at World Church Peace Union, Dr. Henry Atkinson, dies.

1958

Continuing correspondence with Beorse on salt water conversion: Egypt, Dead Sea, Tunisia. May: Nyogen Senzaki dies. Psychiatric sessions with Dr. Baker.

October: completion of "Saladin" epic poem mentioned. Several references in letters to a person he is going to marry. Moves to 772 Clementina St. in San Francisco. Congratulatory letter from President Nasser in Egypt reviewing "Saladin."

December: letter from "Edna" in Karachi (this could be his possible marriage).

1959

Mentions prospective marriage with a lady of English nationality who has lived most of her life in India, a dancer. Attends Rudolph Schaeffer School of Design. March or April: Robert Clifton (Phra Sumangalo) visits Sam, more letters written to State Department.

1960

Travel in Egypt, in Cairo around his birthday (October).

1961

Travel and residence in Pakistan—meeting scientists on land reform and agriculture, meeting saints and Sufis, lecturing on international cultural exchange.

1962

Sent on a peace mission from Pakistan to India. First two days in India, meets with President Radhakrishnan, Swami Maharaj Ranganathananda, and Pir-O-Murshid Hasan Sani Nizami. New Delhi: visit to tombs of Amir Khusrau, Nizamuddin Auliya, Hasan Nizami, Inayat Khan. At dargah of Amir Khusrau, initiated in vision as successor to Mohammed Iqbal in the poetic school of Rumi, also invested with robe that was physically given upon his return to Pakistan.

Visits to Anandashram, with Swami Ramdas and Mother Krishnabai.

Meets Pir Dewwal Shereef, appointed representative of University of Islamabad. Robe given by Pir Barkat Ali, to return to US and begin a mission patterned on the life and career of Moineddin Chisti.

1963

Begins *Lotus and the Universe*. Speaks at Rudolph Schaeffer School with wonderful response (calls this the "turning point in my S.F. story"). Appointed to work on material for the Encyclopedia of Buddhism. Visits Indio, CA to study desert agriculture; gathering material for "How California Can Help Asia." Deaths of Swamis Ramdas and Sivananda. Papers: "The Garden of Allah" project, "Solution of the Palestine Impasse."

1964

Nyogen Senzaki had left a library and manuscripts when he died; Sam was asked to be "librarian" of the "Mentorgarten." Appears in public as a Sufi for the first time at Arabic Cultural Conference. His work is mentioned at Food and Civilization Conference. Reports his brother wishes reconciliation; his two worst enemies have "attritioned themselves." Writing letters about idea of salt-water conversion plants on the Red Sea (Bryn Beorse's ocean thermal plant). Working on Project Prometheus (water problems) and on developing nonpoisonous sprays at City College of San Francisco in response to "Silent Spring." Visits Ruth St. Denis, out of this came "The Dance of Universal Peace." Asked to represent World Buddhist Federation. Attends Master Kyung Bo-Seo from Korea.

1965

Gets scholarship to UC (Berkeley) "Breaking and Freeing" experience: meets three Buddhist masters, one gives him full ordination in Korean and Tibetan schools, later addresses audience to say he is one of the few Americans to attain illumination. In poetical form writes four solutions to Viet Nam; letters to the U.N., Adlai Stevenson, Congressman.

1966

Postcard from Allen Ginsberg—still doing "Allah" chant Sam gave him. June: dispute with his brother Elliot settled, each getting money from Trust. Sidi Abusalem Al-Alawi visits San Francisco, confirms him as a Sufi with baraka, attributes this as a point when his role as teacher of Sufism was hastened toward flowering. Initiates his first disciples of this new wave. Mentions writing of 'Dharma Transmission" in progress. Assists in founding The Holy Order of MANS, a Christian mystical school, in San Francisco, with Father Paul (Earl Blighton).

1967

April: hospitalized for "ptomaine poisoning." God tells him, "I make you spiritual teacher of the hippies." England trip cancelled. June: moves into the Mentorgarten, 410 Precita Ave. in San Francisco with Ed Hunt. August: grand opening house party at Mentorgarten; reports 11 male disciples, 3 women; doing Saturday morning walks class. Receives Senzaki's papers from Lottie Fernandez. Ordained "Zen-shi" by Master Kyung-Bo Seo of Korea.

1968

Met Pir Vilayat Inayat Khan (way prepared by Shamcher Beorse), whose visit and mention of dervish dancing in the East touches off flood of Dances of Universal Peace.

1969

Visits with Vietnamese Buddhist Rev. Thich Thien-An. Meets with Roshi Jiyu Kennett. Doing class on Christian mysticism at Holy Order of MANS.

1970

Visits London and Congress of Temple of Understanding in Geneva. His brother dies. Meets Karmu in Boston. Visits Lama Foundation near Taos, New Mexico. On December 28, shortly before sunrise, slips and falls down the hall steps of his home, suffers a severe concussion. For two and a half weeks is in and out of coma.

1971

January 2: dictates last letter to Sufi Barkat Ali in Pakistan. January 15, dies at age 75. Buried at Lama Foundation, near Taos, NM.

Index

The Sufi Ruhaniat International

The Sufi Ruhaniat International is dedicated to helping individuals unfold their highest spiritual purpose, manifest their essential inner being, and live harmoniously with others, with the hope of relieving human suffering and contributing to the awakening of all of humankind. The organization was founded by Murshid Samuel L. Lewis shortly before he died in 1971. We are in the stream of the ages-old wisdom lineage of Sufism brought to the West in 1910 by Hazrat Inayat Khan under the title "The Sufi Message of Spiritual Liberty" and his disciple Murshid Samuel L. Lewis (Sufi Ahmed Murad Chisti). This work was continued by Pir Moineddin Jablonski, the spiritual successor of Murshid Samuel Lewis, who guided the Ruhaniat from 1971 until his death in 2001. It continues today under the guidance of Pir Shabda Kahn, the successor of Pir Moineddin.

The Ruhaniat family is composed of sincere mureeds (initiated students) who tread the path of initiation and discipleship, seeking the truth of the inner life through personal practice and direct experience—just as the disciples of Christ, Buddha, Muhammad, and other illuminated souls, known and unknown, have done through the ages. Because Sufism is based on experiences and not on premises, we affirm the preciousness of an initiatic relationship of spiritual transmission between initiator and mureed. It is a fundamental principle of the Sufi Ruhaniat International that each mureed have an initiator to serve as friend, guide and reality check. This primary initiatic relationship provides a living matrix within which students as well as teachers may develop in character and spiritual experience. Retreats and classes are open to all, both initiates and non-initiates alike.

Further activities of the Ruhaniat include an Esoteric Studies program, the International Network for the Dances of Universal Peace, the Dervish Healing Order, the Service of Universal Peace and ministerial training, Spiritual Psychology and SoulWork, Ziraat (Sacred Agriculture), Retreat and many other inspired teachings of the leaders and lineage holders of the Ruhaniat.

We have recently crossed the threshold between the old millennium and the new. Many contemporary tools are available to help us in our personal and spiritual growth. At the same time, we represent a tradition that has its roots in prehistory. The sacred practices and teachings that have come down to us from diverse climes and cultures in an unbroken line have been carefully cultivated and prepared for us by innumerable spiritual forebears.

Please contact us through our website **www.ruhaniat.org** or email info@ruhaniat.org